CULTURE, STYLE
AND THE
EDUCATIVE PROCESS

Second Edition

CULTURE, STYLE and the EDUCATIVE PROCESS

Making Schools Work for Racially Diverse Students

Edited by

BARBARA J. ROBINSON SHADE, PH.D.

Professor, Educational Psychology
University of Wisconsin-Parkside
Kenosha, Wisconsin

CHARLES C THOMAS • PUBLISHER, LTD.
Springfield • Illinois • U.S.A.

Published and Distributed Throughout the World by

CHARLES C THOMAS • PUBLISHER, LTD.
2600 South First Street
Springfield, Illinois 62794-9265

© *1997 by* CHARLES C THOMAS • PUBLISHER, LTD.
ISBN 0-398-06747-3   (cloth)
ISBN 0-398-06748-1   (paper)

Library of Congress Catalog Card Number: 96-29595

First Edition, 1989
Second Edition, 1997

With THOMAS BOOKS *careful attention is given to all details of manufacturing
and design. It is the Publisher's desire to present books that are satisfactory as to their
physical qualities and artistic possibilities and appropriate for their particular use.*
THOMAS BOOKS *will be true to those laws of quality that assure a good name
and good will.*

*Printed in the United States of America
SC-R-3*

Library of Congress Cataloging-in-Publication Data

Culture, style and the educative process : making schools work for
  racially diverse students / edited by Barbara J. Robinson Shade. —
  2nd ed.
      p.   cm.
    Includes bibliographical references (p.   ) and index.
    ISBN 0-398-06747-3 (cloth). — ISBN 0-398-06748-1 (paper)
    1. Minorities—Education—United States.   2. African-Americans—
  Education.   3. Mexican Americans—Education.   4. Indians of North
  America—Education.   5. Hmong Americans—Education.
  6. Multicultural education—United States.   7. Cognitive styles—
  United States.   I. Shade, Barbara J.
  LC3731.C85   1997
  371.829'0973—dc21   96-29595
                                                                    CIP
                                                                    Rev.

CONTRIBUTORS

CHRISTINE BENNETT
Indiana University
Bloomington, Indiana

BERTTRAM CHIANG
University of Wisconsin-Oshkosh
Oshkosh, Wisconsin

GRACE C. COOPER
University of the District of Columbia
Washington, D. C.

GEORGE O. CURETON
Medgar Evars College
Brooklyn, New York

MAI DAO
San Jose State University
San Jose, California

STEVEN I. HENRY
Oregon Graduate School of Professional Psychology
Pacific University
Portland, Oregon

BRENT KAULBACK
Canadian Journal of Native Education
University of Alberta
Edmonton, Alberta
Canada

MARJORIE W. LEE
Howard University
Washington, D. C.

VALERIE OOKA PANG
San Diego State University
San Diego, California

FLOY C. PEPPER
Rudolph Dreikurs Institute
Portland, Oregon

OLIVIA SARACHO
University of Maryland
College Park, Maryland

MAUREEN SMITH
University of Wisconsin-Oshkosh
Oshkosh, Wisconsin

JOAN THROWER TIMM
University of Wisconsin-Oshkosh
Oshkosh, Wisconsin

HENRY T. TRUEBA
University of Houston
Houston, Texas

ABLEX PUBLISHING COMPANY
Norwood, New Jersey

AMERICAN EDUCATIONAL RESEARCH ASSOCIATION
Washington, D. C.

ASSOCIATION FOR SUPERVISION AND CURRICULUM DEVELOPMENT
Alexandria, Virginia

ASSOCIATION FOR THE STUDY OF PERCEPTION
Fort Wayne, Indiana

BOARD OF EDUCATIONAL RESEARCH
Howard University
Washington, D. C.

CANADIAN JOURNAL OF NATIVE EDUCATION
University of Alberta
Edmonton, Alberta
Canada

INTERNATIONAL READING ASSOCIATION
Newark, Delaware

KAPPA DELTA PI
Bloomington, Indiana

PRO-ED JOURNALS, INC.
Journal of Learning Disabilities
Austin, Texas

To Oscar, Christina, Kenneth, Patti and Ronnie D.,
Brian, Jason, and Kenny, and
all the STREAM STARS who allowed me to practice these ideas.

PREFACE

An increasing amount of attention is being given to the fact that a large number of students of color are not performing to their maximum potential within the current school setting. Their rejection of and hostility toward school and all of its attendant practices has generated national concern because this country cannot survive if a large portion of its citizens are uneducated, unproductive and noncontributing. The societal and economic implications of such a situation are staggering.

In the examination of this problem, it has become increasingly clear that there are some rather significant differences in student/teacher perceptions of how one becomes educated. These differences seem to be more of a barrier to satisfactory performance than the lack of ability to which this phenomena is usually attributed. This perceptual incongruity leads students from the communities on which this book focuses to report that they believe that schools and teachers are not interested in teaching them, do not like them and do not want them to succeed. The students, as well as scholars and parents, believe that if the educational agents were serious about wanting them to do well, more effort would be made to promote changes in teacher behaviors, changes in the way class is conducted, changes in communication, changes in the way material is presented and changes in the curriculum and methods of assessment.

Although this book focuses on African-American, Mexican-American, American Indians and the Hmong from Southeast Asia because these populations seem to be experiencing the most difficulty, it should be noted that students in general are making similar demands because this generation has become much more visual, much more active, much more technologically based and much more people-oriented than previous generations. Therefore, as one reviews these articles, it is important to keep in mind that the suggestions made for the different racial groups can also have a profound impact on other students because this population cohort is becoming more similar in culture than different. In other words, using these ideas can result in a much more enhanced and enriched classroom for **all** students.

The book is divided into three sections. The first provides a general idea about the cultural styles of the different racial groups. Please do not assume that these characteristics represent all of the people within particular populations. The purpose of this section is to give a sense of the uniqueness of the groups from their perspective as a way of providing some guidelines for observation similar to the identified developmental differences among children. Culture represents the perceptions and meanings attached to ideas as well as accepted behavior which students learn in their communities before they come to school. These characteristics and perceptions of the world are much more important and more representative of the students than their skin color.

The second section concentrates on learning styles with particular attention on how culture affects the way students acquire information. Particular attention is given to the concept of field-independence and field-dependence which is the most popular dimension of cognitive style under discussion. This concept represents a common understanding about how individuals approach reasoning, decision-making and problem solving differently. In other words, it defines an individual's preferred learning style. Educators who understand this dimension can better design instruction in ways which will help all students learn, particularly when their thinking style differs from the one promoted by the school.

The third section provides ideas and suggestions on how to address the differences in cultural orientation if changes in student motivation and attitude toward learning are to occur. Attention to culture facilitates the transformation of the psychological climate which teachers create for learning. This environment sets the stage for the development of student-teacher communication, for developing student self-esteem, and for promoting the belief that the students can succeed. Students who perceive themselves to be in an unfriendly milieu do not believe they have the support or opportunity to learn and are, therefore, unwilling to expend energy on processing the material. As stated by Goleman (1995) continual emotional distress [such as being in an alienating situation] can create deficits in a child's intellectual abilities and cripple their capacity to learn.

The basic premise of this book is: Educators can make a difference in academic performance of students of color if they accept their uniqueness, develop activities which capitalize on the students' preferred styles while teaching them other strategies for learning, and ensure that they feel psychologically comfortable so that they will take the risk of engaging in new and different activities and exploring new ideas. Addressing culture and style is the key to making schools work for racially different students.

REFERENCES

Goleman, D.: *Emotional Intelligence: Why it can matter more than IQ.* New York, Bantam Books, 1995.

Howe, H., & Strauss, B.: *13th Gen: Abort, retry, ignore, fail?* New York, Vintage Books, 1993.

ACKNOWLEDGMENTS

Special thanks to Joan Thrower Timm and Maureen Smith at the University of Wisconsin-Oshkosh who took the time to investigate and write some original chapters for this book. To really address the issues of the various communities, it is important to have scholars who are intimately acquainted with these communities provide the insights.

Thanks also goes to Claudia Melear at the University of Tennessee-Knoxville whose work in African-American learning styles and science will soon become an important contribution to this area; to Carol Mitchell of the University of Nebraska-Omaha for her review; and to all of the educators who continue to use my work as a theoretical basis for their practice.

CONTENTS

Part III. The Educative Process:
Teaching to Cultural Learning Styles

CULTURE, STYLE
AND THE
EDUCATIVE PROCESS

PART I
CULTURAL FOUNDATIONS OF LEARNING

Chapter 1

CULTURE: THE KEY TO ADAPTATION

BARBARA J. SHADE

What is culture? Culture, as Maehr (1974) points out, represents a group's preferred way of perceiving, judging, and organizing the ideas, situations, and events they encounter in their daily lives. It represents the rules or guidelines a set of individuals who share a common history or geographical setting use to mediate their interaction with their environment. As such, culture might involve adherence to a specific religious orientation, use of a certain language or style of communication, as well as preferences for various expressive methods to represent their perceptions of the world, i.e., in art, music, or dance. Culture also determines the guidelines individuals within groups use to select the specific information to which they attend as well as the interpretation given to that information. For Americans of color, culture takes on the added dimension of establishing guidelines for interacting with a society which does not value either their ethnicity, their history and heritage, or their language. Therefore, to truly understand culture, one must understand the process of adaptation.

STYLE AND THE ADAPTATION PROCESS

Adaptation, according to some theorists, is viewed as the behavior which results from an individual's or group's ability to selectively meet the demands of a perceived environment (Allerhand, Weber, Haug, 1970). These scholars suggest that this process represents a two-way interaction between the person and the environment and that successful adaptation occurs when this interaction is accomplished with a limited amount of stress, anxiety, or without exceeding the psychological, financial, or other resources available (Coyne & Lazarus, 1980). The responses involved in making adaptation to the environment involves: the cognitive appraisal or interpretation of the information gleaned in the environment or situation; the affective processing or reappraisal of the situation based upon the person's dominant needs, values, and emotions; and the decision-making or adaptation process in which the individual selects the strategy or action which they believe to be most appropriate. Each person or group proceeds through these steps based upon their own affective state, personal agenda, resources, options, and constraints available to them and the previous experience and understanding of the situation (Wachtel, 1972; Gardner, Jackson, Messick, 1960; Klein, 1970). Consequently, each individual or commune of individuals develops a unique way of coping with life which becomes their cultural style. Let us examine each step in the adaptation process to see the result of this interaction.

Cognitive Appraisal

How an individual or cluster of individuals "sees" the world represents their world view or *Weltanschauung.* This is a set of beliefs about the world which set the stage for the types of inferences individuals make about various ideas, people, actions, or stories they encounter in life. They also become scripts or schemata through and around which cognitive appraisals are made about objects, events, or ideas which help organize the stimuli into some meaningful conceptual pattern. Thus, adaptation is most often defined using the psychological dimension of perception.

The best known studies of the concept of adaptation employing the perceptual process are those done by Herman A. Witkin and his associates who developed the concept of cognitive style using the field-dependence/field-independence construct. In their study of the field-independent/field-dependent dimension of cognitive style, Witkin and his associates (Witkin, Dyk, Paterson, Goodenough et. al., 1962) established the idea that the method in which people approach perceptual tasks determines their approach to the processing of information and ultimately adaptation. Individuals who are able to perceptually disembed the figure from the distracting background are considered to be perceptually differentiated and those who have difficulty are perceptually diffuse. The field-independent or perceptually differentiated individuals seem less interested in people, show and demonstrate more physical and psychological distancing from people and prefer nonsocial situations. Because they are good at cognitive restructuring and information transformation, they tend to rely on their perceptions of the situation to make decisions rather than on external referents. The more perceptually differentiated an individual is, the more capable the individual appears in handling situations which require analysis of abstract ideas and functioning in an impersonal type of situation.

The less perceptually differentiated a person is, the more oriented he or she is to situations with a high number of interpersonal contacts, and a highly structured environment in which carefully contrived directions are given. These individuals who fit these situations are characterized as being interested in people, comfortable in physical closeness, are emotionally open and gravitate toward social situations. In addition, when field-dependent individuals feel that others have the type of information needed to assist them in functioning and making decisions, they are more likely to rely upon them as referents and are more likely to suppress negative feelings or overt expressions of disapproval. Field-dependent individuals typify extraverted personalities.

The use of cognitive style as a reflection of the process of adaptation for ethnocultural groups was studied using cross-cultural research by Witkin and Berry in 1975 to examine how group information processing preferences correlated with their lifestyle. According to their assumptions, the more perceptually differentiated a society, the better the group would be at adapting to a less structured way of living. Both this study and the one by Berry (1976) found that communities which must rely on their entrepreneurial ability to secure food through hunting and migratory movement develop ecological, social, and familial interaction techniques which seem to foster a field-independent or differentiated perceptual style within the group to facilitate adaptation. Societies whose way of life was more sedentary, agricultural, and cooperative, on the other hand, developed behavioral, social, and familial approaches which fostered the field-dependent cognitive style within their community. Witkin (1978) concluded that cognitive styles develop to fit the life situations with which the individual or group must cope. This relationship between cognitive style and adaptation is referred to as cognitive style attunement.

Affective Assessment

The affective dimension of the adaptational process is most evident in studies of cognitive style attunement and individual career choice and satisfaction. In a study by Witkin, Moore, Goodenough, and Cox (1977), the researchers found that individuals with a field-dependent perceptual style were more likely to favor occupations with a "people" emphasis or with high social content and interpersonal relationship requirements. These individuals expressed preferences for such positions as elementary or social-science teaching, business administration, the ministry, social work, personnel work, counselling, or marketing. Individuals whose cognitive style could be labeled as field-independent were more likely to choose career fields such as natural science, mathematics, art, engineering, experimental psychology; the teaching of agricultural or industrial subjects, or working as physicians, dentists, foresters, or farmers. Of particular interest in these studies is the finding that if the cognitive style of an individual and the initial career choice are incongruent, the individual shifts interests or changes positions until a more compatible situation is found and cognitive attunement is reached.

The importance of the style matching worker and role expectations is of growing importance in the business world since it seems to affect productivity and worker satisfaction. One of the first studies in this area was done by McKenney and Keen (1974). They looked at the decision making behavior and cognitive styles of people in different company roles. For example, in examining the working relationship between managers and engineers, stylistic differences were noted. The managers were found to be more intuitive, global, and somewhat field-dependent in their approach to making decisions and handling the tasks while the engineers were more analytical, sequential, and field-independent. These differences in decision-making and task completion efforts created conflict and hampered the completion of projects when the two groups were asked to collaborate.

How stylistic differences influence the working relationships in other business climates is being pursued by such researchers as Jean Lipmen-Blumen who is looking at the personal administrative style of women in administration and by David Wok who works with communication style differences. Within the educational domain, attention is being given to the importance of the leadership style of the principal. As Guild et al. (1985) point out, cognitive style affects the leadership competencies of principals and subsequently has a significant effect upon the culture of the school, the interaction and morale of the faculty and, ultimately, the academic achievement of the students. From these studies one concludes that cognitive style attunement has an affective as well as a cognitive dimension which facilitates or hampers adaptation.

Situational Adjustment

The final step to successful adaptation to an environment is the ability to make the correct decision about appropriate coping strategies. Again, cognitive style becomes a major factor. For example, Witkin (1978) found that individuals apparently select others to share important situations in their life by determining whether or not they have similar cognitive styles. An example of this is the study in which the cognitive style compatibility of college roommates and dating partners was compared. They found that roommates or partners who were considered to be most compatible were those who shared a similar cognitive style profile (Witkin, 1978).

Whether or not cognitive style attunement is important in one of society's most important institutions, i.e., the school, is still under debate. The research attempts to investigate this by matching the style of the teacher in the classroom with the style of the learner. The results of the studies are mixed. There is some possibility that the inconsistent findings about whether or not the match and mismatch of teacher and learner styles is important to academic success may be due to the examination of the wrong variables. In most studies of cognitive style congruence, the compatibility is determined by matching the style with the environmental expectations rather than the styles of other individuals within the situation. If this is the case, perhaps a better indicator of the importance of style congruence for teachers and learners is in the examination of the match between the culture of the school as a setting and the style of the learner. The merit of this approach is demonstrated in a study matching students with law schools by Smith (1979). He found that students did better when their cognitive style was congruent with the culture of the law school they attended. One school examined was a school in which a strict interpretation of the law was advocated. The cognitive style best suited for this situation was one which was more cognitively rigid, less tolerant of ambiguity, and accepting of an authoritarian climate. Smith called this a *monopathic* style. The other school was one which tended toward a less strict interpretation of the law and, therefore, best tolerated students who were creative, cognitively flexible, tolerant, and needed less structure or guidance. This was the *polypathic* cognitive style according to Smith. The students who were most successful at each school were those whose style best matched the organizational climate rather than instructor style.

SUMMARY

The selection of appropriate adaptational strategies depends, in large measure, upon the individual's perception of the environment, and this perception is based upon past history and previous socializing experiences, i.e., culture. Culture, through the mediating process called cognitive style, determines the affective and cognitive behaviors which an individual selects to meet environmental demands. As environmental psychologists have been able to suggest, situations in which individuals find themselves tend to solicit the behavioral patterns necessary for survival within the confines of that situation. As such cognitive style has a significant impact upon an individual's competent performance in various behavioral settings.

These are the underlying assumptions of this book. The reviews and studies presented examine the cultural perspective which accompanies the three dominant groups of color to the school and attempts to demonstrate the manner in which this cultural style ultimately influences their responses to the school setting. For example, Christine Bennett vividly portrays the conflict which often results because educators do not have knowledge of the cultural filter through which the children and their community view the school, its curriculum and its expectations. The examples she presents are timeless as a trip into any classroom with African-American, Hispanic-American, and Native American children will attest. This suggests that she is not describing incidents which relate to specific individuals and their traits. Instead, it would appear that we are talking about behavior and perceptions which are contextually and culturally-based oriented and which have a major influence on school-pupil adjustment of children of color.

REFERENCES

1. Allerhand, M. E., Weber, R. E., & Haug, M.: *Adaptation and Adaptability*. New York, Child Welfare League, 1970.
2. Berry, J. W.: *Human Ecology and Cognitive Style: Comparative Studies in Cultural and Psychological Adaptation*. New York, John Wiley & Sons, 1976.
3. Coyne, J. C., & Lazarus, R. S.: Cognitive style, stress perception and coping. In Kutash, I., Schlesinger, L. B., & Associates (Eds.): *Handbook on Stress and Anxiety: Contemporary Knowledge, Theory and Treatment*. San Francisco, Jossey Bass, 1980.

4. Gardner, R. W., Jackson, D. N., & Messick, S. J.: Personal organization in cognitive controls and intellectual abilities. *Psychological Issues, 2,* 1960.
5. Guild, P. B., & Garger, S.: *Marching to Different Drummers.* Alexandria, Association of Supervision and Curriculum Development, 1985.
6. Klein, G. S.: *Perception, Motives, and Personality.* New York, Alfred Knopf, 1970.
7. Maehr, M. L.: *Sociocultural Origins of Achievement.* Monterey, Brooks/Cole, 1974.
9. McKenney, J. L., & Keen, P. G. W.: How managers' minds work. *Harvard Business Review,* May/June:79–90, 1974.
10. Smith, A. G.: *Cognitive Styles in Law Schools.* Austin, University of Texas Press, 1979.
11. Wachtel, P. L.: Cognitive style and style of adaptation. *Perceptual and Motor Skills, 35:*779–785, 1972.
12. Witkin, H. A.: *Cognitive Styles in Personal and Cultural Adaptation.* Hartford, Clark University Press, 1978.
13. Witkin, H. A., & Berry, J. Psychological differentiation in cross-cultural perspective. *Journal of Cross-Cultural Psychology, 6:*5–87, 1975.
14. Witkin, H. A., Dyk, R. B., Paterson, H. F., Goodenough, D. R., & Karp, S. A.: *Psychological Differentiation.* New York, Wiley and Sons, 1962.
15. Witkin, H. A., Moore, C., Goodenough, D. R., & Cox, P. W.: Field dependent and field independent cognitive styles and their educational implications. *Review of Educational Research, 47:*1–64, 1977.

Chapter 2

CULTURE AND LEARNING STYLE WITHIN THE AFRICAN-AMERICAN COMMUNITY*

BARBARA J. SHADE

How do children obtain knowledge? The scholars who have examined this question suggest that the learning process involves interpreting sensory events, categorizing the information into familiar categories, searching memory for similar experiences and ideas to which the information relates, and manipulating ideas, images, and concepts. Exactly what information is learned, however, is determined by the interests, needs, and background of the individual. More important, as Cole and Scribner (1974) point out, a child's method of perception, memorization, thinking, and using any type of knowledge are inseparately bound to the patterns of activity, communication, and social relations of the culture to which he/she is a member. This chapter examines the cultural dimensions of the African-American community which have a significant impact on the learning behaviors of its members.

CULTURAL FOUNDATIONS OF AFRICAN-AMERICAN LEARNING STYLE

Culture may be defined as standards and definitions used by members of a human community to organize their experiences. These definitions influence their perceptions, judgments, and actions and set the stage for how members of that cultural group adapt to their social and physical environments. Although this broad definition of culture is generally used when studying less industrialized societies, it is also a definition which can be used to study African-Americans. Of course, many people will argue that African-Americans are really only "typical" Americans and subscribe to the tenets of mainstream American culture. Others,

---

*Some segments from Shade, Barbara J. African-American cognitive style; A variable in school success? *Review of Educational Research, 52*:219–234. Used with permission.

however, argue that African-Americans have a distinct culture based upon their inability to fully participate in the majority culture and the recognition by them that American society is color-coded. Charles Keil (1966) suggests that this situation produces a culture best defined as "experiential wisdom" that provides African-Americans with a unique outlook on life that cannot be shared by nonblacks.

This unique outlook emanates from three major sources. In addition to those aspects acquired from European-oriented mainstream society and those which are adaptations of the various Africanisms, Americans of African descent have also acquired ways of thinking, feeling, and acting which are typical of oppressed or colonized people (Staples, 1976). It is the combination of the modes of actions, artifacts, and behaviors from these three sources which constitute African-American culture.

Mainstream American Culture

In 1955, Mason examined major studies done on acculturation by anthropologists to determine exactly what constituted "mainstream" culture in America. Mason defined this culture as European, Caucasian, and primarily operative in the western hemisphere. The identified beliefs, values, customs, desired behaviors, and dispositional factors are those which McClelland (1961) and others have since defined as necessary for achieving in American society. They are very often referred to as national characteristics.

Based upon these analyses, the "typical" American is supposedly exposed to learning which emphasizes: (1) the role of the individual rather than the group, (2) the idea that nature must be controlled and harnessed for man's advantage and, (3) the ultimate successful personality as one which is self-reliant, industrious, thrifty, highly motivated, and certainly competitive. Punctuality, future orientation, direct action, and order are also valued as are freedom of expression, equal opportunity, and social democracy. While it is recognized that some of the professed values conflict with the idea of individual interests and success, Mason (1955) suggests that this, too, is a part of the American culture, i.e., making choices and tolerating ambiguities and inconsistencies. For the most part, these authors suggest that the idea of individuality prevails.

The contact with this prevailing attitude has influenced African-Americans as it has other immigrant groups. As the domestic servants or slaves to those individuals or families who epitomize the very essence of this view, African-Americans observed and imitated these behaviors and beliefs. In addition, African-American and Euro-American scholars inundated the African-American community with the idea that the adherence to this life-style and view point would alleviate the difficulties being perpetuated by prejudice, segregation, and "Jim Crowism." Evidence of the inculcation of these views is noted in the recorded orientations of African-American individuals who worked as house slaves or those who became professionals and leaders of the African-American community (Blassingame, 1979; Quarles, 1969).

African Survivalisms

In spite of this cultural onslaught from the mainstream, the development of separate communities both in the slave quarters and in cities and the need to join forces against the color-caste system, provided the impetus and the opportunity for remnants of the African culture to remain. Cultural artifacts such as art forms, musical rhythms, scales, instruments, dances, folk tales, myths, and riddles, and some aspects of religion were among the first aspects of African culture identified as having been transmitted to this country (Goldstein, 1971; Blassingame, 1979; Pasteur & Toldson, 1982). In recent years both African and African-American writers have concentrated on the belief and attitudinal system which seems to have survived. Wade Nobles (1980) identifies these as beliefs which emphasize group communality and a sense of unity with particular emphasis on the idea that the individual should subordinate the interests of "self" to the survival of the group and that cooperation is better than competitiveness. Also important is the idea that nature is not an aspect of the environment to be conquered but one in which there must be integration and interdependence between the individual and nature.

The Culture of Oppression

To these preceding cultural perspectives must be added the culture of inferiority in which every African-American is submerged, i.e., the idea that only ideas, views, and attitudes which are of northern European origin are acceptable and those with an African origin are unacceptable. Ascribers to these values give the highest value possible to white skin color, Caucasoid facial features, straight hair, and other physical characteristic, while the lowest value possible is assigned to black skin color, Negroid features, curly hair, etc. The accompanying belief is that those possessing the less desired traits are concomitantly intellectually inferior.

Ogbu (1978) and Howard (1980), using other societies around the world as comparison, suggest that this type of environment produces the type of psycho-behavioral modalities common to colonized or caste-dominated people. Among these are self-hatred, over-identification with those in power, anxiety, hostility, aggression, and a general inadequate development of the motivational, cognitive, and intellectual skills necessary for that society. A cultural byproduct of this situation is a preoccupation and group focus on the concepts of *freedom* and *equality.*

From the African, European, and colonized experiences, African-Americans developed a perspective of life, mechanisms of survival, a view of the world, and expressions of individual personality which have come to be recognized as unique cultural patterns. Although the totality of this pattern has yet to be clearly identified, a number of authors have elaborated on some aspects of it. Staples (1976), for example, suggests that African-American cultural patterns consist of unique customs, rituals, aesthetic appreciation, social organizations, language structures, and values which stress group unity, solidarity, and mutual aid. Jones (1979) indicates African-American cultural components contain a group-specific perspective of time, work, rhythm, and spirituality, and that African-Americans have a unique propensity for improvisation, spontaneity, and a preference for oral expression.

In studies of these dimensions Alper (1975) found that African-American perspectives of work differed from whites with blacks rating job satisfaction and job climate as being more important than white workers thought them to be. Additional cultural elements identified include preference of religiousness (Malpass & Symond, 1974), the value of solidarity and group consciousness (Walker, 1976), and an appreciation of color intensity and certain garment and other aesthetic preferences (Jenkins, 1983; Schwartz, 1963). Several scholars suggest that African-Americans differ from other groups in their preference for a toleration of a high noise level and need for vividness and multiplicity of stimuli which Boykin refers to as "verve" (White, 1980; Boykin, 1979). Other authors enumerate kinesthetic preference, the kinship system, the ability to handle contradictions, a different perspective on the role and type of cultural hero, verbal and nonverbal communication patterns, orientation toward work, and a healthy suspicion of people within the environment as important African-American cultural components. Of these cultural components, the kinship system, worldview, and social interactive behaviors have the greatest impact on learning style.

The Kinship System

The Americans from Africa arrived with an already enlarged sense of community, having lived in a highly-structured commune and society in which the members depended upon each other for physical protection, mutual support, and assistance in economic ventures. Within their new environment, a similar configuration developed, both in the slave community on each plantation as well as among the African-Americans in cities (Blassingame, 1979; Meier & Rudwick, 1970). This time, however, the bond was predicated upon color and experiential communality rather than on tribal connections. Throughout history, whether working as a share-cropper, migrating to the North or West, or living in the confines of the ghettos, the need for network assistance continued. This kinship network, sometimes described as an extended or augmented family and composed of either relatives, friends, and neighbors, became and remains an integral aspect of the African-American community.

The African-American kinship network is a multigenerational social network of relatives, friends, and neighbors (Aschenbrenner, 1973; MacAdoo, 1977; Martin & Martin, 1978; Stack, 1974). Although previously viewed as a less than desirable structure, recent research efforts have found it beneficial to African-Americans in that this network acts as a buffer for individuals against negative ecological forces and serves as a cultural facilitator and mediator (Comer, 1976). Through this network, African-American individuals and their nuclear family system are able to give and receive emotional, physical, psychological, and social support.

As members of this kinship system, African-Americans are trained in the concept of collective responsibility and the importance of the authority of a dominant family figure. At the same time, members of the group are encouraged to seek and move toward independence of the unit (Martin & Martin, 1978; Aschenbrenner, 1972). However, the extent that this is tolerated depends upon the economic plight and other needs of the network. As in the Barry, Child, and Bacon (1959) study, the greater the need for mutual support to insure financial and economic survival, the greater the pressure for kinship support and less independence. Thus, this support may, as Stack (1974) points out, take the form of economic assistance as it does in many lower class families, or it may take the form of the social and emotional support for the socially alienated middle-class family members (MacAdoo, 1977).

It is this sense of mutual responsibility which promotes the practice of informal adoption of dependent children, or the inclusion of financially insecure elderly relatives of a single-parent family as a part of a household. This collective consciousness, however, does not stop at relatives, but extends as well to any person who is accepted by the group and has the need and/or desire to be included. Even in present times when more family members are moving away to new locations, many young adults find themselves developing a pseudo-kinship system among friends who come from similar backgrounds or being "adopted" by other families, thus, still participating as a part of some network. Almost from the beginning, the majority of African-Americans come to know the world within the confines of what Cohen (1969) calls a shared-function group. According to Cohen, shared-function groups promote a cooperative approach to learning and these individuals are more likely to engage in relational rather than analytical thinking styles.

Social Interactive Behaviors

As a part of this group orientation, or perhaps as a result of it, African-Americans seem to develop a unique affective or personal orientation which manifests itself in a unique approach to: social cognition, interpersonal interaction, meanings attached to words, use of nonverbal communication, and reliance on external referents for information and advice.

Social Cognition: In studies in which groups were compared on their attentiveness to cues in the faces of other people, African-Americans were found to focus on very different cues than Euro-Americans and subsequently developed different recognition patterns. In a study using black and white females, Hirschberg, Jones, and Haggerty (1978) found that the African-American subjects paid much more attention to the affective characteristics of the pictures of male faces than to the physical characteristics. In other studies of this phenomena, it was found that although both groups seem to pay closer attention to the faces of people of their own racial group (Galper, 1973; Chance, Goldstein, McBride, 1975; Luce, 1974), African-Americans seemed better at discerning facial emotions displayed by individuals regardless of their race (Gitter, Black et al., 1972).

Not only are African-Americans better at attending to facial cues, they also appear to detect different social reactions and nuances. A study done by Hill and Fox (1973) of a military situation found that African-American and Euro-American squad leaders had entirely different perceptions about the climate and interrelationships of the people in their squads. Euro-American squad leaders reported more of a perceived need to give reprimands to subordinates of their own race and better performance ratings to subordinates of other racial groups. African-American squad leaders did not make these types of distinctions and also reported perceptions of better relationships between themselves and their subordinates.

A similar study conducted in a school environment reported similar differences in interpersonal perceptions. When teachers were questioned about staff relationships in a recently desegregated school, African-American teachers indicated a perception of more teacher-to-teacher conflict than Euro-American teachers. At the same time, they also reported having a better rapport with the nonacademic staff as well as the students (Witmer and Ferinden, 1970). As in the previous situation, racial differences in perceptions of social interactions seemed to polarize along a continuum with African-Americans responding more to the people in the situation and the Euro-Americans responding more to the task requirements.

Verbal Interpretations: This difference is also found in studies of the social meaning assigned to words. Landis et al. (1976) studied a group of African- and Euro-American middle-class males and hard-core unemployed males by asking them to respond to a word list on a semantic differential scale. Regardless of class, racial differences emerged in the values attached, emotional reactions generated, and the potency assigned to the words. For example, the most highly valued words for African-Americans and not for Euro-Americans are quality-of-life words such as *progress, success, future,* and *money.* Words having the most positive response and value for Euro-Americans and not for African-Americans were words such as *marriage, work,* and *hope.* In the personal relationship category, words such as *truth, respect* and *sympathy* were valued highly by African-Americans while Euro-Americans preferred such words as *love.* On the other hand, Euro-Americans responded with more emotion and negativism to words such as *battle, danger, trouble, crime,* and *confrontation* while African-Americans showed not only less emotion, but neutrality.

In another study of differences in social perceptions Szalay and Bryson (1973) found that words representing themes of racial integration, individual needs, and social problems were perceived as having higher value by African-Americans while Euro-Americans preferred word domains representing various "isms," national loyalty, and health concerns. The response variation apparently represents differences in attached affective meanings.

Social Distance: Perhaps the area in which differences in interpersonal style is most evident is that of social distance. Social distance involves the expanding and contracting physical space surrounding the individual (Liebman, 1970). The perception of social cues, ideas, and attitudes is affected by the amount of physical separation demanded by the individual for social interaction. Those who permit individual to come close gather one sort of information while those who demand greater separation receive other types of cues (Hall, 1966). The result is a manifestation of different social cognitive behavior.

Studies using adult-samples noted a closer social distance preference among African-Americans. Bauer (1973) found this to be true for college students as did Hall (1966), Connally (1974), and Liebman (1970). Willis (1966) reported the opposite finding for older African-American adults; however, the significance level chosen for potential error determination was extremely high. This finding, thus, had a high probability of being a chance occurrence based upon the situation and should probably be disregarded.

When compared to other ghettoized, high-involvement groups, Jones (1971) found little difference in African-American social distance requirements, at least in a street-meeting situation. However, this was not true in a study done by Baxter (1970) in which African-Americans seem to prefer greater social distance than Mexican-Americans. This study would appear to be measuring the axis or degree in which individuals faced each other rather than face-to-face social distance as in other studies as the dyads were observed while watching animals in a zoo. If this is the case, then the Baxter findings are not inconsistent with the trends previously noted, for while African-Americans seem to interact at a closer distance than others, they do seem to face each other less directly.

The differences noted for African-Americans on this dimension seem to depend upon the situation in which the proxemic research was conducted. In studies of children in grades one through four, African-Americans tend to stand closer for purposes of communication than other ethnic groups observed (Duncan, 1978; Aiello & Jones, 1971; Jones & Aiello, 1973). Scherer (1974) studied the same age group using photographs of interacting dyads. Although no significant difference was found, the trend was in the expected direction. However, Zimmerman and Brody (1975) observed fifth and sixth grades and this time found that

Euro-American children of this age group permitted closer social distance than African-American children. Unlike the other studies, these
children did not know each other and came to the experimental situation from different neighborhoods. The fact that this study was done in a
laboratory situation rather than a naturalistic setting, as were the others,
probably accounts for the difference in the results. In a later study, again
the closer personal space among African-American elementary school
children was found (Willis, Carlson, & Reeves, 1979).

When individuals of other races are involved in the social interaction,
some difference in social space preference seems to be noted as well. For
Euro-Americans the choice of interpersonal space requirements seems to
be based upon sex, with Euro-American females being more cautious of
involvement with males regardless of race (Liebman, 1970). For African-
Americans, race seemed to be a determining factor. While African-
Americans seemed willing to invade others' space more often (Dick,
1976), they did appear to prefer African-Americans rather than Euro-
Americans (Sherif, 1973; Liebman, 1970). Thus, it would appear that
African-Americans seem to prefer closer social contact but particularly
with other African-Americans.

Communication Style: Cultural variation in social contact is also noticed
in the nonverbal communication patterns of African-America. Not only
are blacks more likely to touch each other in conversation than whites
(Willis et al., 1978), they are also more likely to engage in the reading of
body language. In his analysis of the various communication styles,
Cooke (1972) found that messages were sent between individuals or
groups; hand gestures, body stances, styles of walking, as well as hairstyles
or attire.

External Referents: Social sensitivity in interpersonal relationships
has also been defined using the area of social referent preference or
determination of the locus of control. Some individuals appear to have
an orientation toward people and are thus considered externally-oriented
as they rely heavily on them for judgments, ideas, values. Those individuals who are less interested in information provided by others or in high
involvement with people or social situations and seem to be aloof,
withdrawn, and independent in their judgment are considered more
impersonal and are often labeled as internally-oriented individuals.

Although it is an often repeated assumption that African-Americans
are more externally-oriented in their social referent preference, there is
little empirical data to support this conclusion. Among the first studies

looking at ethnic differences in this dimension was the one by Battle and Rotter (1963). In this study middle-class blacks and middle-class whites were compared with lower-class blacks and whites. When social class was controlled, no significant differences were found. However, when middle-class Euro-Americans were compared with lower-class African-Americans, a significant difference merged with Euro-Americans being more internally-oriented and African-Americans more externally-oriented. Unfortunately, this difference is often reported as a racial difference rather than an economic role difference.

Scott and Phelan (1969), studied unemployed adult males between the ages of 20–28, and racial-differences did emerge in the same directions as found in the Battle and Rotter (1963) study. Again, however, these differences may still be a function of the economic role of the groups. Gurin and her associates (1969) and Gurin and Epps (1975) noted that African-Americans seem to have a higher ability than more groups to differentiate between situations in which they have control and those in which other people have the most influence. Studies by Ducette and Wolk (1972) and Kinder and Reeder (1975) seem to support this. Thus, the differences found by Scott and Phelan may merely reflect the greater understanding of African-American males who are unemployed about the realistic plight of their situation and epitomizes the African-American view of the world.

Person Perception: Social sensitivity also may be the result of the fact that individuals who are a part of African-American culture are taught at an early age to be wary of people and systems within their environment (Shade, 1978; Wubberhorst, et al., 1971). This lack of trust and suspiciousness often shows up on measures of personality. McClain (1967) found, for example, that college students in the South were more likely to be more suspicious, and apprehensive than whites in the standardization sample of the 16PF personality form. Similar findings were reported by Triandis (1976) in his study of lower-class, hardcore unemployed African-Americans and for those in prisons or in counseling (Berman, 1976; Wright, 1975). Although the subjects of many of the studies were those who were having problems, the idea of distrust or having a healthy suspicion of Euro-Americans as well as other African-Americans seems to be considered a trait rather typical of African-Americans in general (Halpern, 1973; White, 1980). This suggests that there is a basic cultural consensus as to what represents trustworthiness and, as one author points out, African-Americans appear to determine this on nonverbal behavior rather than on verbal cues (Roll, Schmidt, Kaul, 1972; Switkin, Gynther, 1974; Terrell & Barrett, 1979). The idea that the people within one's environment should be approached with caution, wariness, and a sense of distrust is vital to the survival of a group of people who live in an urban society and in a society with dislikes predicated on skin color. It is, as Perkins (1975) points out, a way of insuring that the individual does not become a "victim." Prohibiting victimization also requires an ability to manipulate the system or individuals with whom one comes in contact in order to achieve certain desired goals. It is, thus, not surprising that many counselors and observers of African-American individuals report the presence of manipulative behavior or the development of a high level "con-artist" which within the African-American community is known as a "hustler."

To really understand this social sensitivity, Yarian (1974) suggests that one must examine the heros of that group which are in essence cultural emblems of the group's perspective and valued behavior. Within African-American folklore and music there are the tales of the animal or slave trickster who manages to talk or literally trick his oppressors or captives into letting him escape. Other heros are those who are just simply so tough and formidable that they literally bully their way through life, even if it requires violence. Perhaps, however, the most prevalent hero is the one which Levine (1977) calls "the moral hard man" which represents the hero who literally beats society using society's own rules. Within Jerome Taylor's (1980) typology of African-American heros, this "moral hard man" might well be the "splendid performer," the "man of integrity," the "independent spirit," or the "group leader." As noted in the studies, the ideas of wariness, trust, manipulation, and survival dominate.

To summarize, the cultural environment from which African-American children come to school seems to encompass the following attributes: (a) An aesthetic appreciation of bright colors, fashionable clothing, and hairstyles; (b) a deep respect for spirituality and humanness which is often manifested in a religious orientation; (c) a spontaneity and ability for improvisation and rhythmic orientation which is shown in body movements, music, art forms, verbal, and nonverbal communication patterns, and other artistic expressions; (d) a value system which incorporates not only the desire for success but also group unity, freedom, and equality; (e) a unique perspective about time, work, heros, and people; (f) socialization experiences from a shared-function, supportive, and often extended kinship system; (g) an unusual ability to correctly perceive the affective dimensions of situations and people. As a result, African-American learning seems to be influenced by the:

- people with whom they interact in the learning process;
- the social situation in which learning occurs;
- the degree of relevance and applicability of the material;
- both the verbal and nonverbal communication means used to interpret the material;
- the preference for deductive rather than inductive reasoning; and
- the preference for active involvement rather than passive receptivity.

Of particular importance is that this apparent orientation toward social cognition rather than the physical and abstract world seems to have an impact upon the type of information African-Americans prefer to learn.

The degree to which individuals ascribe to these cultural orientations and preferred learning style, of course, depends upon the social-class lifestyle in which the person is reared.

Social Class

Social class is itself a culture as it represents a way of life which specifies social expectations in the areas of family life, use of leisure time, use of economic resources, church participation, friendship patterns, civic activities, and attitudes toward life (Loeb, 1961). In spite of the general stereotype of homogeneous class structure, the African-American community is as socially heterogeneous as the Euro-American community (Billingsley, 1968; Blackwell, 1975).

Although the African-American upper class is relatively small, comprising approximately 10 percent of the population, it contains two strata—one with long-established members and the other composed of the newly arrived. The established upper class is characterized by individuals and families with a long established tradition of educational achievement, respectable occupations, dependable income, and an enduring family name. Prior to the 1940s, this group largely represented an aristocracy of light skin color. The newer numbers of the upper class are those who have attained their position through achievement rather than ascription. Thus, this class is reminiscent of the achievement of the "American Dream" based on the attainment of some prominence, fame, or success in business. Together both groups encompass a life-style which includes participation in certain religious denominations, membership in specific social groups, and a life-style which mirrors their Euro-American counterpart.

The delineation of the strata within the African-American middle-class always has been difficult. Willie (1974) attributes this to the lack of understanding by many social scientists of the criteria for stratification used within the black community. In addition, although a differentiation of subgroups can be made based upon occupation, church denomination preference, educational attainment, political behavior, and residential patterns, Blackwell (1975) points out that the middle-class professional white collar worker and skilled blue collar worker share a common life-style and value orientation. These commonalities include a strong orientation toward mainstream culture particularly in the area of high achievement motivation, family stability, activism, social striving, and consumerism. Ulf Hannerz (1969) calls this group the "mainstreamers."

The lower class within the African-American community is composed of the working nonpoor, the working poor, and the underclass. Again, as in the other groups, life-style, friendship circles, leisure time activities, and church attendance become the major differentiators of the subgroups in this strata. While it is the lower class most often used in studies of African-American behavior, it is the underclass group whose life style is best described in the "cultural deprivation" literature.

Together the major components of African-American culture and the social stratification system serve as the transmitters of the cognitive and affective entry behaviors which come with the child to school. If these entry behaviors are not those schools perceive are necessary for handling learning tasks, as many scholars suggest, conflict is bound to occur which interrupts the learning process and subsequently affects school achievement. From all indications, this is exactly what seems to occur.

REFERENCES

1. Aiello, J. R., & Jones, S. E.: Field study of the proxemic behavior of young school children in three subcultural groups. *Journal of Personality and Social Psychology, 19:*351–356, 1971.
2. Alper, W.: Racial differences in job and work environment priorities among newly hired college graduates. *Journal of Applied Psychology, 60:*132–134, 1975.
3. Aschenbrenner, J.: Extended families among Black Americans. *Journal of Comparative Family Studies, 3:*257–268, 1973.

4. Barry, H., Child, I., & Bacon, M.: Relation of child training to subsistence economy. *American Anthropologist, 61:*51–63, 1959.
5. Battle, E. S., & Rotter, J.: Children's feelings of personal control as related to social class and ethnic group. *Journal of Personality, 31:*482–490, 1963.
6. Bauer, E.: Personal space: A study of blacks and whites. *Sociometry, 36:*402–408, 1973.
7. Baxter, J. C.: Interpersonal spacing in natural settings. *Sociometry, 33:*444–456, 1970.
8. Berman, J. J.: Parolees' perception of the justice system: Black-white differences. *Criminology, 13:*507–520, 1976.
9. Billingsley, A.: *Black Families in White America.* Englewood Cliff, Prentice-Hall, 1968.
10. Blackwell, J. E.: *The Black Community: Diversity and Unity.* New York, Dodd, Mead & Co., 1975.
11. Blassingame, J.: *The Slave Community.* New York, Oxford University Press, 1979.
12. Boykin, A. W.: Psychological/behavioral verve: Some theoretical explorations and empirical manifestations. In Boykin, A. W., Franklin, A. J. and Yates, J. F. (Eds.): *Research Directions of Black Psychologists.* New York, Russell Sage Foundation, 1979.
13. Chance, J., Goldstein, A., & McBride, L.: Differential experience and recognition memory for faces. *Journal of Social Psychology, 97:*243–253, 1975.
14. Cohen, R.: Conceptual styles, culture conflict, and nonverbal tests of intelligence. *American Anthropologist, 71:*828–856, 1969.
15. Cole, M., & Scribner, S.: *Culture and Thought: A Psychological Introduction.* New York, John Wiley & Sons, 1974.
16. Connally, P. R.: An investigation of the perception of personal space and its meaning among Black and White Americans. Unpublished doctoral dissertation, University of Iowa, 1974.
17. Cooke, B. G.: Nonverbal communication among African-Americans: An initial classification. In Kochman, T. (Ed.): *Rappin' and Stylin' Out: Communication in Urban Black America.* Urbana: University of Illinois Press, 1972.
18. Dick, W.: Invasion of personal space as a function of age and of race. *Psychological Reports, 39:*281–282, 1976.
19. Ducette, J., & Wolk, S.: Locus of control and levels of aspiration in black and white children. *Review of Educational Research, 42:*493–504, 1972.
20. Duncan, B.: The development of spatial behavior norms in black and white primary school children. *Journal of Black Psychology, 5:*33–41, 1978.
21. Galper, R. E.: Functional race membership and recognition of faces. *Perceptual and Motor Skills, 37:*455–462, 1973.
22. Gitter, A. G., Black, H., & Mostofsky, D.: Race and sex in the perception of emotion. *Journal of Social Issues, 28:*63–78, 1972.
23. Goldstein, R. (Ed.): *Black Life and Culture in the United States.* New York, Thomas Crowell, 1971.

24. Gurin, P., & Epps, E.: *Black Consciousness, Mobility, and Achievement.* New York, John Wiley and Sons, 1975.
25. Gurin, P., Gurin, G., Lao, R., & Beattie, M.: Internal-external control in the motivational dynamics of Negro youth. *Journal of Social Issues, 25:*29–53, 1969.
26. Hall, E.: *The Hidden Dimension.* New York, Doubleday, 1966.
27. Halpern, F.: *Survival: Black/White.* New York, Pergamon Press, 1973.
28. Hannerz, U.: *Soulside: Inquiries Into Ghetto Culture and Community.* New York, Columbia University Press, 1969.
29. Hill, W., & Fox, W.: Black and white marine squad leader's perceptions of racially mixed squads. *Academy of Management Journal, 16:*680–686, 1973.
30. Hirschberg, N., Jones, L., & Haggerty, E.: What's in a face: Individual difference in face perception. *Journal of Research in Personality, 12:*488–499, 1978.
31. Howard, J. H.: Toward a social psychology of colonialism. In Jones, R. (Ed.): *Black Psychology.* New York, Harper & Row, 1980.
32. Jenkins, H. C.: *Black Aesthetics: Cognition in a Cultural Context.* Unpublished doctoral dissertation, University of Wisconsin, Madison, 1983.
33. Jones, J. M.: Conceptual and strategic issues in relationship of black psychology to American social science. In Boykin, A. W., Franklin, A. J., and Yates, J. F. (Eds.): *Research Directions of Black Psychologists.* New York, Russell Sage Foundation, 1979.
34. Jones, S. E.: A comparative proxemic analysis of dyadic interaction in selected subcultures of New York City. *Journal of Social Psychology, 84:*35–44, 1971.
35. Jones, S., & Aiello, J.: Proxemic behavior of black and white first-, third-, and fifth-grade children. *Journal of Personality and Social Psychology, 25:*21–27, 1973.
36. Keil, C.: *Urban Blues.* Chicago, University of Chicago Press, 1966.
37. Kinder, D. R., & Reeder, L. G.: Ethnic differences in beliefs about control. *Sociometry, 38:*261–272, 1975.
38. Landis, D., McGrew, P., Day, H., Savage, J., & Saral, T.: Word meanings in black and white. In Triandis, H. C. (Ed.): *Variations in Black and White Perceptions of the Social Environment.* Urbana, University of Illinois Press, 1976.
39. Levine, L. W.: *Black Culture and Black Consciousness.* New York, Oxford University Press, 1977.
40. Liebman, M.: The effects of sex and race norms on personal space. *Environment and Behavior, 2:*208–246, 1970.
41. Loeb, M.: Social class and the American social system. *Social Work, 6:*12–25, 1961.
42. Luce, T. S.: The role of experience in interracial recognition. *Personality and Social Psychology Bulletin, 1:*39–41, 1974.
43. MacAdoo, H.: The ecology of internal and external support systems of black families. Paper presented at the Conference on Research Perspectives in the Ecology of Human Development, Cornell University, 1977.
44. McClain, E. W.: Personality characteristics of Negro college students in the South. *Journal of Negro Education, 36:*320–325, 1967.

45. McClelland, D. C.: *The Achieving Society,* New York, Van Nostrand, 1961.

46. Malpass, R. S., & Symond, J.: Value preferences associated with socioeconomic status, sex, and race. *Journal of Cross-Cultural Psychology, 5:*28–300, 1974.

47. Martin, E., & Martin, J. M.: *The Black Extended Family.* Chicago, University of Chicago Press, 1978.

48. Mason, L.: The characterization of American culture in studies of acculturation. *American Anthropologist, 57:*1264–1277, 1955.

49. Myrdal, G.: *An American Dilemma: The Negro Problem and Modern Democracy.* New York, Harper & Row, 1944.

50. Meier, A., & Rudwick, E.: *From Plantation to Ghetto.* New York, Hill & Wang, 1970.

51. Nobles, W. W.: African philosophy: Foundations for Black psychology. In Jones, R. (Ed.): *Black Psychology,* New York, Harper & Row, 1980.

52. Ogbu, J.: *Minority Education and Caste.* New York, Academic Press, 1978.

53. Pasteur, A. B., & Toldson, I. L.: *Roots of soul: the Psychology of Black Expressiveness.* Garden City, Anchor Press/Doubleday, 1982.

54. Perkins, E.: *Home is a Dirty Street: The Social Oppression of Black Children.* Chicago, Third World Press, 1975.

55. Quarles, B.: *The Negro in the Making of America.* New York, Collier Books, 1969.

56. Roll, W. V., Schmidt, L. D., & Kaul, T. J.: Perceived interviewer trustworthiness among black and white convicts. *Journal of Counseling Psychology, 19:*537–541, 1972.

57. Scherer, S.: Proxemic behavior of primary school children as a function of their socioeconomic status and subculture. *Journal of Personality and Social Psychology, 29:*800–805, 1974.

58. Schwartz, J.: Men's clothing and the Negro. *Phylon, 24:*224–231, 1963.

59. Scott, J. D., & Phelan, J. G.: Expectancies of unemployable males regarding source of control and reinforcement. *Psychological Reports, 25:*911–913, 1969.

60. Shade, B. J.: The social-psychological characteristics of achieving black children. *Negro Educational Review, 29:*80–86, 1978.

61. Sherif, C. W.: Social distance as categorization of intergroup interaction. *Journal of Personality and Social Psychology, 25:*327–334, 1973.

62. Stack, C.: *All Our Kin.* New York, Harper & Row, 1974.

63. Staples, R.: Black culture and personality. In Staples, R.: *Introduction to Black Sociology.* New York, McGraw-Hill, 1976.

64. Switkin, L., & Gynther, M.: Trust, activism and interpersonal perception in black and white college students. *Journal of Social Psychology, 94:*153–154, 1974.

65. Szalay, L., & Bryson, J. A.: Measurement of psychocultural distance: A comparison of American blacks and whites. *Journal of Personality and Social Psychology, 26:*166–177, 1973.

66. Taylor, J.: Dimensionalization of racialism and the black experience: The Pittsburg Project. In Jones, R. (Ed.): *Black Psychology.* New York, Harper & Row, 1980.

67. Terrell, F., & Barrett, R.: Interpersonal trust among college students as a

function of race, sex, and socioeconomic class. *Perceptual and Motor Skills,* *48:*1194, 1979.

68. Triandis, H. C. (Ed.): *Variations in Black and White Perceptions of the Social Environment.* Urbana, University of Illinois Press, 1976.

69. Walker, R.: *Society and Soul.* Unpublished doctoral dissertation, Stanford University, 1976.

70. White, J. L.: Toward a black psychology. In Jones, R.: *Black Psychology* (2nd edition). New York, Harper & Row, 1980.

71. Willie, Charles V.: The black family and social class. *American Journal of Orthopsychiatry, 44:*50–60, 1974.

72. Willis, F. N.: Initial speaking distance as a function of the speakers' relationship. *Psychoanalytic Science, 5:*221–222, 1966.

73. Willis, F., Carlson, R., & Reeves, D.: The development of personal space in primary school children. *Environmental Psychology and Nonverbal Behavior, 3:*195–205, 1979.

74. Witmer, J., & Ferinden, F.: Perception of school climate: Comparison of black and white teachers within the same schools. *Journal of the Student Personnel Association for Teacher Education, 9:*1–7, 1970.

75. Wright, W.: Relationships of trust and racial perceptions toward therapist-client conditions during counselling. *Journal of Negro Education, 44:*161–169, 1975.

76. Wubberhorst, J., Gradford, S., & Willis, F.: Trust in children as a function of race, sex, and socioeconomic group. *Psychological Reports, 29:*1181–1183, 1971.

77. Yarian, S.: *The Comic Book Hero: A Cultural Fantasy.* Unpublished doctoral dissertation, Adelphi University, 1974.

78. Zimmermann, B., & Brody, G.: Race and modeling of influences on the interplay patterns of boys. *Journal of Educational Psychology, 67:*591–598, 1975.

Chapter 3

AMERICAN INDIAN CULTURE: A DEVELOPMENTAL PROCESS

MAUREEN E. SMITH

There are over 400 American Indian tribes in the United States. Each of these tribes have their own distinctive culture. However, there are some similarities that teachers need to know and understand (Kasten, 1992). As Little Soldier (1992) noted, "there are certain core beliefs that transcend these tribal differences and that are shared by the majority of Native American people" (pg. 16).

The basic function of a society's value system is to provide its members with a shared purpose in life. This purpose is demonstrated in custom, ritual, and symbols. Culture provides a society with a shared world view that addresses the basic categories of understanding of common concepts. Pivotal elements in any culture, according to Attneave (1982) can be defined in five specific orientations: (a) relationship of humans to the environment; (b) time orientation; (c) interactions with people; (d) idealized state of being; and (e) the inherent nature of humankind. Using this frame of reference, the author compared the Native American traditional value preference with that of European-American middle class.

Relationship with Nature: In spite of tribal diversity, there appears to be a general metaphysical belief system which prevails throughout most of North America which serves as the basis for American Indian culture. This belief system is based upon the idea of living in harmony with nature and within the tribe. While most tribes have a strong sense of tribalism, there is a humble sense of the tribe in relation to the natural environment along with a concept of the importance of Mother Earth and the Creator. These beliefs in harmony, along with a humbled sense of self allow the American Indian society to function in an orderly and controlled manner (Bopp & Bopp, 1984).

American Indians try to live in harmony with nature while "mainstream" values stress the controlling and harnessing of the environment. As a part of this view, American Indians contend that the idealized state of being is simply to be—to exist in the here and now. This perception sets the stage for their time orientation.

Time Orientation: The time orientation for American Indian students is very different than mainstream culture. In mainstream culture, the future is of paramount importance with past being least important. Native cultures look first to the present, then to the past, and finally toward the future. Therefore, students often will not be very concerned about the future. In addition, there is the concept of "Indian time." When one attends an American Indian function such as a pow-wow, it is rare if it begins exactly when it is scheduled to start. Indian time lacks the exactness of mainstream societal standards. Thus, it is not uncommon for Native American students to be late for school or a meeting. This tardiness is often viewed as a sign of indifference or disrespect to the mainstream observer.

Inherent Nature of Mankind: Atteneave (1982) found that Native societies seem to view humankind as inherently good with evil as the last preferred value while mainstream culture seems to view humans as both good and evil, with good being the last preferred characteristic. In addition, there is also the belief that everything is interrelated—both animate and inanimate. As such change is ongoing and one can only understand change if one views the whole context. To illustrate this point, the symbol of a medicine wheel is often used to explain the critical relationships with which most humans live and interact. The medicine wheel has four points which represent different qualities of the human being. The first representation is the four cardinal directions and each direction symbolizes an important human quality. The four points on the wheel can also represent the four races of humanity—white, yellow, black and red—with each race being equal and necessary for the whole. The points also represent the four states of being, i.e., mineral, animal, vegetable, and human or the four states of being—physical, emotional, mental, and spiritual. Finally, the wheel is also perceived as reflection to the four domains of human learning: action, reflection, belief and vision. The important aspect of the wheel is that it represents the necessity for balance in all things. Thus, Native peoples learn that opposites exist, nothing is inherently good or bad, and that an individual should take things as they are (Bopp & Bopp, 1984).

Social Interaction Style: Native people place a high value on being polite to other people. For example, if an individual is offered something— gift or good, it is rude not to accept. Therefore, if offered something to eat, whether hungry or not, Native people will accept and eat it. It is also impolite to leave an individual to which one is talking to meet some schedule, so individuals remain until they are certain the conversation is over.

American Indian society considers the roles of kinship very important. However, the idea of an extended family and kinship is broadly defined. Rather than perceiving the relationship as only those who are part of the immediate family, the family consists of cousins, aunts, uncles, grandparents, siblings, in-laws, and even close friends. This again represents interrelatedness.

American Indian tribes have a rich oral tradition which facilitates the successful transmission of stories and necessary information. Because American Indians often regard time, space and motion differently than do non-Natives, their writings and oral presentations may seem to be disorganized, wandering or lack of goal direction. This is the result of the perception of time, the world and space as circular and reciprocal rather than linear. Getting to the point is not a particularly prized value in many Native American communities (Brown, 1982; Pipes, et al., 1993).

Traditionally, Native individuals who need to ask for something often do so in a very indirect and ambiguous manner. It is viewed as inappropriate behavior to come out and directly ask for something one desires. Part of the rationale for this approach is to save face—both of the one making the request as well as the one to whom the request is made. If the ambiguous request is ignored, neither party feels embarrassed for either asking or refusing the request. The result is that social harmony is preserved.

An important part of communication style of Native people is the tolerance for silence. In fact, silence is seen as a virtue as well as an expectation. Talking constantly is seen as odd and inappropriate. If one has nothing to say, one should be quiet. If a question appears to be sufficiently answered by another, generally there is a perception that there is little need for additional input.

Another aspect of communication and one which creates cultural confusion is in the area of eye contact. Native people perceive direct eye contact as inappropriate and a sign of disrespect. While it is true that eye contact is different, it is not absent. For many Native people, the amount and intensity of eye contact is much less than that used in mainstream culture. As Pipes and associates note, Native Americans do not demonstrate an absence of eye contact. Rather the culture reinforces a different schedule and patterning of making visual contact.

Because each person is interdependent with the tribe, group cooperation is paramount. Therefore, it is important that individuals avoid expressing disapproval. Instead they may engage in ridicule and ostracism. Overt hostilities among members of the tribe must be avoided at all costs. When they do occur, it is blamed on some outside supernatural force to preserve tribal unity.

Cultural Norms: The necessary values, mores and norms were taught to the young by extended family members or knowledgeable members of the tribe who functioned effectively in their prescribed roles through oral history, songs and legends. Because there is a shared community, a shared spirituality, a shared language, a common past and shared customs, all participants in the community understand the expectations and needs of the tribe (Szasz, 1983; Whiteman, 1986). These values provide the foundation of the socialization process of Native children within their culture. First, children are taught using a competency-based perspective to ensure that they discover ideas, acquire the elementary skills before proceeding to more complex ones, and through this process develop a sense of harmony and a sense of self. In addition, the education within the community is based upon real-life problems. Children are given utilitarian and pragmatic training which is experientially based (Whiteman, 1986).

Begishe (1992) describes the socialization process which leads to the development of Native American children within the Navajo tribe as an example of the enculturation of the children:

Stage 1. *One Becomes Aware (Hani Hazlii).* Between the ages of 2 and 4, the individual, no longer considered a baby, is aware of the current environment and begins to develop his/her own life story. One begins to remember.

Stage 2. *One Becomes Self-Aware (Adaa Akozhniidzii).* Between the ages of 4–6, a child is learning his/her gender role and begins to imitate the elders. Storytelling is an important mechanism for teaching the child about Mother Earth, the relationships with others and nature, and all living things.

Stage 3. *One Begins to Think and Do Things (Nitsidzikees Dzizlii).* Between the ages of 6–9, the child begins to practice the lessons learned from the elders. He/she learns to make sacrifices and begins to assume adult responsibilities in accordance with one's gender identity.

Stage 4. ***One's Thought Begins Existing (Hanitsekees Niliinii Hazlii).*** Between the ages of 10 and 15, the individual is expected to remember and demonstrate an accurate understanding of the stories about the correct way to live. It is the time for orientation and rite of passage to adulthood. During this period the individual is taught about the sacredness of land, home, and thought.

Stage 5. ***One Begins to Think for Oneself (Ada Nitzidzikees Dzizlii).*** The period between ages 15–18 represent the movement toward independence. Social and physical training is complete and the culture and values of the tribe should be fully understood and internalized.

Stage 6. ***One Begins to Think about All Things (Taa Attsoni Baanitsidzikees Dzizlii).*** In this stage, the individual is assumed to have mastered all life skills necessary for survival and should be ready for marriage.

These are the perspectives which come to school with American Indian children today. There is a sense of autonomy, a high regard for group cohesion, and a sense of self, time and space which needs to be recognized and incorporated into the current instructional process. Unless this is done, the success of Native children is undermined as they are not being taught within their traditional learning context.

REFERENCES

1. Attneave, C.: American Indians and Alaska Native families: Emigrants in their own land. In McGoldrick, M., Pearce, J. & Giordano, J. (Eds.): *Ethnicity and Family Therapy.* New York, Guilford Publications, Inc., 1982.

2. Begishe, K.: Nitsahakees Bee Haho'dilyaa (One's Development Through Thoughts). Rough Rock Demonstrate School Chart by Shirley Begay, 1982.

3. Bopp, M., & Bopp, J.: *Four Winds Development Project.* Lethbridge, Alberta, 1984.

4. Brown, J.: *The Spiritual Legacy of the American Indian.* New York, Crossroads, 1982.

5. Bryde, J.: *Modern Indian Psychology.* Vermillion, South Dakota, Institute of Indian Studies, 1971.

6. French, L.: *Psychocultural Change and the American Indian.* New York, Garland Publishing, Inc., 1987.

7. Kasten, W.: Bridging the horizon: American Indian beliefs and whole language learning. *Anthropology and Education Quarterly,* 23:100–119, 1992.

8. Little Soldier, L.: Working with Native American children. *Young Children,* 47:15–21, 1992.

9. Pipes, M., Westby, C., & Inglebret, E.: Profile of Native American Students. In

Clark, L. (Ed.) *Faculty and Student Challenges in Facing Cultural and Linguistic Diversity.* Springfield, Ill: Charles C Thomas Publisher, 1993.

10. Szasz, M.: *American Indian Education.* Norman, OK: University of Oklahoma Press, 1983.

11. Whiteman, H.: Historical review of Indian education: Cultural policies United States position. *Wicazo Sa Review,* 2:27–31, 1986.

Chapter 4

THE CULTURE AND STYLE OF MEXICAN-AMERICAN SOCIETY

Barbara J. Shade

One of the fastest growing ethnocultural groups in the United States is the Mexican-American population. According to census reports, individuals with Mexican backgrounds currently comprise 8 percent of the people in America, with the majority of them residing in California, Arizona, New Mexico, Colorado, Texas, and New York (Trueba, 1988).

Like African-American and Native American populations, the history of the group is one replete with discrimination, economic exploitation, and geographical containment (Weinberg, 1977). In addition, because of America's preoccupation with the melting pot theory, Mexican-Americans are exhorted to relinquish their values, language, and lifestyles and accept styles and processes which are not only alien to them but have not proven to be adequate replacements for what they are asked to ignore. As Vela (1980) points out, being a Mexican-American is equated with a deficit which has to be corrected.

Communities reinforce their perceptions of Mexican-American inferiority by placing the students with this ethnocultural and linguistic orientation in schools which are in poor, dilapidated neighborhoods and held in low esteem or regard by the district administration. Like the inner city schools within other urban areas, schools with a large percentage of Mexican-American children seem most often to be staffed by new or weak educators with inadequate materials and technology to assist in the code switching and adequate development of children who can communicate in both Spanish and English.

For those children who are in districts where fewer Mexican-American children reside, the designation of a disability is enhanced through placement of Mexican-American children in special schools or special classes for bilingual children. If Mexican-American children are in regular classes, they are often ignored by the teacher, given less opportunity for leadership and less opportunity to make the necessary transitions to

35

facilitate communication. Most recently, three states with a large linguistically different population passed an amendment which declared English as the official language, and citizens with a bilingual and bicultural orientation are facing punitive measures for using their native tongue. These and other incidents transmit a clear message that persons with linguistic and cultural variations cannot be tolerated.

What are the cultural variations which have been identified as incompatible with Eurocentric patterns?

MEXICAN-AMERICAN CULTURE

Culture, as previously indicated, represents the guidelines and rules groups develop to guide their interaction with the world. These guidelines emanate from a set of shared historical experiences and which finally coalesce into a set of shared values and concepts. The basic components of Mexican-American culture are: an agrarian background which has been coupled with a strong commitment to Catholicism, and the development of many family structures which are based on clear and rather rigid sex role differentiation rules (Ramirez & Castaneda, 1974; Weinberg, 1980). These experiences appear to have generated some rather common values such as:

1. Individuals should identify very closely with their community, family, and ethnic group.

2. Individuals should be very sensitive to the feelings of others.

3. Status and role definitions within the community and family are clearly delineated and should be respected.

4. Achievement or success is highly dependent upon the cooperative efforts of individuals rather than competitive individualism (Rameriz & Casteneda, 1974).

These values, of course, influence personality development and the *Weltanschauung* through which individuals socialized within this culture perceive ideas, concepts, people, and events. In studies cited by Martinez (1977), the modal personality traits most often manifested by individuals of Mexican-American heritage seem to be a tendency toward orderliness, less aggressive interaction, active internal control, and the need to have close interpersonal relationships. To this must be added an association of the male within the family with the traits and dimensions of power while women are most closely associated with the concept of love and belonging as well as religiosity. Rameriz and Castenada (1974) combined these dimensions and labeled the cultural preferences as **field sensitivity** which was a way of indicating that Mexican-Americans are field-dependent in their perceptual processing and very social in their interactional style. Many scholars objected to this type of labeling and studies which followed consistently asked the question as to whether or not Mexican-Americans were field-dependent based upon one test without examining the issue of their behavior and interactional style. For the purposes of this chapter, we will separate the concepts of perception and social behavior.

Field-Dependence

In the studies of African-Americans, a definite pattern has been established which suggests that individuals within this cultural group tend to perceive lines, drawings, other spatial visualization tasks from a field-dependent perspective. The measures used to discern this are generally types of tasks which require the use of visual information processing. When these same tasks are given to individuals within the Native American population, the results indicate that this group tends toward field-independence. This suggests that Native American culture emphasizes the perception or use of visual information in a different way than used with the African-American society. This type of finding cannot be established for the Mexican-American population as the measures used in the studies of perception were kinesthetic processing tasks. Rameriz and Castenada (1974), Buriel (1975), Kagan and Zahn (1975), and Figueroa (1980) all used the Rod-and-Frame Test which is a measure requiring differentiation of the body from the environment rather than visual perception. Based upon these studies, Mexican-American individuals do appear to be field-dependent when assessing their physical or social relationship to the environment, but this may not be true in the examination of the visual perception which is the primary modality used in the school and testing situation.

Social Interaction

The enhancement of and relationship to the group is an important cultural value which seems to generate the need for students and individuals from the Mexican-American community to be involved in collective or cooperative efforts rather than individualized efforts. It is a value which surfaces in classroom interaction. Teachers of Mexican-American children report that Mexican-American children attempt to work together on tasks. This behavior results in teacher complaints that they are copying from their neighbor and are, thus, dishonest and slothful. Delgado-Gaitan and Trueba (1985), however, interpret this propensity to copy and work together as an effort on the part of Mexican children to collectivize their learning experience and maximize their intellectual exchange and knowledge acquisition. This, according to these authors, is consistent with their socialized value system. Sierra (1973) comments further on the importance of interpersonal relationships and cooperative efforts as well as the fact that Mexican-American children prefer to work with some classroom authority rather than working alone. These preferences, of course, differ significantly from the competitive, individualistic classrooms usually promoted.

Bilingualism

Kagan and Zahn (1975) suggests that the culture of Mexican-Americans cannot be clearly understood without considering the accompanying language orientation. The Spanish spoken by the Mexican-American community is the vehicle used in socialization and contains the content of learning. It is through the use of this language that Mexican-American children construct their perceptions of social reality and ultimately manipulate and handle abstract concepts and processes which they encounter. If Vygotsky (1962) is correct, the language used by individuals is representational of their thought processes—a concept with important implications for Mexican-Americans.

When you acquire a new language, as many people do when they take foreign language instruction and as is being asked of Mexican-American and other linguistically diverse children in American schools, the thought processes and social reality must take on different dimensions. As Valdman (1966) points out, learning a different language means incorporating a different culture, a different perspective of the world, particularly the sociocultural system, and, in general, a different cognitive style to handle and adequate processing of information in that language.

Mexican-American children are under a great deal of pressure to relinquish their language and the information processing style which accompanies it. For many children this creates severe culture conflict, particularly when viewed from their value of group unity, group cooperation, and group involvement. The request is akin to asking individuals to ignore and destroy portions of their self identity and more importantly, to renounce or abandon segments of their family and community to which they have a great attachment. The alternative is, of course, to become not only bilingual, but also bicultural in orientation and style (Rameriz & Castenada, 1974).

How the Mexican-American community and its children address the issue of bilingualism is a major sociocultural decision which can be made only by members of their community. For the most part, the majority of the community continues to advocate and transmit the importance of the use of Spanish. This is the language most often used in homes, family gatherings, neighborhoods, and churches as lower socioeconomic individuals are more likely to be economically and socially isolated within their own community and this seems to promote the maintenance of Spanish and the inadequate mastery of English. Although English is perceived as the language of social mobility, even the well educated and upwardly mobile individuals make efforts to maintain Spanish as a matter of ethnic pride and cultural continuity and identity (Penalosa, 1980).

The cultural conflict which results from variation on these three dimensions is an underlying dilemma for Mexican-American and other linguistically diverse students as they enter the school setting. How they respond to it individually often determines their academic success. The inability of the school to accommodate these differences may be one of the major factors which exacerbates the academic and social failure of a large portion of the Mexican-American population.

REFERENCES

1. Buriel, R.: Cognitive styles among three generations of Mexican Americans. *Journal of Cross Cultural Psychology,* 6:417–429, 1975.
2. Delgado-Gaitan, C., & Trueba, H. T.: Ethnographic study of participant structures in task completion: Reinterpretation of "handicaps" in Mexican Children. *Learning Disabilities Quarterly,* 8:67–75, 1985.
3. Figueroa, R. A.: Field dependence, ethnicity, and cognitive styles. *Hispanic Journal of Behavioral Sciences,* 2:35–42, 1980.
4. Kagan, S., & Zahn, L.: Field dependence and school achievement gap between Anglo-American and Mexican American children. *Journal of Educational Psychology,* 67:643–650, 1975.
5. Martinez, J. L.: *Chicano Psychology.* New York, Academic Press, 1977.
6. Penalosa, F.: *Chicano Sociolinguistics.* Rowley, Newbury House Publishers, 1980.
7. Ramirez, M., & Castaneda, A.: *Cultural Democracy, Bicognitive Development and Education.* New York, Academic Press, 1974.
8. Sierra, V.: Learning style of the Mexican American. In Bransford, L. A., Baca,

L., & Lane, K.: *Cultural Diversity and the Exceptional Child.* Reston, Council for Exceptional Children, 1973.

9. Trueba, H.: English literacy acquisition: From cultural trauma to learning disabilities in minority students. *Linguistics and Education, 1:*125–152, 1988.

10. Valdman, A.: *Trends in Language Teaching.* New York, McGraw-Hill, 1966.

11. Vela, J. E.: Assimilation and the Chicano. *Lifelong Learning, June:* 10–12, 1980.

12. Vygotsky, L. S.: *Thought and Language.* Cambridge, MIT Press, 1962.

13. Weinberg, M.: *A Chance to Learn.* Cambridge, Cambridge University Press, 1977.

Chapter 5

ASIAN-AMERICAN CHILDREN: A DIVERSE POPULATION*

VALERIE OOKA PANG

To many teachers, Asian-American students seem to look and be alike—they are model minority students. Like many other stereotypes, this perception is easier believed than carefully examined. In fact, most Asian-American students are neither "super brains" nor "gang members." They do represent many cognitive strengths and weaknesses, have diverse ethnic roots, live in many parts of the United States, and range from being newly immigrated to having roots over 200 years old (Cordova, 1983). Without basic knowledge of the diversity of the particular population, schools cannot provide an equal chance for all to develop their intellect and skills (Kitano, 1983).

Asian-Americans encompass a number of highly diverse groups, including those of the Cambodian, Chinese, East Indian, Filipino, Guamanian, Hawaiian, Hmong, Indonesian, Japanese, Korean, Laotian, Samoan, and Vietnamese heritages. In toto, Asian-Americans make up the fastest growing minority group in the United States. From 1970 to 1980, the Asian population increased by approximately 143 percent. *(Editor's note: The U. S. Census Bureau projects that by 2050, the Asian population will be 8.2%.)*

Before getting into the general discussion of Asian-American population, a word must be said about the label, "Oriental." Though this term is often used in education to identify students with Asian roots, its use in reference to U. S. Citizens and residents ignores the negative connotations of an outgroup status, of foreigners, and perhaps even of "yellow peril." Asian-Americans have resided in the United States for over 200 years, some being able to trace their roots back over ten generations. Also, soldiers from the Filipino-American community fought in the War of 1812 (Cordova, 1983). It is more appropriate to call individuals within

---

*Excerpted from Pang, Valerie Ooka. Asian-American Children: A Diverse Population. *The Educational Forum*, 55:49–66, 1990. Reprinted with permission of Kappa Delta Pi. All rights reserved.

this population "Asian-American" or, more inclusively, "Asian and Pacific Islander-American."

Factors Contributing to Diversity

Asian-American students, native or immigrant. An important variable when dealing with Asian-American population is place of birth, American-born or immigrant. The experiences of the two groups may differ greatly, and so does the manner in which they identify themselves. Though it is dangerous to overgeneralize across individuals within a group, American-born students are likely to be more assimilated into the mainstream, especially those who do not reside in ethnic communities (Sue, Sue & Sue, 1983; Cabezas, 1981). For example, many Japanese-American students who live in middle-class suburban neighborhoods may not choose to identify themselves along ethnic lines (Kitano, 1976). Matute-Bianchi (1986) found such high school students from central California identify themselves through their school activities like student government and social clubs, rather than through ancestry. They did not want to engage in school activities that were ethnically tied. For example, though attempts had been made at one school to establish a club focusing on Japanese history, no student of Japanese descent joined the group.

However, many American-born, limited English proficient students may readily identify themselves through ethnic lines, and even boast, "I can be President of the United States." These children may come to school unable to speak English because they have spoken their ancestral languages all their lives. Kindergarten could be the very first setting requiring them to use English. On the other hand, many American-born students speak only English. They can be categorized as being bicultural and they may look positively at ethnic membership and life in an environment that mixes both mainstream and traditional Asian values (Sue, Sue & Sue, 1971). These children may be family-oriented, respect elders, and value education, while at the same time participate in mainstream after-school activities like football or ballet. They may not choose to take part in Asian-American activities at school, but can be members of a local Buddhist temple, participating in ethnically specific activities in that context (Matute-Bianchi, 1996).

Like their American-born counterparts, immigrant students clearly demonstrate a wide range of approaches to their background. There are highly assimilated ones who feel compelled to blend into American society and so relinquish ancestral cultural values, behaviors, and traditions. They may, for example, refuse to speak their first language and view their ethnic ties as obstacles to being accepted into the mainstream. In contrast, there are those who are extremely proud of their background. The parents of these children speak their ancestral language at home and the children may attend a special Saturday or after-school language school built to ensure that the values, beliefs and language of the originating culture remain in the community (Guthrie, 1980).

Possible Intragroup Conflicts. Many Asian-Americans have found themselves with increasing feelings of marginality. Marginality refers to conflicting attitudes that may develop when a member of a minority group finds himself or herself at cultural odds with the dominant society. As a result the person can develop personality traits of insecurity, hypersensitivity, and excessive self-consciousness. Within the Asian-American population itself, those students whose families have old roots within the United States may not feel comfortable with new immigrant students. They may fear being identified with the immigrants who, they feel, are old fashioned, "nerds," or "weird" in dress and behavior. When new immigrants are being harassed by other students, the better established ones may feel the pressure to "join in" so as not to be perceived as being associated with the newcomers. Or they may ignore the harassment without trying to discourage the taunting.

The second source of intragroup conflict may lie in the past, "old country" animosities. Many new immigrant students find themselves placed in classes with others from groups that, historically, have been fierce enemies. Antagonism has cropped up in some schools involving Asian-American students battling each other. In one instance, a teacher who had Vietnamese-American and Cambodian-American students learned about these animosities in a peer teaching situation. The Vietnamese-American student had lived in the United States for about seven years and spoke English well. The Cambodian-American student had been in the United States for only three years and was having some difficulties understanding the material. The teacher mistakenly assumed that they would be happy to work with each other since they had similar refugee experiences. He asked the Vietnamese youth to help the Cambodian. Since such students generally have a high regard to teachers, they were rather reluctant to speak out, but the Vietnamese student explained diplomatically that he did not think the other student would accept his help. This greatly surprised the teacher, but the prediction of the student was confirmed when the Cambodian student said, "I do not want to accept help from a Vietnamese." These feelings were worked through, but even then it was difficult for the students who had been in adversarial roles to view the situation in a new light.

Of course, immigrant and American-born youth may not generally form close friendships with each other. There can exist a mutual feeling of mistrust, reflecting a lack of understanding of each other's values and beliefs. Sometimes language barriers contribute to the distance. Those born in the U. S. who do not speak an ancestral language may feel unable to communicate with immigrants who are speaking a first language other than English. And, on their part, immigrant youngsters may not understand English sufficiently well to feel comfortable participating in peer group conversations.

Socialization of Children

Parental attitudes and child rearing practices definitely impact the development of children. Though quite a few studies have examined general tendencies of Asian-Americans as one group, only two large projects could be located that compared varying practices within that large group. One study, conducted by Cabezas (1981), examined the early childhood development of 233 Asian-American families (Chinese, Japanese, Korean, & Vietnamese) from the San Francisco-Oakland metropolitan area, focusing upon parent values, child rearing, and interactional styles. He found, in Asian-American mothers born both here and overseas, a predominance of question-asking behavior in comparison to modeling, cueing, or direct commands, even though American-born ones showed a higher incidence than those born elsewhere. Chinese and Filipino mothers born overseas used more direct commands and were more authoritarian in their beliefs than the other mothers. In those families where mothers asked more questions, the children also responded with more questions and sought more verbal approval from their mothers. The results of this study seem to be in conflict with the belief that Asian-American students do not have the verbal skills to involve themselves in an interactive school setting. An Asian-American child's failure to participate may reflect a lack of encouragement to engage in interaction rather than lack of ability. If these children are not being consistently included in class discussions, they may feel reticent about participating because of strong respect for authority. If they go into the school with strong verbal interaction skills, but these skills are not being developed in classrooms, they could become less apt to participate as they progress through the educational system.

The second study was by Rumbaut and Ima (1988) who examined parent-child relationships of the Southeast Asian-American refugee community in the San Diego City Schools. Extensive data were collected on 579 youth, while general comparative information was collected on 1485 junior and senior high school students. Lao and Khmer parents were found to stress academic discipline and pressure youth to achieve less than Vietnamese, Chinese-Vietnamese, and Hmong parents. In addition, there was a less sense of obligation toward elders and parents in Lao and Khmer communities. Vietnamese, Chinese-Vietnamese, and Hmong parents had stronger parental controls and domination over their children and they emphasized the importance of collective survival. In contrast, the Lao and Khmer, rural in origin and less educated, seemed to value a more individualistic adjustment to American life (e.g., in moving out as quickly as possible from shared living arrangements). Yet their communities also had a fatalistic point of view toward life, which seemed to manifest itself in the lack of an aggressively competitive attitude toward academic success. The Lao of the upper-class background are more likely to have migrated to France, and many of the Khmer elite were killed in Kampuchea. Therefore, many of the refugees who settled in the United States have had fewer resources and hold values that do not advance a strong desire for "success."

The Vietnamese-American community, in particular, seemed to have more strict control over their children than Khmer and Lao parents, regardless of social class. Vietnamese-American students are more likely to feel familial obligation and to be competitive in school. In elite Vietnamese families, a complex bicultural manner of resolving conflicts with children was found—though the word of parents was highly respected, children were permitted in some instances to explain, in a polite tone, their perspective in the conflict situation. Parents wanted children to feel that they had some control over their own existence. Meanwhile people in the Hmong community, whose agrarian roots did not include high levels of education, have adapted nicely to the American school system [behaviorally]. The discipline parents have instilled in the children coupled with a strong respect for authority seems to result in high levels of motivation. These students demonstrate great tenacity and discipline in their school work. Unfortunately, though many Hmong students do well in high school, very few continue studies on the college level. There is a great deal of pressure to have a family and many Hmong youth marry young.

Sociopsychological and Academic Needs

To many school personnel, Asian-American students appear to have fewer and less severe personal problems than other students. Though teachers are often aware of the academic problems of those from Southeast Asia, the needs of other students may not be readily apparent. It is easy for teachers to spot problems of language proficiency, but it is much more difficult to identify internal conflicts in students.

Needless to say, Asian-American students must deal with the stresses of racism and the existence of conflicting cultural messages communicated by frequently portrayed images of Asian-Americans. One of those images is the "model minority" classification, which can be accompanied by the belief that they are the students who raise the grading curve. They are usually not the football starts or cheerleaders and they may be perceived as "nerds." Students who do well must cope with this social image and it is not always an asset to stand out academically, to be considered "eggheads." Yet, they oftentimes come from families in which education is highly valued. Parents will sacrifice material comfort in order to provide the best educational experience for their children (Mordkowitz & Ginsburg, 1986). Some parents expect not only "good" grades but also "exceptionally high" grades from their offspring. Thus, students who feel pressure from their families must deal with possible rejection from their peers.

On the other hand, there are Asian-American children who are not intellectually gifted and cannot reach the high academic standards which parents or teachers have set for them. These students have a difficult time dealing with negative feelings of being a "loser." One *sansei* (third generation Japanese-American) high school student said about himself, "My folks just gave up on me because I didn't get into college." Unfortunately, this message was also reiterated by his teacher who told the student, "Your sister was an A student—how come you only get C's? You're not trying." The model minority image can be a terrible liability for those students who are not academically inclined, especially when teachers assume that children from certain Asian-American groups will be top achievers. These students are trying to deal with the powerful process of assimilation and mixed messages regarding their acceptance into mainstream society can be a heavy burden for them to carry.

The impact of being a member of a visibly different minority group can also have a forceful effect on the fragile and developing self-image of children. The findings of a study examining the self-concept of Asian-American youth show a disturbing pattern of generally lower levels of self-esteem than Caucasian and black American youngsters (Tidwell, 1980). Another study reported Vietnamese-American students to score lowest on overall self-concept in comparison to non-Vietnamese-Asian, Caucasian, black American and Mexican-American students (Oanh & Michael, 1977). Similarly, Korean-American and Chinese-American students may not feel as positive about their physical self-image as black or white American students (Chang, 1975; Fox & Jordan, 1973). In yet another study of the general self-concept of Japanese-American students in the fourth through sixth grades, lower physical self-concept scores were seen offset by high academic self-image scores to make the general scores less than revealing (Pang, Mizokawa, Morishima & Olstad, 1985). These findings may be surprising to many teachers who believe Asian-American students are well-adjusted, competent students. Such studies point to the need for schools to take steps to help Asian-American students develop more positive perceptions of themselves.

Impact of Prejudice and Ethnic Bias. The impact of ethnic prejudice as an influential factor on the socio-psychological development of Asian-American children must also be addressed. There are enough reports of the frustrations Asian-American students have in dealing with prejudicial attitudes and remarks. For instance, Kim (1978) found 30 percent of the Korean-American children she studied reporting discrimination at school in the form of harassment or name-calling. Such incidents involved not only other students but also some school personnel. She recounted an incident in which a five-year-old boy said, "They [his classmates] call me Chinese!" Apparently, this child was disturbed by his Korean-American identity and angry about his bicultural existence. Similar concerns were expressed by Japanese-American high school students in central California. They were upset because of the perceived image their peers had of Japanese-Americans. As one ninth grader said: "They [the school community] think we are all smart and quiet. We're not but they think we are." Another student indicated that Japanese-American "students have a reputation for being really good in science and math." And another student said he was not particularly "good" in math but "the teacher expected me to do good in it."

To understand the experiences of Southeast Asian-American students in the San Diego City Schools in California, the district surveyed 521 junior high students and found strong resentment against Southeast Asian-Americans. Approximately 30 percent of the nonrefugee students made disturbing remarks such as: "Get rid of the Cambodians."

"I think the blacks and whites get along great but it's the Vietnamese we can't stand."

"Move some Nips to other schools" (Rumbaut & Ima, pg. 59, 1988). Vietnamese-American students were greatly offended by derogatory remarks which abusers considered to be casual statements. In addition, some Southeast Asian-American youth felt that some teachers were biased against them, making negative statements about Vietnam or giving them unfair punishment.

These biases found in school experiences can greatly affect the emerging bicultural identity of Asian-American youth. The teaching staff must begin to understand the choices and dilemmas such students face in the cultural assimilation process and assist them in developing the personal confidence and coping skills to deal with ethnic prejudice that they may encounter. Students may withdraw from the school community or fight back, verbally or physically if they feel powerless to deal with prejudicial situations.

SUMMARY

The inaccurate model minority myth and belief in the homogeneity of the Asian-American often deters the development of programs that fully address their varied needs. New perspectives on these children should be adopted by school personnel.

One area of concern in self-concept of which a global view may not be sufficient to clarify their feelings of specific inadequacies. Asian-American children may also suffer from test anxiety and pressures for high academic achievement. Some appear to be highly influenced by a desire to please their parents, an impetus potentially stronger than direct parental pressure. Additionally, teachers may be unconsciously contributing to the heightened anxiety in students by assuming most Asian-American students to be high achievers. Another important concern is the inability of many school staff to recognize feelings of depression, frustration, and desperation in these students.

There is also the need for schools to institute educational programs to help Asian-American children become confident in communication skills, both oral and written. Because these students often exhibit competencies in technical and scientific fields, school personnel may overlook their lower grades in English, creative writing, or composition. There are some Asian groups whose children are dropping out of school at a very high rate, and the effects can be devastating on the economic and political survival of their communities.

There are high numbers of "at-risk" students in certain groups which calls for a balanced view of Asian-American students and their families. Like any other group, they have strengths and needs. We are still saddled with an educational system that has difficulty dealing with children who come to school with varying values, languages, and motivational backgrounds. Understanding the great diversity within the group is crucial, otherwise, their needs may continue to be overlooked. Asian-American students cannot have equal educational opportunity when their educational experience is shaped by inaccurate information and naive beliefs.

REFERENCES

1. Cabezas, A.: *Early Childhood Development in Asian and Pacific American Families: Families in Transition.* San Francisco, Asian, Inc. 1981.
2. Cordova, F.: *Filipinos: Forgotten Asian-Americans.* Dubuque, Iowa, Kendall/Hunt Publishing Co., 1983.
3. Fox, D., & Jordan, V.: Racial preference and identification of American Chinese. Black and White children. *Genetic Psychology Monographs,* 88:220–286, 1973.
4. Guthrie, G.: *A School Divided.* Hillsdale, N.J.: Lawrence Erlbaum Associates, 1985.
5. Kim, B.: *The Asian-Americans: Changing Patterns, Changing Needs.* Montclair, N.J., Association of Korean Christian Scholars in North America, 1978.
6. Kitano, H.: *Japanese Americans: The Evolution of a Subculture.* New Jersey, Prentice-Hall, 1976.
7. Kitano, M.: Early education for Asian-American Children. In Saracho, O., & Spodek, B.: *Understanding the Multicultural Experience in Early Childhood Education.* Washington, D. C., National Association for the Education of Young Children, 1983.
8. Matute-Bianchi, M.: Ethnic identities and patterns of school success and failure among Mexican-descent and Japanese-American students in a California high school: An ethnographic analysis. *American Journal of Education,* 94: 233–255, 1986.

9. Oanh, N. T., & Michael, W. B.: The predictive validity of each of ten measures of self-concept relative to teacher's ratings of achievement in mathematics and reading of Vietnamese children and of those from five other ethnic groups. *Educational and Psychological Measurement* 37:1005–1016, 1977.
10. Pang, V., Mizokawa, D., Morishima, J., & Olstad, R.: Self-concepts of Japanese-American children. *Journal of Cross-Cultural Psychology,* 16:99–109, 1985.
11. Rumbaut, R., & Ima, K.: The adaptation of Southeast Asian refugee youth: A comparative study. A report prepared for the U. S. Department of Health and Human Services, Office of Refugee Resettlement, Washington, D. C., 1988.
12. Sue, D., Sue, D., & Sue, D.: Psychological development of Chinese-American children. In Powell, G. (Ed.) *Psychological Development of Minority Group Children.* New York, Brunner/Mazel Publishers, 1983.
13. Tidwell, R.: Gifted students' self-images as a function of identification process, race, and sex. *Journal of Pediatric Psychology,* 5:57–69, 1980.

Chapter 6

ACCULTURATION ISSUES FOR AT-RISK SOUTHEAST ASIAN–AMERICAN STUDENTS*

MAI DAO

Despite the general image of Asian students as the "model minority," there exists students who are educationally at risk. Students described as "educationally at risk" are those students who are in danger of dropping out of school or leaving school without adequate skill levels (Slavin, Karweit, & Madden, 1989). Factors associated with being at risk include poverty, underachievement, poor attendance, peer pressure, drug and alcohol abuse, behavior problems, low socioeconomic status and the effects of traumatic exodus.

There is a growing, diverse group of Southeast Asian-American students who are at risk of dropping out of school due to the previously mentioned factors. There has been a certain amount of well-publicized achievement by students from Chinese, Korean, Japanese, and Vietnamese backgrounds; however, children from minority families who have limited English proficiency and are impoverished have historically done poorly in school. Such children are not only more likely to perform poorly in academic areas, they are also more likely to complete fewer years of education and drop out of school. Without changes in public intervention approaches, these trends are very likely to continue. Recent research suggests that the factors that cause children to be educationally at risk are rapidly increasing (Catterall & Cota-Robles, 1988; Kirst, 1989); the number of limited-English speaking children has increased [and] the number of minority children from families living in poverty increased. Specifically, in regard to Southeast Asian refugee families, reports indicate that they are not just at the nation's poverty threshold, they are significantly below it (Rumbaut, 1987). Among the Mien and Hmong

---

*Previously published under the title, Designing assessment procedures for educationally at-risk Southeast Asian-American students by Mai Dao, *Journal of Learning Disabilities*, 24:594–601. Copyright 1991 by PRO–ED, INC. Reprinted by permission.

refugees, for example the unemployment rate is 90 percent (Takaki, 1989).

ACCULTURATION ISSUES

The majority of Southeast Asian-American students come from refugee backgrounds. The critical difference between immigrants and refugees is that immigrants come to America voluntarily; refugees are forced to flee for their lives. Immigrants choose, and thereby are psychologically prepared, to migrate to a new land, whereas refugees are abruptly uprooted. Immigrants have passed the stage where survival is an immediate concern; refugees have to face survival problems: language handicaps and barriers of poverty, prejudice, minority status, and pervasive uncertainty (Rumbaut, 1985). In addition, they have to struggle with the process of coming to terms with the loss of country, home, family, friends, social status, material possessions, and other meaningful aspects of life. This can cause severe psychological distress even under the best of circumstances (Rumbaut, 1985).

Another distinction to be made is between urban and rural backgrounds. Generally, people from urban areas have been exposed to and are more or less accustomed to the cultures and languages of the industrialized Western societies. They can, therefore, adjust more easily to Western ways. On the other hand, rural people come from highly traditional agricultural societies. Except for bombs, guns, and planes, many of them (such as the Hmong and other tribal people) have previously had little contact with cultures of the industrialized West. Therefore their transition to mainstream America can be a traumatic experience and involve a long and difficult adjustment process.

The adjustment concerns of previous Anglo-European immigrant and refugee groups were confined merely to variations within Western cultures. The adjustment process for the Southeast Asian-American groups, however, is much more difficult, because there is a great difference between Eastern and Western cultures. A poem by Tran (1987) reflects the underlying philosophical differences between East and West and serves to illustrate the continuum of the adjustment process of many Southeast Asian people in America.

Along this continuum, there are those who are capable of adapting

East	West
We live in time.	You live in space.
We are always at peace.	You are always on the move.
We are passive.	You are aggressive.
We like to contemplate.	You like to act.
We accept the world as it is.	You try to change it according to your blueprint.
We live in peace with nature.	You try to impose your will on her.
Religion is our first love.	Science is your passion.
We delight in thinking about the meaning of life.	You delight in physics.
We believe in freedom of silence.	You believe in freedom of speech.
We lapse into meditation.	You strive for articulation.
We marry first, then we love.	You love first, then marry.
Our marriage is the beginning of a love affair.	Your marriage is the happy end of a romance.
It is our indissoluble bond.	It is a contract.
Our love is mute.	Your love is vocal.
We try to conceal it from the world.	You delight in showing it to others.
Self-abnegation is the secret to our survival.	Self-assertiveness is the key to your success.
We are taught from the cradle to want less and less.	You are urged everyday to want more and more.
We glorify austerity.	You emphasize gracious living and enjoyment.
Poverty is to us a badge of spiritual elevation.	It is to you a sign of degradation.
In the sunset years of life, we renounce the world and prepare for the hereafter.	You retire to enjoy the fruit of your labor.

— Tran, 1987.

Figure 6-1. EAST–WEST CULTURAL DIFFERENCES

quickly and easily, those who can adapt to a limited extent, and those who cannot adapt. Refugees who cannot adapt easily may become confused and depressed, thereby affecting the young ones around them. For example, maternal depression level has been correlated with the low achievement of some southeast Asian refugee students (Rumbaut & Ima, 1987).

Refugee parents, particularly those from rural areas, may also be culturally and linguistically unprepared to provide academic assistance to their children, because the American school system is different from the traditional Southeast Asian educational system. They may have attitudes and values toward schooling that are at variance with those of the American school (Te, Chhim, & Laungpraseut, 1989).

Families newly arrived in the United States face adjustment problems that affect their emotional, physical, and financial status, even if they have been exposed to Western industrial societies. Overwhelmed by these stressors, parents are left with few resources with which to nurture their children. However, cultural and linguistic differences do not automatically result in, or necessarily cause, educational risks among Southeast Asian-American students. One must observe and be sensitive to signs of maladjustment in the families that could affect the child.

CONDITIONS OF EDUCATIONAL RISK AMONG SOUTHEAST ASIAN-AMERICAN STUDENTS

Lack of Educational Experiences:

One group of at-risk Southeast Asian-American students are those who lack educational experiences. Unlike established immigrant populations in California who have achieved English language proficiency and performed well and consequently have attained economic and financial security, new waves of refugees come from educationally disadvantaged and/or impoverished conditions in their war-torn lands. Many refugee children come from rural villages or have grown up in jungles or in refugee camps. These children have had limited experience with schooling.

In 1986, less than half of the southeast Asians entering the United States had levels of education equivalent to elementary school (Chinn & Plata, 1986). War prevented children in Cambodia and Laos from receiving any education. Rural schools are virtually nonexistent in Laos and only one fourth of the Laotian population can be considered literate. The Hmong appear to have the lowest level of education of all southeast Asian-Americans: 41 percent of the population has no formal education and another 40 percent has educational levels equivalent to elementary school. At the other extreme, Vietnamese-Americans have the highest level of education—28 percent of the population having at least two years of postsecondary education.

The Illiterate Adolescent:

Another refugee issue involves the adolescent student who is illiterate in his or her own native language. This student may be a Cambodian child who grew up in the jungle before escaping to Thailand, or a Vietnamese child who grew up in refugee camps. Such a child may begin school at high school age and yet lack what for a kindergartner would be considered reading skills (e.g., knowing how to hold a pencil). This student needs to learn the rudimentary aspects of American daily life and school life before he or she can acquire basic learning skills and benefit from English as a second language instruction.

Traumatizing Experiences:

Another group of at-risk students are traumatized children. For example, many refugee children from Cambodia have witnessed the beating to death of their father or other loved ones. Some have lived near fields of cadavers. Others have witnessed the death of their siblings at sea.

In the classroom, these refugee children may be withdrawn for 1 to 2 years; or they may exhibit disruptive behaviors that are extremely hard for school staff to understand. Instead of interpreting the child's behaviors or problems based on the idea of social maladjustment in the usual American context (e.g., problems of growing, reality testing, school entrance or puberty) (Bower, 1969), the [educator] must realize that the behaviors of these children are responses to trauma resulting from extraordinary circumstances.

Many of the traumatized refugee children need appropriate interventions to help them overcome their emotional difficulties before they can benefit from instruction. This is an important issue for educators to consider who now are more and more concerned with "Why aren't they learning English?" (Dao, 1990).

Related to this point is the critical need to involve trained bilingual and bicultural personnel in the assessment process. For example, an 11-year-old child who had witnessed the rape and killing of his mother by Thai pirates was referred for not making progress in school; he was perceived by regular staff as withdrawn, noncooperative, and at times defiant (Dao, 1988). The regular school staff had no idea what kind of suffering the child had been suppressing. It was with the assistance of a sensitive, trained resource teacher from the same cultural and linguistic background that the child opened up and demonstrated the need for an opportunity to grieve. Subsequently, this child's behavior changed. Given insight into the nature of the problem, school personnel were then able to identify appropriate ways to help him participate and learn.

Refugee children's traumatizing experiences have undoubtedly left emotional scars of various degrees of severity. As a result, these children are not emotionally ready to benefit from instruction. [Educators] must identify this barrier to academic progress that has to be removed and dealt with in order to be effective in helping the child learn.

Lack of Natural Family Support:

"Unaccompanied minors" are another source of concern. Because of the high cost of clandestine escape out of the Southeast Asian countries, families often pool all their resources in order to send their children out of the country alone, hoping they will have a better education and future in some free country of asylum. In many cases, these children are sent to Anglo-American foster homes; the children's adjustment problems and the foster parents' limited knowledge of Southeast Asian cultures often result in conflict that leads to very difficult situations (Mortland & Egan,

1987). In other cases, unaccompanied minors live with relatives who are barely out of adolescence themselves and ill-equipped to provide a stable home. Consequently, these children are now growing up with little adult supervision and without the guidance and support of their natural families. Moreover, the problems associated with growing up, unlike those of normal children, are compounded by problems related to their sense of guilt and their self-imposed obligation to support the "ones left behind," as well as the pressure to succeed in school. "Such youths often experience intense feelings of loneliness, homesickness, and a longing for parental nurturance. They are vulnerable to feelings of confusion, shame, and generalized despair" (Nidorf, 1985, p. 413). They are believed to be at significantly higher risk for suicide than their peers because of their lack of a well-defined family structure to provide guidance. They are also at risk for gang activity because the gang offers them a sense of belonging. Identifying these minors and providing guidance to ensure their academic success is critical.

Health Problems:

Another type of risk effects a significant number of refugee children who have suffered conditions such as malnutrition, unsanitary conditions, disease, physical injuries, and lack of medical care. For example, prenatal malnutrition or the effects of drugs in infancy (given during clandestine escape in order to keep the infant from crying) need to be detected because these factors have demonstrated correlations with behavioral and learning problems (Wei, 1986).

Miseducation in the United States:

Another increasingly serious problem is the direct outcome of the failure of American schools to provide appropriate educational programs for adolescent refugee students. For instance, a 16-year-old boy with no English skills and only a couple of years of education in Vietnam has been placed in an American high school because of his chronological age. Unable to meet the demands of high school, he becomes discouraged and drops out of school, onto the streets, where he meets other at-risk youths. At the age of 18, these youths lose all public assistance benefits and therefore the opportunity to finish vocational or high school. Without adequate job skills, fluency in English or family or community support, they have little chance to find employment. Faced with this situation, many of these youths turn to street gangs, the only available (if maladaptive) support system (Freeman, 1989).

Southeast Asian-American students' academic performance is affected by inadequate English language development programs. Specifically these students suffer academically because of hasty reclassification from "limited-English-proficient" to "fluent-English-proficient" status. Most of the reclassifications take place 1 to 3 years after a student has entered the American school system (i.e. the student is mainstreamed into the regular program without further language development support). Very few remain designated as limited-English-proficient beyond 5 years. Yet according to research, it takes 3 to 7 years for limited-English-proficient students to reach the level of academic English language proficiency sufficient to succeed in the academic setting (Cummings, 1981). Therefore, [educators] need to evaluate the student's English language proficiency level, and determine the length of time the child has been [and should be] provided language development support.

Problems of Second Language Acquisition:

Southeast Asian-American students who are in the process of acquiring English as a second language may be demonstrating learning or behavior problems that are related to loss of their first language and incipient development of English as a second language. That is, their first language is declining while their English proficiency is still low, resulting in communication difficulties that affect their academic performance. Assessors must be able to distinguish between these problems and true learning disabilities.

Cultural Differences:

Many Southeast Asian-American students come from highly authoritarian family backgrounds, wherein they are often expected to do as told and not voice their opinions. In addition, they are also accustomed to heavy rote learning that is part of their traditional educational practices. As a result, they do not often exhibit the kind of participatory behaviors expected by American teachers. [Educators] must be able to distinguish between two underlying causes of lack of participation: (1) the child has a learning problem or (2) the child is a reflective learner (and is very bright). School personnel have recognized that many of these students are passive and want to encourage them to discuss and participate more in class. However, they have not recognized that these students need to be taught how to discuss and lead discussion groups.

A related aspect is that many Southeast Asian-American students tend to perceive things globally; as field-sensitive learners, they are not used to separating the whole into its parts or analyzing things out of context. In contrast, field-independent teachers in the American school system tend to emphasize analysis of the parts. Consequently, once Southeast Asian-American students have been taught to participate in discussions, teachers need to be aware that their contributions will tend to reflect their global perspectives. This approach, if acknowledged, will enrich classroom discussions. However, if this type of contribution is misperceived and rejected, there will be a risk of destroying students' motivation. In other words, teachers will be more effective if they address the learning styles of both the field-sensitive and field-independent students.

While it is important to recognize the value of these students' learning styles, teachers must also help Southeast Asian-American students to develop their analytical skills. Therefore to guide intervention, [educators] must identify the students' underlying cognitive learning styles. (Editor's note: *Attention to the cognitive learning styles of this group are addressed in the next section by Timm and Chiang.*)

REFERENCES

1. Bower, E. M.: *Early Identification of Emotionally Handicapped Children in School.* Springfield, Ill., Charles C Thomas, 1969.
2. Catterall, J. & Cota-Robles, E.: The educationally disadvantaged: Demographics, consequences, and policy prospects. Paper presented at the Conference on Accelerating the Education of At-Risk Students, Palo Alto, Ca., 1988.
3. Chinn, P. C., & Plata, M.: Perspectives and educational implications of Southeast Asian students. In Kitano, M. K., & Chinn, P. C. (Eds.) *Exceptional Asian Children and Youth.* Reston, VA: Council for Exceptional Children, 1986.
4. Cummins, J.: The role of primary language development in promoting educational success for language minority students. In California State Department of Education (Ed.) *Schooling and Language Minority Students: A Theoretical Framework.* Los Angeles, CA: Evaluation, Dissemination and Assessment Center, 1981.
5. Dao, M.: A survey of the current situation of special education services for Vietnamese-American refugee children in a California school district. Unpublished manuscript, 1988.
6. Dao, M.: Issues in assessment of learning disabilities in ESL students. Paper presented at the conference of the National Association of Teachers of English to Speakers of Other Languages, San Francisco, 1990.
7. Freeman, J.: *Hearts of Sorrow.* Stanford, CA, Stanford University Press, 1989.
8. Kirst, M. W.: *Conditions of Children in California.* Berkeley: Policy Analysis for California's Education, 1989.
9. Mortland, C. A., & Egan, M. B.: Vietnamese youth in American foster care. *Social Work,* 240–244, 1987.

10. Nidorf, J. F.: Mental health and refugee youths: A model for diagnostic training. In Owan, T. C., Bliatout, B., Lin, K–M., Liu, W., Nguyen, T. D., & Wong, H. D. (Eds.) *Southeast Asian Mental Health: Treatment, Prevention, Services, Training, and Research.* Washington, D. C., U. S. Department of Health and Human Services, 1985.

11. Rumbaut, R. G.: Mental health and the refugee experience: A comparative study of Southeast Asian refugees. In Owan, T. C., Bliatout, B., Lin, K–M., Liu, W., Nguyen, T. D., & Wong, H. C. (Eds.) *Southeast Asian Mental Health: Treatment, Prevention, Services, Training, and Research.* Washington, D. C., U. S. Department of Health and Human Services, 1985.

12. Rumbaut, R. G.: From Southeast Asian to San Diego: An analysis of the economic, cultural and psychological adaptation of Indochinese refugees. Proceedings of Service Delivery Models for Outreach/Prevention/Intervention for Southeast Asian Refugee Infants, Children, and their Families. Washington, D. C., National Maternal and Child Health Clearinghouse, 1987.

13. Rumbaut, R. G. & Ima, K.: *The Adaptation of Southeast Asian Refugee Youth: A Comparative Study.* Washington, D. C., Government Printing Office, 1987.

14. Slavin, R. E., Karweit, N. L., & Madden, N. A.: *Effective Programs for Students At Risk.* Boston, Allyn & Bacon, 1989.

15. Takaki, R.: Another look at Asian "Success." *San Francisco Chronicle,* August 24, 1989.

16. Te, H. D., Chhim, S–H., & Luangpraseut, K.: *Introduction to Vietnamese Culture; Introduction to Cambodian Culture; Laos, Culturally Speaking.* San Diego, Multi-functional Resource Center, 1989.

17. Tran, V. M.: East-West cultural differences. In Dao, M. (Ed.). Vietnamese to Vietnamese American: Selected Articles. San Jose, CA, Division of Special Education and Rehabilitative Services, San Jose State University, 1987.

18. Wei, D.: Strategies for assessing and identifying Southeast Asian children. Paper presented at San Jose State University Summer Institute for Personnel Working with Southeast Asian Students with Special Needs, San Jose, CA, 1986.

PART II
COGNITIVE STYLE:
Cultural Ways of Knowing

Chapter 7

COGNITIVE STYLE: WHAT IS IT?

Barbara J. Shade

The term *cognitive style* is a relative newcomer to psychological literature and one which stimulates a great deal of skepticism and controversy. Some of this difficulty, of course, may relate to the fact that there are numerous definitions of the term as well as several different perspectives from which the construct is viewed. However, Vernon (1973) points out that in spite of the variety of definitions, there is a general overall consensus that *cognitive style* represents a superordinate construct which accounts for individual differences in a variety of cognitive, perceptual, and personality variables which influence the method of perceiving, organizing, and interpreting information.

Because cognitive style is a highly individualized way of using the various cognitive, perceptual, and symbolic modes of learning, it is often considered to be a part of an individual's personality system. In fact, in the early studies of the concept, Gardner, Holzman, Klein, Linton, and Spence (1959) defined cognitive style as a superordinate level of control within the personality system. In conceptualizing cognitive style in this way, it becomes a tool used by individuals to learn to cope with or adapt to the various environments in which they find themselves.

Guilford (1980) took a somewhat expanded view and suggested that cognitive style represented an individual's executive system which served as the initiator and controller of intellectual functioning. This view suggests that cognitive style performs a metacognitive process as identified by Campion and Brown (1978) to guide individuals through their perceptual and interpretive activity when learning. Regardless of the approach, however, both views of the concept indicate that it represents individual preferences for processing information (Ausburn & Ausburn, 1978; Coop & Sigel, 1971; Bieri, 1971).

Cognitive style as described by various dimensions under the concept, generally takes on a bipolar value to describe variations of use by different individuals. The dimensions seem to be divided into three basic categories: those which are identified based upon their perceptual processing orientation; a second group which identifies the type of representation or organization of the information while the third group addresses the allocation and monitoring of the processing strategies.

Cognitive styles which might be closely related to the first group include the *field independence and field-dependence* dimension of Witkin and his associates (1962) and Paivio's (1971) *visualizer vs verbalizer* styles which appears to be indicative of the identification, selection, and representation processes. A similar stylistic dimension is described by Vernon (1973) of Jaenichian's *integrated vs disintegrated* styles in which differences in perceptions of images are considered to be dissociated and inflexible or integrated and flexible. Other styles described by Vernon which might fit this category are Messmer's *synthetic and analytic* types, Neumann's *diffusive vs fixative* styles which examine individual preference for whole or detailed information and Santesfaneo's *levelling and sharpening* style which concentrates on attention deployment.

The cognitive styles which seem to identify the representation, or information organizational processes involved in information processing include those of Pettigrew's (1958) *broad vs narrow* thinkers, Kagan, Moss and Sigel's (1963), conceptual differentiation styles, i.e., *description, relational, and inferential,* as well as Goldstein and Scherer's (1941) idea of styles which focus on either the *abstractness or concreteness* of information. While the previous are more likely to examine the choice of representation of the information being perceived, the following styles examine the sequencing and allocation of the strategies to processing the information. This includes Kagan's (1966) *reflectivity and impulsivity* style which identifies the speed with which the processing is done and strategies selected and Hudson's (1966) *convergent vs divergent* thinkers and Pask's (1969) *holistic vs serialistic* styles which identify the sequencing approach individuals usually take to the thinking process.

The selection of the appropriate adaptational strategies depend, in large measure, upon the individual's perception of the environment. This perception is based upon past history and previous socializing experiences of the individuals. Based upon these perceptions, individuals develop both the intellectual and the behavioral responses which serve as a bridge between them and an environment and produce the least amount of stress and anxiety possible. These strategies become coping mechanisms.

Studies of cognitive styles as adaptational approaches have identified, in addition to the dimension of field-independence and field-dependence, such dimensions as: Jung's (1923, 1949) concept of *extraversion-intraversion;* Kretschmer's (1925) *dissociate vs integration* attention style, and Harvey, Hunt, and Schroder's (1961) conceptual systems theory which delineates an individual's ability to differentiate and integrate information in a *complex or simple* manner. These styles seem to concentrate on how much attention the individual gives to the environment from which the information is coming and determines how the individual will adapt.

Other stylistic dimensions in the study of individual adaptational approaches concentrate on the extent to which individuals are bound by their own ideas, values, beliefs, culture, and experiences. Cognitive style dimensions used in studies from this perspective include Rokeach's (1960) *open-mindedness vs intolerance of ambiguity or closed mindedness,* Klein's (1970) *constricted vs flexible control,* Kelly and Bieri's concept of cognitive complexity or cognitive simplicity (Goldstein & Blackman, 1978), and Parlett's (1970) *syllabus-bound vs syllabus free* style. These stylistic dimensions represent the ways in which individuals file and process information so that the environment takes on some type of psychological meaning.

COGNITIVE STYLE AND INTELLECTUAL ABILITY

Many theorists suggest that cognitive style is only a synonym for intellectual ability (Widiger, Knudson & Rorer, 1980). Frederico and Landis (1980), based upon their correlational studies, disagree. They found that cognitive processing habits or preferences were very discrete entities and accounted for different segments of the variance in intellectual performance. Other examinations of the issue seem to confirm this hypothesis.

Eagle (1965) identified five cognitive style dimensions and correlated them with intelligence test scores at two grade levels to determine if there was a relationship between style and intellectual ability. He found that, although boys and girls seem to have different patterns of cognitive styles, IQ and style were apparently independent variables. Eagle found that 9.4 percent of the variance on IQ tests was accounted for by cognitive style of boys and 7.3 percent was accounted for in girls.

Blaha, Fawaz, and Wallbrown (1979) made a similar discovery. In testing children on frequently used psychometric measures of cognitive control, personality, and psychomotor coordination, they found that information processing accounted for 16 percent of the variance in performance while intelligence based upon IQ accounted for 9 percent.

In another study, DuBois and Cohen (1970) investigated the relationship between intellectual ability and the field-independence/field-dependence dimension. Although they reported a relationship, it was apparently a negative one as all correlations between the two concepts were in the opposite direction. Coates (1975) examined this relationship for preschool children using the WPPSI. Two major factorial dimensions were found to be present in the WPPSI, namely perceptual analytical skills and verbal comprehension. In her analysis, she found that the underlying process required to perform on the tasks which assess field dependence/independence was the same one required for performance on various intellectual measures such as the Block Design and Picture Completion tasks. She labeled this process as "perceptual analytical ability." She concluded, as did Witkin and his associates (1977) that the results individuals obtain on various measures of ability may be influenced by their particular cognitive style, since this element serves as a mediator between the individual and the environment and represents the manner in which individuals approach various mental tasks. Snow and Lohman (1984) equate these mediational skills or what we have termed cognitive style with **aptitude.**

Aptitude is defined as a readiness to learn from a particular instructional approach. Individual differences in aptitude emanate from three major components: (a) learning rate, or the speed and efficiency with which individuals can acquire the concepts; (b) stylistic preferences or strategies used to perform the learning tasks; and (c) the means selected for monitoring or adapting their cognitive processes to the task requirements (Snow & Lohman, 1984). High aptitude individuals are those whose cognitive response pattern is highly congruent with the response pattern required by a particular environment. Low aptitude students are those in which there is a mismatch between the required responses and their use of the various response components.

Examination of the types of aptitudes which seem most prevalent and rewarded within the academic environment include: the ability to think in a linear, sequential pattern; the ability to link cause and effect; the ability to attend to and receive visual and auditory information with a particular emphasis on the print modality; the ability to reflect and inhibit movement or responses; the possession of a wealth of information as a part of long-term memory and the ability to retrieve it early; the ability to differentiate the important and needed information from unimportant and irrelevant cues.

It would, thus, appear that cognitive style must be both an adaptational and an information processing control. It serves as the foundation to the individual's personal adjustment by determining the information to which they will attend, the intellectual mediating processes in which the individual will engage and the responses which will be selected as appropriate behavior. As such, this important tool must have a significant impact upon an individual's competent performance within various behavioral settings. One of the most important settings which influences competence in this society is the school or educational setting and the groups which appear to have the most difficulty demonstrating their ability to perform competently are ethnic minorities and in particular African-Americans.

The readings in this section use the concept of cognitive style to attempt to answer the following questions:

1. Do African-Americans and other ethnic minorities have a unique cognitive style which influences their adaptation and intellectual performance?

2. Is this style different from Euro-Americans and the style generally perpetuated in this society?

3. If so, how does this style effect competent performance in one of the most important social institutions in America, i.e., the school?

REFERENCES

1. Ausburn, L. J., & Ausburn, F. B.: Cognitive styles: Some implications and information for instructional design. *Educational Communication and Technology: A Journal of Theory, Research and Development, 26:*337–354, 1978.
2. Bieri, J.: Cognitive structures in personality. In Schroder, Suedfeld, H. M. (Eds.): *Personality Theory and Information Processing.* New York, Ronald Press, 1971.
3. Blaha, J., Fawaz, N., & Wallbrown, F.: Information processing components of Koppitz errors on the Bender-Gestalt. *Journal of Clinical Psychology, 35:*784–790, 1979.
4. Campion, J. C., & Brown, A. L.: Toward a theory of intelligence: Contributions from research with retarded children. *Intelligence, 2:*279–304, 1978.
5. Coates, S.: Field independence and intellectual functioning in preschool children. *Perceptual and Motor Skills, 41:*251–254, 1975.
6. Coop, R. H., & Sigel, I. E.: Cognitive style: Implications for learning and instruction. *Psychology in the Schools, 8:*152–161, 1971.

7. Dubois, T. E., & Cohen, W.: Relationship between measures of psychological differentiation and intellectual ability. *Perceptual and Motor Skills, 31:*411–416, 1970.

8. Eagle, N.: The relation of five cognitive variables to change in IQ between grades 3–4 and grade 8. *Psychology in the Schools, 2:*143–149, 1965.

9. Frederico, P. A., & Landis, D. B.: Are cognitive styles independent of ability and aptitudes? Paper presented at annual meeting of the American Psychological Association, 1980.

10. Gardner, R. W., Holzman, P. S., Klein, G. S., Linton, H. B., & Spence, D. P.: Cognitive control: A study of individual consistencies in cognitive behavior. *Psychological Issues,* Monograph #4. New York, International University Press, 1959.

11. Goldstein, K. M., & Blackman, S.: *Cognitive Style: Five Approaches and Relevant Research.* New York, John Wiley & Sons, 1978.

12. Goldstein, K., & Scherer, M.: Abstract and concrete behavior: An experimental study with special tests. *Psychological Monographs, 53:*1–239, 1941.

13. Guilford, J. P.: Cognitive styles: What are they? *Educational and Psychological Measurement, 40:*715–735, 1980.

14. Harvey, O. J., Hunt, D. E., & Schroder, H. M.: *Conceptual Systems and Personality Organization.* New York, John Wiley & Sons, 1961.

15. Hudson, L.: *Contrary Imaginations.* London, Methuen, 1966.

16. Jung, C.: *Psychological Types.* London, Routledge & Kegan Paul (1923) [Translated by H. Godwin Baynes, 1949.]

17. Kagan, J.: Reflection-impulsivity: The generality and dynamics of conceptual tempo. *Journal of Abnormal Psychology, 71:*17–24, 1966.

18. Kagan, J., Moss, H. A., & Sigel, I.: Psychological significance of style of conceptualization. In Wright, J. C. & Kagan, J. (Eds.): Basic cognitive processes in children. *Monographs of the Society for Research in Child Development, 28:*73–112, 1963.

19. Klein, G. S.: *Perception, Motives and Personality.* New York, Alfred Knopf, 1970.

20. Kretschmer, E.: *Physique and Character.* London, Kegan Paul, 1925.

21. Paivio, A.: *Imagery and Verbal Processes.* New York, Holt, Rinehart, & Winston, 1971.

22. Parlett, M. R.: The syllabus-bound student. In Hudson, L. (Ed.): *The Ecology of Human Intelligence.* New York, Penguin Books, 1970.

23. Pask, G.: Strategy competence and conservations as determinants of learning. *Programmed Learning,* October: 250–261, 1969.

24. Pettigrew, T.: The measurement and correlates of category width as a cognitive variable. *Journal of Personality, 26:*532–544, 1958.

25. Rokeach, M.: *The Open and Closed Mind: Investigations Into the Nature of Belief Systems and Personality Systems.* New York, Basic Books, 1960.

26. Snow, R. E., & Lohman, D. F.: Toward a theory of cognitive aptitude for learning from instruction. *Journal of Educational Psychology, 76:*347–376, 1984.

27. Vernon, P.: Multivariate approaches to the study of cognitive styles. In Royce, J. (Ed.): *Multivariate Analysis of Psychological Theory.* New York, Academic Press, 1973.

28. Witkin, H. A., Dyk, R. B., Paterson, H. F., Goodenough, D. R., & Karp, S. A.: *Psychological Differentiation.* New York, John Wiley & Sons, 1962.

29. Witkin, H. A., Moore, C. A., Goodenough, D. R., & Cox, P. W.: Field-dependent and field-independent cognitive styles and their educational implications. *Review of Educational Research, 47:*1–64, 1977.

Chapter 8

AFRICAN-AMERICAN COGNITIVE PATTERNS: A REVIEW OF THE RESEARCH

Barbara J. Shade

Cognition, in its broadest definition, represents the act of knowing. Within the act are the processes of perception, memory, mental elaboration, and reasoning. Although, as Cole and Scribner (1974) point out, the processes are basically the same for all individuals, differences are noted in the way the processes are used. The basis of these variations is found in the demands of a specific ecocultural environment (Thompson, 1969; Berry 1976). The purpose of this chapter is to examine the patterns of knowing which have been developed and transmitted within the African-American community. Such a search is built on the premise that Americans of African descent have developed a unique culture as the result of coping with and adapting to a color-conscious society, and a part of that culture includes specific and unique cognitive strategies.

Identifying African-American differences is a perilous task in that the identified variations are generally interpreted as being deficient and negative. In spite of this difficulty, differences in the use of cognitive processes will be explored with the hope that these will be viewed as preferences or stylistic dimensions rather than badges of inferiority.

In this exploratory effort, questions undoubtedly will be raised about the wisdom of depicting African-Americans as a monolithic group. This occurs for several reasons. First, there is the recognition that "color" affects the environmental responses of all African-Americans, regardless of social class. In addition, at this point in history there still remains a viable social-cultural system which transmits both the African-American worldview and cognitive-behavioral patterns to all levels of the community (Blackwell, 1975). The third reason there is an assumption of homogeneity is based upon the study by Stodolsky and Lesser (1967). They found that, although class differences were present in levels of performance, an ethnic group's overall pattern was essentially the same.

70

There are, of course, reasons to believe that there may be developmental and gender differences within the African-American community as there are in other groups. Unfortunately, the current studies of African-American cognition have neglected these variables, thus, individual differences are difficult to ascertain. Within the studies reviewed here, neither social class nor gender differences were identifiable.

The studies chosen for this review will deal with school-aged children 3–21 who are native-born African-Americans. Studies using international samples of individuals with African heritage were not selected as it was felt that the ecological demands are not equivalent in both societies; therefore, cognitive patterns might not be similar. Also, the patterns to which we allude are not seen as innate characteristics, but socialized environmental behavior.

A second, and equally important, characteristic of the subjects in the studies chosen for review is that they represent a "normal" population. As Bruner (1968) points out, "Our insights into mental functioning are too often shaped by the observations of the sick and the handicapped. It is difficult to catch...man's mind...at its best" (p. 15). It was this reviewer's wish to understand African-American cognition at its best, not after it had succumbed to the pressures of the environment.

With these general guidelines in mind, let us return to the examination of the important question: Do African-Americans have a unique pattern of cognitive strategies or a cognitive style? To determine the answer, it is necessary to use the information processing paradigm and examine the way in which African-Americans perceive, encode, represent, and analyze information.

The Information Processing Paradigm

The information processing model which has emerged in the last decade assumes that man's internal structure performs certain behavioral processes (Strom & Bernard, 1982). More important, the paradigm assumes an interaction between the environment and the organism rather than a reaction.

There are numerous models which have emerged to depict the process (Gagne, 1977; Das, Jarmon & Kirby, 1975; Anderson, 1980). In general as depicted in Figure 8-1, the model suggests that:

1. The information is registered through the preferred sensory modality or modalities and preferred cues are selected for attention.
2. The information is then placed in short-term memory for recognition and labeling.

INFORMATION PROCESSING

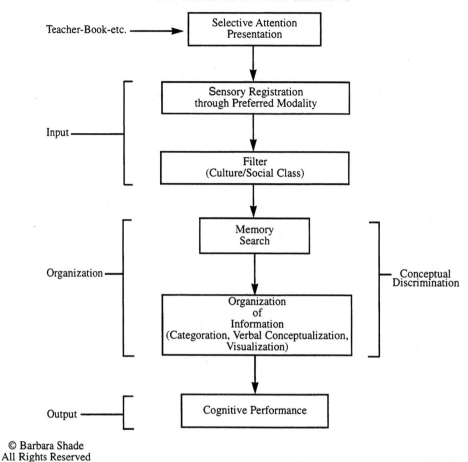

Figure 8-1.

3. The information is sorted, classified, and organized.

4. Following organization, the information is analyzed and incorporated; then performance requirements specified.

5. The individual decides to act or respond on the basis of the analysis of the information.

The major variation in this processing of information which seems to be uniquely African-American occurs in the preprocessing and central processing stage, e.g., in their patterns of perception.

AFRICAN-AMERICAN PATTERNS OF PERCEPTION

Perception is the basic process of cognition as it is the process through which the living organism maintains contact with the environment (Travers, 1982). Based upon the research in the area, perception is heavily influenced by one's socialization and past experiences. As J. J. Gibson (1950) points out, individuals are taught to "see the world." This process of "seeing" involves not only the sensation or reception of the sensory stimuli, but also involves an analytical process. There is reason to believe that the perceptual process of African-Americans differs in style from other groups.

The question of a unique perceptual style with the African-American community has been around for some time. It was first raised by Tyler in 1956 and again by Mandler and Stein in 1977. Mandler and Stein (1977) point out in their examination of this issue that the question has been reinterpreted as a truism without any substantial empirical documentation. Although it is an issue which has not been confronted directly, it is one which seems to continually manifest itself as we look for a pattern which represents how African-American culture trains its children to learn.

Sensory Modality Preference

One of the first variations noted in African-American perceptual style is in the preference of modalities for receiving information. Information present in the environment is registered in all six sensory channels. However, there appears to be a hierarchy of development which leads to the efficient and preferential use of the channels. According to Barsch (1971), the younger child makes the most efficient use of the gustatory, olfactory, and tactual senses. However, as learning occurs and cognitive effectiveness increases, the kinesthetic, auditory, and visual modes become the most heavily relied upon. As we examine the mode most emphasized in mainstream American culture, we note that emphasis is placed on perceiving via the visual channel.

The majority of the information in our society is transmitted through the visually-oriented material. Vision is seen as the "queen" of the sensory registration modes and is the medium through which we attempt to assess learning ability and other aspects of cognition. If one examines the instruments on which many judgments about individuals are made such as the Raven's Progressive Matrices, the Bender-Gestalt Test, the Thematic Apperception Test, the Group Embedded Figures Test and the performance tasks of the intelligence tests, one notes that these are predominantly, and almost exclusively, visual information processing tasks.

It is, however, an error to assume that all individuals have the same modality preference or the same efficiency in use. Barbe and Swassing (1979) found that individuals have a modality through which they prefer to receive information and that the preferred modality may not be vision. Wober (1966) agrees and further suggests that the demands of the environment develop this preference.

To prove his point, Wober worked with the Embedded Figures Test, the Rod-and-Frame Test, the Kohs Block Design and the Raven's Progressive Matrices. In addition to the visually oriented versions, the tests were converted into tactile and proprioceptive versions as well. The results demonstrated that the style of processing information in one modality does not correlate highly with the ability to process information in one modality. Individuals who had performed at the lower end of the continuum on the visually oriented tasks, did better on the kinesthetic/tactile versions of the instrument. Wober concluded that there are different *sensotypes*. By sensotypes, Wober means the modality pattern preferred by the child for perceiving the world and upon which the child develops his/her abilities. This concept is much the same as Barsch (1971) processing mode hierarchy which is said to represent the rank order of the sensory modes in which individuals prefer to receive information.

The idea of an individual preference in modality dominance is another resurrected idea. Fernald presented the same hypothesis in 1912 and later conducted a study to identify visual learners, auditory learners, and kinesthetic learners (Fernald, 1943). Like Barsch and Barbe, Fernald promotes the belief that, while all modalities are active, individuals find some modalities more effective and efficient than others. This premise leads to the question: Is there a more effective modality for learning than vision for African-Americans?

Charles Keil (1966) noted in his book, *Urban Blues*, that there are certain modes of perception more characteristic of the black community than the white community. In his explication of the various cultural components of the community, Keil writes: " . . . its modes of perception and expression, its channels of communication are predominantly auditory and tactile rather than visual and literate . . . the prominence of the aural perception, oral expression, and kinesic codes . . . sharply demarcate the culture from the white world . . . " pp. 16–17.

Other indications that African-Americans may have a different modality preference come from the ethnographic study done by Pavenstedt and her associates of thirteen low-income children from problem families. In the report (Pavenstedt et al., 1967), the observers commented that the children were rather advanced in their motor development and seemed to use visual perception differently than usually observed. Malone (1967) noted in his part of the study that the children used vision as ways of protecting and orienting themselves in the environment rather than for gathering information.

Although the aural mode is undoubtedly a very important channel in African-American culture, it seems very probable that the kinesthetic mode is the primary mode of information induction for the majority of the members of the community. This supposition is made based upon the literature in the field of motor learning. The evidence has been around for some time that African-Americans have a high motoric capability due to their apparent sensorimotor precocity (Morgan, 1981). They also appear to use kinesics more than most groups. Guttentag (1972), for example, studied the difference in the number and variety of movements of African-American and Euro-American four year olds. She found that African-American children emitted a significantly greater movement responses and a greater variety. Van Alstyne and Osbourne (1937) examined the rhythmic responses of black and white children between the ages of two and six. African-American children were found to be 50 percent better than Euro-American children in following rhythms. In a similar study, Stigler (1940) compared the capacity of the two groups to perceive minute body movements by attaching a kinestemeter to study peripheral acuity. African-Americans were superior in their ability to perceive the slightest body movements. One might conclude from these studies that African-Americans are adept at gathering, using, and analyzing kinesthetic information.

In his book, *The Mind's Eye,* Sommers (1978) details the characteristics of individuals who are high in kinesthetic imagery. These individuals can take in and elaborate in great detail spontaneous motoric responses. The description presented by Sommers closely parallels the descriptions often noted by sociologists and anthropologists of African-American rhythm, spontaneity and movement as exhibited in walks, stance, dance, and athletic encounters (Pasteur & Toldson, 1982; Kochman, 1972).

Apparently, imagery is one of the best ways to study modal preferences. For example, Colvin and Meyer (cited in Barsch, 1971) read a story comprised of visual, auditory, and motor words to a group of children. The children were then asked to write the story on the next day. The number of words recalled in each modality was judged to indicate the primary modal preference. Perhaps the closest use of this approach to study African-American modalities is the work done by Kochman (1972) in black idiom. In his study of the communication pattern, to which most African-Americans revert when interacting with one another, Kochman found that there was a preponderance of words which possess the quality of rapid and unrestricted movement or have the potential for such movement. Conversely, words which suggest static or impeded movement have unfavorable connotations. Kochman (1972) goes on to suggest that patterns such as the identified kinetic quality of the language have a significant influence on the minds and habits of the speakers. We assume that this pattern of kinetic preference also is operating within the African-American perceptual process.

Cue Selection

The number and types of information to which an individual is exposed is massive; therefore, choices must be made about the cues or information an individual can address. Thompson (1969), Gibson (1969), and others suggest that a culture trains its children to tune in on certain types of information and filter out others. In his theory on person-environment interaction, Little (1976) postulates that in the early stages of experiencing the environment, the child construes persons as things and things as persons. However, socialization practices seem to produce a developmental change which leads to a specialization in attention which causes the affective, cognitive and behavioral systems of the child to focus on development a better understanding of the nonsocial or the physical world—thus becoming a thing specialist or to focus on the social and personal world by becoming a person specialist. When Yarrow, Rubenstein, and others (1971) examined this preference for African-American infants in terms of human and inanimate objects, they found that the two aspects of the environment were strikingly independent.

In studies which examined this developmental sequence in the African-American community, Young (1970, 1974) found that the child-training practices used by African-American families in both the North and the South seemed to emphasize attending to person rather than nonperson cues. She observed that the mothers tended to use status-oriented pressure and inconsistent discipline which forced children to learn to judge the moods of people in authority in order to avoid punishment or aversive reactions. But in addition, the child's life from infancy to around age three seemed to be filled with a great deal of body contact and touching. Young (1974) contends that this type of training seems to frustrate the child's interest in the "object" world and refocus the child's attention to people stimuli.

Carpenter (1970) and associates also examined the response style of African-American infants by exposing them to three types of stimuli: the mother, a mannikin, and an abstract picture. The authors noted that the mother, as the most familiar stimulus, received less of the child's attention than the other two. This response was interpreted as the result of familiarity and less color. Of the other two presentations, it was noted that these infants attended more and for a longer period of time to the mannikin or human-like face than the abstract stimuli. One might speculate that this is another situation in which African-American children choose social over nonsocial cues.

Although their study was not oriented to the examination of racial differences per se, Lewis and Wilson (1972) did examine the mother-child relationship of 32 twelve-week-old infants, of which a large portion of the sample were African-Americans. They found that lower socioeconomic mothers were more likely to touch their children, hold them more, and smile at them, which was interpreted as exhibitions of behaviors which would strengthen attachment bonds rather than instituting "distancing." Distancing behaviors were interpreted as those which help the child separate *self* from the immediate environment and move toward the achievement of representational thought. Bruner et al. (1966) describes this developmental phenomena as an important for cognitive growth. As a child moves from the stage in which action and objects are fused to the point of being able to represent objects independent of the actions taken toward them, they are developing their skills in memory and representational thought. More important, the children are setting the stage for learning to handle abstract concepts.

Evidence of this "person" cue preference of African-American children is found in several studies. Damico (1983) examined the person-vs-object hypothesis by permitting black and white sixth-grade children the opportunity to photograph school as they perceived it. Although the findings were apparently an artifact or secondary finding of a larger study, the significant difference in the types of photographs taken to depict the meaning of school seemed to support the hypothesis. African-American children chose to include people such as teachers or classmates in their pictures while the Euro-American children depicted objects or physical settings. Damico concluded that African-American children were significantly more people-oriented than object-oriented.

In another study, Eato and Lerner (1981) asked 183 African-American sixth graders to indicate their perceptions of their physical school environment and their social environment in the school. The researchers were attempting to determine which of the factors seemed to influence the children's adaptive behavior. The major factor that seemed to be most important to all children were the people in the environment, in particular the teachers. The physical environment seemed important only to the males and at a fairly minimum level.

Other indications that African-Americans seem to have a preference for social and people cues is found in the literature on recognition of faces and emotions. It has been found that not only are African-Americans better able to recognize faces and emotions than groups to which they are compared (Galper, 1973; Chance, Goldstein, McBride, 1975; Luce, 1974; Gitter, Black, Mostosoky, 1972) but they also are extremely sensitive to social situations nuance (Hill & Fox, 1973; Witmer, Ferinden, 1970).

This attention to social nuances may have led to the results which Sherif (1973) observed about the differences in categorization of situations. In this study African-Americans and Euro-American students were asked to analyze and sort situations which were acceptable for participation in terms of interracial interactions and those which were unacceptable. African-American students were found to make their decisions based upon the interpersonal demands and the possible social effects on the person while Euro-American students categorized situations based upon the formal demands of the settings. Again, for African-Americans people took precedence over rules and context.

Other indications that the interpersonal domain has a primary spot in African-American attention is found in the research on learning styles. African-Americans seem to prefer affective materials to facilitate their learning (Rychlak, 1975), warm and supportive teachers (St. John, 1971), and a socially interactive environment (Slavin, 1983; Cureton, 1978). As Morgan (1981) points out in his examination of the learning style of African-American children, "It appears as though the social interaction model provides an atmosphere in which black children can do well."

This information preference pattern probably is best represented in the behavioral dimension as *extraversion*. Although there are many interpretations of the extraversion-introversion dimensions, the one which seems to best fit the information processing paradigm is the conceptualization by Carl Jung. According to Jung (1923), extraversion represents a preference for and attention to the external world rather than the internal world of ideas, concepts, or insights (intraversion). The choice manifests itself in the preference for action, for involvement and for being a part of the human scene (Myers, 1980). The Myers-Briggs Type Indicator measures extraversion based upon Jung's interpretation.

Using a group of 758 undergraduates at Howard University, Levy, Murphy, and Carlson (1972) administered the Myers-Briggs Type Indicator at two different times in order to establish the test's reliability for their population. A comparison of the 146 males of the sample with a Euro-American sample from Amherst revealed that a larger percentage of the African-American population fell in the extraverted category than in the intraverted categories than occurred with Euro-American males. A similar finding emerged in a recent study of ninth-grade students done by this author (Shade, 1983). When viewed *in toto,* both the African-American and Euro-American groups were extraverted. However, when divided by achievement level, the African-American high achievers and the Euro-American low achievers were extraverted, while the Euro-American high achievers and the African-American low achievers preferred their internal world.

When Morris (1979) reviewed the literature on extraversion-introversion, he noted that, in general, most children are externally oriented until around ages 12 and 13 and up to that point extraversion is highly correlated with school achievement. After that age, students who do well become more introverted and introversion becomes more highly correlated with achievement. For African-Americans, it is interesting to note that the developmental change occurs only for the high-risk students who are not finding much success in school while African-American students who manage to succeed maintain their orientation toward social interaction and involvement.

Farley (1974), in his studies of cue preference and motivation has proposed that extroverts are individuals seeking stimulation from their outside world and in their search look for a variety of stimuli, complexity, novelty, and activity. Although he uses a different terminology, it appears that this is the same description Boykin (1979) gives of African-American children in his discussion of psychological and behavioral verve. According to Boykin, African-American children seem to prefer and need a variety of information at a constantly changing pace and seem to have little tolerance for monotonous or low-level activity. Euro-American children, on the other hand, seem to be able to tolerate a more low-keyed and less varied type of activity.

An interesting by-product of this orientation, according to Farley (1981), is that this preference for high stimulation or extraversion is believed to be predictive of creative performance and a highly creative personality. Perhaps it is. In a study of the performance of 70 African-American eighth-grade students in Northeast Georgia on various creative and cognitive measures, Richmond (1971) found that African-Americans were superior to Euro-Americans on the test of figural elaboration. This task is seen as a test of ability to elaborate, embellish, and develop ideas and a high sensitivity in observation. It is one of Torrance's tests of creativity. While the evidence that this group of students was extraverted comes from the author's own observation of their intensity and personal involvement in the testing situation and their friendliness toward the examiners, the finding does raise the question of the possibility of a relationship between African-American cue preference and creativity as suggested in Farley's theory.

If the orientations toward the social as opposed to the nonsocial world are independent as Little suggests, it would appear that the development of the cognitive strategies needed for person and social cognition would prohibit the development of the other strategies needed in handling the skills as defined by Bruner (1966).

INFORMATION RETRIEVAL AND RECOGNITION

To handle the many types of information with which individuals are bombarded, it is necessary to learn to discriminate and group the various bits of data into broad and generalizable categories. This segmentation and division of the world is quite arbitrary, and many theorists suggest that the categorization of information is rooted in the cultural dimension of the individual (Rosch, 1975). Those individuals who are able to do this will have material lodged in their long-term memory in such a manner as to allow easy retrieval and use in performing other cognitive tasks. Factors which affect the memory process include the organization of the information, the meaning attached to it, its position in the presentation of the information and the context in which it was presented.

The evidence about African-American encoding patterns is rather limited with the majority of the evidence found in the studies of conceptual differentiation. Of the studies available, it appears as though African-Americans group information about objects, as well as people and events, differently than other groups. Sigel, Anderson, and Shapiro (1966), for example, found that African-Americans tended to categorize objects based upon pictorial representations of those objects in a more relational or holistic manner rather than an analytical or detail oriented manner. Orasanu, Lee, and Scribner (1979) found that African-Americans tended to sort word lists on the basis of their functional use while Euro-Americans used a more taxonomic, descriptive approach. As previously mentioned, Sherif (1973) found that African-Americans categorized situations differently than Euro-Americans.

Examination of the inclusiveness of categories suggest that individuals tend to have a broad or narrow approach to the development of classifications. Those individuals who put concepts into many categories based upon only a few attributes are considered to be narrow categorizers while those who use many attributes and, thus, end up with few categories are broad conceptualizers (Pettigrew, 1958; Gardner, 1983). In a study by Carlson (1971) African-American elementary and middle school children seemed to be broad based classifiers while Euro-American children were more narrow in their conceptualizing. Wilcox (1971), however, studied the associations made by college students and found that African-Americans tended to be more narrow in their associations while Euro-American college students were more broad in their associative style. In a study using ninth grade students in an urban area, Shade (1983) found that African-American students were more likely to create more categories for concepts, thus being narrow classifiers, while Euro-American students were more likely to create fewer and be broad categorizers. This was particularly true for those students who were classified as low achievers. One can conclude, based upon these studies, that African-Americans tend to be narrow in their conceptualization of similarities of concepts.

An accompanying factor in categorization is, of course, the attributes which appear to be the most salient to the perceiver and which are used to develop the classifications. In a study of the categorization behavior of Navaho, Spanish, and Anglo-American children in New Mexico, Tagatz,

Lee, Layman, and Garrison (1971) noted ethnic differences in the processing of information for forming categories. In spite of these differences, however, the recall performance was similar.

In another study Franklin (1979) examined female adolescents under the assumption that words which could be clustered around cultural-specific units would be more readily recalled. He found that both the African- and Euro-American groups tended to have better recall of words which related to the Euro-American cultural orientation but that the most important mediating variable was the ability to identify and classify words into discrete categories. In another study with adolescents, Franklin and Fulani (1979) found that no sex difference or recall differences existed between the ethnic groups. However, it was noted that blacks tended to cluster the words more than whites and recalled more of them in later trials. Similar findings were reported by Orasanu, Lee and Scribner (1979) in their investigation using 210 elementary children distributed by race and socioeconomic status. Although no difference was noted in the amount of recall, a significant difference was noted in the types of categories created for organizing the information to be recalled. African-American children and lower socioeconomic children tended to categorize concepts based upon functional attributes or the use of the object rather than around particular physical or conceptual similarities. It would also appear that words or objects which have a positive affective impact on students also facilities conceptual transformation and helps in the recall of information. Rychlak, Hewitt, and Hewitt (1973) found that African-American students performed better with paired associate words they liked than those they disliked. A similar finding was reported by August and Felker (1977) and Rychlak (1975).

INFORMATION ANALYSIS AND EVALUATION

The difference manifested in the sorting behavior of African-Americans may be a difference in cognitive strategies with African-Americans apparently proceeding with a top-down processing approach rather than the bottom-up approach most often used in teaching (Anderson, 1980). On the other hand, this variation noted in perceptual analysis and organization may be based upon "what" is being discriminated. This is to say that the types of tasks used to assess categorization behavior may not be registering a difference in processing but rather in what is being perceived (Cole, Gay, Glick, & Sharp, 1971).

Sigel, Anderson, and Shapiro (1966) noted, for example, that while class and IQ did not seem to make a difference in the sorting behavior manifested, the method of presentation did have an effect. Some children within their sample did not respond to pictorial representations of the objects at all, but did very well in response to the objects themselves. In research by this author, only a slight difference was noted between African-American and Euro-American students on the Clayton-Jackson Object Sorting Task which is a written list of objects to be categorized. A highly significant difference was noted, however, in a pictorial task in which the students were asked to discern similar characteristics of objects and select another which was comparable (Shade, 1983).

There is a general assumption that any mode of presentation will elicit the same type of information processing behavior (Sigel, Anderson, Shapiro, 1966). This may not be the case.

Mangan (1978), Kennedy (1974) and Hagan and Jones (1978) point out that interpretations of visual images are learned within the cultural milieu of the individual. Images which may have cultural interpretations include photographs, images representing spatial information, geometric forms, and line drawings. Teaching the decoding of these representations is analogous to teaching children to read the written word (Mangan, 1978). Thus, a pictorial image should not be expected to convey the same information to all individuals or groups. If we assume, then, that the pictorial representations as found in the Matching Familiar Figures Test, the Raven's Progressive Matrices, the Bender-Gestalt Test, and other such instruments are *not* the nonsymbolic representations of the world they are purported to be, we can also assume that African-American children may be seeing and registering different information from these tasks than expected.

The possibility that variation in performance on pictorial psychometric tasks is due to processing differences rather than ability differences was the basis for the study conducted by Blaha, Fawz and Wallbrown (1979). These researchers administered the Bender-Gestalt, the Goodenough Draw-A-Person Test and the Matching Familiar Figures Test to 74 middle-class African-American students in the first grade. The tasks were then correlated on the basis of the subprocesses involved in the information processing paradigm and IQ. The results demonstrated that 9 percent of the variance in performance was accounted for by intelligence, 6 percent of the variance by visual-motor integration and coordination, 3 percent by the response time, and the remaining variance, or 16 percent, was accounted for by the perceptual process in the information processing model.

Using the supposition that there may be a difference in what is being perceived when the information appears in pictorial form, previous studies of African-American cognitive patterns were reexamined by identifying the task requirements of the tasks African-American students were asked to complete.

In the study of various ethnic groups, Stodolsky and Lesser (1967) used four tasks. A verbal ability task which required memorization of verbal labels; a reasoning task which required the formation of concepts; a number facility task in which students used various arithmetic processes; and a space conceptualization task which required students to interpret pictures by visualizing movement, spatial relationships, or size. Results indicated that African-Americans did best on the verbal, than the reasoning and number tasks, and ended up as the lowest of the four ethnic groups on the space conceptualization task. This pattern was found for both the middle and lower class sample as well as in the sample from another city.

Rohwer (1971) also examined the cognitive patterns of African- and Euro-American children who were five to eight years of age. Large differences were found between the groups on the pictorial vocabulary task (the Peabody Picture Vocabulary Test) and the Raven's Progressive Matrices, a test which requires the completion of a pictorial pattern series. Little, if any, difference was found on the learning proficiency task which required the learning and transformation of verbal pairs. This same type of disparity is found throughout the literature with African-Americans doing as well, if not better, than their age group on tasks using aural perception, but poorly on tasks requiring visual picture perception (Hall & Kaye, 1977; Guinagh, 1971).

Backman (1972) in her study of patterns of cognitive abilities of talented youngsters from four racial groups in the ninth through the twelfth grades compared the groups using several achievement tests, a visual reasoning task, a task measuring perceptual-motor coordination and memory. The results reported indicated that African-Americans, regardless of socioeconomic status, had high scores on the perceptual speed and accuracy task but ended up as the lowest of all the ethnic groups on the visual reasoning task.

In their review of the perceptual difference manifested by people of African-American heritage, Mandler and Stein (1977) point out that this same pattern between verbal and pictorial representations appears in the literature on intelligence test performance. When the verbal and performance IQ scores are compared, little, if any, difference is noted on the verbal subtests, but consistently lower scores are found on the visual-spatial performance tasks, i.e., the Block Design Test, the Object Assembly, and the Picture Completion tasks (Young & Bright, 1954; Davidson, 1950; Teahan & Drews, 1962). A similar pattern emerged in a study done by Vance, Hankins, and McGee (1979) using the WISC–R. Farnham-Diggory (1970) reported similar findings in her examination of information processing by young children. She found that African-American children did well in the processing and synthesizing of verbal material, but poorly on visual material which required analysis and organization.

A similar pattern of verbal and pictorial processing differences was found in the study by A.R. Jensen (1973). Children at the fourth, fifth, and sixth grades representing three ethnic groups were given a rather extensive battery of standardized tests. Rather than identify differences on each measure, basic underlying processes were factored out, and three factors emerged. Factor one was found to load heavily on all of the verbal-type tests in the battery; factor two was represented in the pictorial type tasks; and factor three included those tests requiring memorization. Although Jensen labeled each factor as a type of intelligence, they could just as easily have been labeled as types of information to be processed.

In addition to the intelligence measures and such tests as the Raven's Progressive Matrices, attention must also be paid to tests such as the Bender-Gestalt, the Thematic Apperception Test, and the Rorschach. In studies using each of these measures which require pictorial/visual information processing, African-Americans end up with lower or different than expected performances (Henderson, Butler, & Goffeney, 1969; Albott and Gunn, 1971; Marmorale & Brown, 1977). It is also interesting to note that the Alpha and Beta tests used by the Army as the first classification test and which set the stage for the consistent labeling of African-Americans as inferior beings also contained a substantial number of subtests which required visual information processing (Jenkins & Paterson, 1961).

Finally, attention must also be given to the test most often used to study cognitive style, i.e., the Embedded Figures Test, another visual processing task. As with the instruments, African-Americans end up with lower scores, suggesting that they are more likely to be field-dependent (Perney, 1976; Ritzinger, 1971; Schratz, 1976; Gamble, 1971; Shade, 1986).

For each of these instruments a less than expected performance by African-Americans has been interpreted as some type of a deficit. Mandler and Stein (1977) suggest that a deficit approach is inappropriate. A more plausible explanation may be that African-Americans have merely been taught to perceive, that is to visually transform, the world differently.

CONCLUSIONS

How do African-Americans come to know the world? From all indications their knowledge is gained most effectively through kinetic and tactile senses, through the keen observation of the human scene, and through verbal descriptions. This difference in perception manifests itself, not only in worldview, but also in modality preference, cue selection, and pictorial perception. Although our examinations of the effect of melanine may lead to an additional factorial contribution to the difference in the perceptual process (Pasteur & Toldson, 1982; Stewart, 1981), at this point in time culture appears to be the major "progenitor" of this variation.

The evidence that these patterns exist, while sufficient to produce a strong intuitive argument, is really insufficient to produce the types of changes necessary in the teaching-learning process and in the assessment of skills. There is an overwhelming need for a cadre of scholars to examine these issues in the laboratories and in the field in an effort to support these propositions. With substantiation, it would then be possible to encourage a more concentrated and positive look at modality-based instruction, a less value oriented approach to the differences in cognitive style, and perhaps, a process, rather than ability, orientation to the concept of intelligence.

The type of learner described by these patterns who can tolerate and live with diversity and variety, who can conceptualize the world as a whole rather than just in its parts, who is personable and an exceptional observer and interactor with society is exactly the type of person Toeffler (1980) suggests will do well in "The Third Wave" civilization. If this is the case, these traits not only epitomize African-Americans but will be the type of cognitive patterns promoted for society in general. Understanding these dimensions, then, becomes not only a defense against past judgments, but also and more importantly, the basis for the development of the capacity to adapt to our future existence.

REFERENCES

1. Albott, W.L., & Gunn, H.E.: Bender-Gestalt performance by culturally disadvantaged first graders. *Perceptual and Motor Skills, 33:*247–250, 1971.
2. Anderson, J. R.: *Cognitive Psychology and Its Implications.* San Francisco, W. H. Freeman, 1980.
3. Backman, M. E.: Patterns of mental abilities: Ethnic socioeconomic status and sex differences. *American Educational Research Journal, 9:*1–12, 1972.
4. Barbe, W. B., & Swassing, R. H.: *Teaching Through Modality Strengths: Concepts and Practices.* Columbus, Zaner-Bloser, 1979.
5. Barsch, R. H.: The processing mode hierarchy as a potential deterrent to cognitive efficiency. In Hellmuth, J. (Ed.): *Cognitive Studies: 2: Deficits in Cognition.* New York, Brunner/Mazel, 1971.
6. Berry, J. W.: *Human Ecology and Cognitive Style: Comparative Studies in Cultural and Psychological Adaptation.* New York, John Wiley & Sons, 1976.
7. Blackwell, J. E.: *The Black Community: Diversity and Unity.* New York, Dodd, Mead, 1975.
8. Blaha, J., Fawz, N., & Wallbrown, F.: Information processing components of Koppitz errors on the Bender-Gestalt. *Journal of Clinical Psychology, 35:*784–790, 1979.
9. Boykin, A. W.: Psychological/behavioral verve: Some theoretical explorations and empirical manifestations. In Boykin, A. W., Franklin, A. J., & Yates, J. F. (Eds.): *Research Directions of Black Psychologists.* New York, Russell Sage Foundation, 1979.
10. Bruner, J. S.: *On Knowing: Essays for the Left Hand.* New York, Atheneum, 1968.
11. Chance, J., Goldstein, A., & McBride, L.: Differential experience and recognition memory for faces. *Journal of Social Psychology, 97:*243–253, 1975.
12. Cole, M., Gay, J., Glick, J., & Sharp, D. W.: *The Cultural Context of Learning and Thinking.* New York, Basic Books, 1971.
13. Cole, M., & Scribner, S.: *Culture and Thought: A Psychological Introduction.* New York, John Wiley & Sons, 1974.
14. Cureton, G. O.: Using a black learning style. *The Reading Teacher, 1:*751–756, 1978.
15. Damico, S. B.: The two worlds of school: Differences in the photographs of black and white adolescents. Paper presented at the annual meeting of the American Educational Research Association, Montreal, 1983.
16. Das, J. P., Kirby, J., & Jarmon, R. F.: Simultaneous and successive syntheses: An alternative model for cognitive ability. *Psychological Bulletin, 82:*87–103, 1975.
17. Davidson, K. S.: A preliminary study of Negro and white differences on form I of the Wechsler-Bellevue scale. *Journal of Consulting Psychology, 6:*489–492, 1950.
18. Eato, L. E., & Lerner, R. M.: Relations of physical and social environment perceptions to adolescent self esteem. *Journal of Genetic Psychology, 139:*143–150, 1981.
19. Farley, F. H.: A theoretical-predictive model of creativity. Paper presented at

the annual meeting of the American Psychological Association, New Orleans, August, 1975.

20. Farley, F. H.: Basic process individual differences; A biologically based theory of individualization for cognitive, affective and creative outcomes. In Farley, F. H., & Gordon, N. J. (Eds.): *Psychology and Education: The State of the Union.* Berkeley, McCutchan, 1981.

21. Farnham-Diggory, S.: Cognitive synthesis in Negro-white children. *Monograph of the Society for Research in Child Development, 35,* #4., 1970.

22. Fernald, G. M.: Diagnosis of mental imagery. *Psychological Review,* Monograph Supplement, #58, 1912.

23. Fernald, G. M.: *Remedial Techniques in Basic School Subjects.* New York, McGraw-Hill, 1943.

24. Gagne, R. M.: *The Conditions of Learning* (3rd ed). New York, Holt, Rinehart & Wilson, 1977.

25. Galper, R.: Functional race membership and recognition of faces. *Perceptual and Motor Skills, 37:*455–462, 1973.

26. Gamble, J. F.: Cognitive and linguistic style differences among educationally advantaged and disadvantaged eighth-grade boys. Doctoral dissertation, University of Tennessee, 1971.

27. Gibson, E. J.: *Principles of Perceptual Learning and Development.* New York, Appleton-Century-Crofts, 1969.

28. Gibson, J. J.: *The Perception of the Visual World.* Boston, Houghton-Mifflin, 1950.

29. Gitter, A. G., Black, H., & Mostofsky, D.: Race and sex in the perception of emotion. *Journal of Social Issues, 28:*63–78, 1972.

30. Guinagh, B. J.: An experimental study of basic learning ability and intelligence in low socioeconomic status children. *Child Development, 42:*27–36, 1971.

31. Guttentag, M.: Negro-white differences in children's movement. *Perceptual and Motor Skills, 35:*435–436, 1972.

32. Hagan, M. A., & Jones, R. D.: Cultural effects on pictorial perception: How many words is one picture really worth? In Walk, R. D., & Pick, H. L. Jr. (Eds.): *Perception and Experience.* New York, Plenum Press, 1978.

33. Hall, B. C., & Kaye, D. B.: Patterns of early cognitive development among boys in four subcultural groups. *Journal of Educational Psychology, 69:*66–87, 1977.

34. Henderson, N. B., Butler, B. W., & Goffeney, B.: Effectiveness of the WISC and Bender-Gestalt test in predicting arithmetic and reading achievement for white and non-white children. *Journal of Clinical Psychology, 25:*268–271, 1969.

35. Hill, W. H., & Fox, W. M.: Black and white marine squad leaders' perception of racially mixed squads. *Academy of Management Journal, 16:*680–686, 1973.

36. Jenkins, J. J., & Paterson, D. G.: *Studies in Individual Differences: The Search for Intelligence.* New York, Appleton-Century-Crofts, 1961.

37. Jensen, A. R.: Level I and Level II abilities in three ethnic groups. *American Educational Research Journal, 10:*263–276, 1973.

38. Jung, C.: *Psychological types.* London, Routledge & Kegan Paul, 1923 [Translated 1949 by H. Goodwin Baynes].

39. Keil, C.: *Urban Blues.* Chicago, University of Chicago Press, 1966.
40. Kennedy, J. M.: *A Psychology of Picture Perception.* San Francisco, Jossey-Bass, 1974.
41. Kochman, T.: The kinetic element in black idiom. In Kochman, T. (Ed.): *Rappin and Stylin Out: Communication in Urban Black America.* Urbana, University of Illinois Press, 1972.
42. Levy, N., Murphy, C., & Carlson, R.: Personality types among Negro college students. *Educational and Psychological Measurement, 32:*641–653, 1972.
43. Luce, T. S.: The role of experience in interracial recognition. *Personality and Social Psychology, 1:*39–41, 1974.
44. Malone, C. A.: Developmental deviations considered in the light of environmental forces. In Pavenstedt, E. (Ed.): *The Drifters: Children of Disorganized Lower-Class Families.* Boston, Little, Brown, 1967.
45. Mandler, J. M., & Stein, N. L.: The myth of perceptual defect: Sources and evidence. *Psychological Bulletin, 84:*173–194, 1977.
46. Mangan, J.: Cultural conventions of pictorial representation: Iconic literacy and education. *Educational Communication and Technology Journal, 26:*245–267, 1978.
47. Marmorale, A., & Brown, F.: Bender-Gestalt performance of Puerto Rican, white and Negro children. *Journal of Clinical Psychology, 33:*224–228, 1977.
48. Morgan, H.: Factors concerning cognitive development and learning differentiation among black children. In Harrison, A. E.: (Ed.) *Conference on Empirical Research in Black Psychology, 6:* 14–22, 1981.
49. Morris, L. W.: *Extraversion and Introversion: An Interactional Approach.* Washington, Hemisphere, 1979.
50. Myers, I. B.: *Gifts Differing.* Palo Alto, Consulting Psychological Press, 1980.
51. Orasanu, J., Lee, C., & Scribner, S.: Free recall: Ethnic and economic group comparisons. *Child Development, 50:*1100–1109, 1979.
52. Pasteur, A. B., & Toldson, I. L.: *Roots of Soul: The Psychology of Black Expressiveness.* Garden City, Anchor Press/Doubleday, 1982.
53. Pavenstedt, E. (Ed.): *The Drifters: Children of Disorganized Lower-Class Families.* Boston, Little, Brown & Co., 1967.
54. Perney, V. H.: Effects of race and sex on field dependence-independence of children. *Perceptual and Motor Skills, 42:*975–980, 1976.
55. Richmond, B. O.: Creative and cognitive abilities of white and Negro children. *Journal of Negro Education, 40:*111–116, 1971.
56. Ritzinger, F. C.: Psychological and Physiological differentiation in children six to eleven years of age. Doctoral dissertation, Washington University, St. Louis, 1971.
57. Rohwer, W. D.: Learning, race, and school success. *Review of Educational Research, 41:*191–211, 1971.
58. Rosch, E.: Universals and cultural specifics in human categorization. In Brislin, R. W., Bochner, S., & Lonner, W. J. (Eds.): *Cross Cultural Perspectives on Learning.* Palo Alto, Sage Publications, 1975.

59. Rychlak, J. F.: Affective assessment, intelligence, social class, and racial learning style. *Journal of Personality and Social Psychology, 32:*989–995, 1975.
60. St. John, N.: Thirty-six teachers: Their characteristics and outcomes for black and white pupils. *American Educational Research Journal, 8:*635–648, 1971.
61. Schratz, M.: A developmental investigation of sex differences in perceptual differentiation and mathematic reasoning in two ethnic groups. Doctoral dissertation, Fordham University, 1976.
62. Shade, B. J.: Afro-American patterns of cognition. Unpublished manuscript. Madison, WI: Wisconsin Center for Educational Research, 1983.
63. Shade, B. J.: Is there an Afro-American cognitive style? *Journal of Black Psychology, 13:*13–16, 1986.
64. Sherif, C. W.: Social distance as categorization of intergroup interaction. *Journal of Personality and Social Psychology, 25:*327–334, 1973.
65. Sigel, I. E., Anderson, L. M., & Shapiro, H.: Categorization behavior of lower and middle-class Negro preschool children. *Journal of Negro Education, 35:*218–229, 1966.
66. Slavin, R. E.: *Cooperative Learning.* New York/London, Longman Press, 1983.
67. Sommers, R.: *The Mind's Eye: Imagery in Everyday Life.* New York, Delacore Press, 1978.
68. Stewart, M. D.: Sensori-motor abilities of the African-American Infants: Implications for development screening. Doctoral dissertation, George Peabody College for Teachers of Vanderbilt, 1981.
69. Stigler, R.: Comparison of the capacity to perceive minute movements in the visual periphery in whites and Negroes. *Biological Review, 30:*114–126, 1940.
70. Stodolsky, S., & Lesser, G.: Learning patterns in the disadvantaged. *Harvard Educational Review, 37:*546–593, 1967.
71. Strom, R. D., & Bernard, H. W.: *Educational Psychology.* Monterrey, Brooks/Cole, 1982.
72. Teahan, J. E., & Drews, E. M.: A comparison of northern and southern Negro children on the WISC. *Journal of Consulting Psychology, 26:*292, 1962.
73. Thompson, L.: *Secrets of culture: Nine community studies.* New York, Random House, 1969.
74. Toeffler, A.: *The Third Wave.* New York, William Morrow, 1980.
75. Travers, R. M. W.: *Essentials of Learning* (5th ed.). New York, Macmillan, 1982.
76. Tyler, L. E.: *The Psychology of Human Differences* (2nd ed.). New York, Appleton-Century-Crofts, 1956.
77. Van Alstyne, D., & Osbourne, E.: Rhythmic responses of Negro and white children two to six. *Monographs of the Society for Research in Child Development, 2,* #4, 1937.
78. Vance, H., Hankins, N., & McGee, H.: A preliminary study of black/white differences on the revised Wechsler Intelligence Scale for Children. *Journal of Clinical Psychology, 35:*815–819, 1979.
79. Witmer, J., & Ferinden, F.: Perception of school climate: Comparison of black and white teachers within the same schools. *Journal of the Student Personnel Association for Teacher Education, 9:*1–7, 1970.

80. Wober, M.: Sensotypes. *Journal of Social Psychology, 70:*181–189, 1966.

81. Young, M. F., & Bright, H. A.: Results of testing 81 Negro rural juveniles with WISC. *Journal of Social Psychology, 39:*219–226, 1954.

82. Young, V. H. Family and Childhood in a Southern Negro Community. *American Anthropologist, 72:*269–288, 1970.

83. Young, V. H.: A black American socialization pattern. *American Ethnologist, 1:*405–413, 1974.

Chapter 9

STYLES OF LEARNING AMONG NATIVE CHILDREN: A REVIEW OF THE RESEARCH*

BRENT KAULBACK

One of the more recent attempts to improve the delivery of educational programs in schools has been to try to match the methods of instruction to the individual perceptual strengths or preferences of the child. Recent research in the fields of neurology, education, and behavioral psychology has confirmed that many children differ in the ways they learn and process information. Children have been classified according to their performance on visual, auditory, and kinesthetic perceptual tests. Some children, it appears, learn best when visual input is presented and they are able to abstract principles from images and pictures. Others have keen auditory abilities and such children can generally remember details and information presented through oral lesson formats. Kinesthetic learners, in contrast, tend to utilize their sense of touch and these children learn best when allowed to write down information and manipulate tactile objects.

The assumption behind matching teaching to sensory modality in this way is that one sensory channel, either visual, auditory, or kinesthetic, will function more effectively than the other two for the purposes of processing information. It is argued that instruction keyed to a child's perceptual strength will considerably enhance and facilitate his ability to learn. Conversely, those taught without any regard for individual differences in learning style may experience great difficulty and even face school failure if they lack the strategies to efficiently process and retain information presented in a particular manner.

Some researchers view this mismatch between learning style and

*From Kaulback, Brent. Styles of learning among Native children: A review of the research. *Canadian Journal of Native Education*, 11:27–37, 1984. Used with permission.

instructional methods as a prime cause of school failure among Native children (Havinghurst, 1970; Kleinfeld, 1970). Kleinfeld (1970), for instance, presented the hypothesis that Inuit children often possess unusual perceptual strengths which are seldom recognized or tapped within formal school programs. She speculated that educational programs and methods designed to utilize and complement the perceptual strengths of these children would enhance their academic progress. Similarly, Havinghurst (1970) suggested that instructional methods employed by teachers of Indian children are not always effective owing to the distinct needs and perceptual abilities of these children. It was his contention that a careful analysis of the methods being used by teachers of Native children could become the basis for more adequate instructional techniques.

In the light of this research, which has questioned the effectiveness of certain teaching practices in Native education, and in view of our need to constantly upgrade and improve the delivery of educational programs, I propose to review the research and literature which has revealed pertinent information about the perceptual abilities or learning styles of both Indian and Inuit children. Following this review, I will attempt to identify those factors which may account for the distinct learning styles of these children. It is my hope that this review and discussion will provide teachers with a strong base from which they can examine their own teaching practices and begin to develop modality-based programs and materials which may enhance the academic progress of Native children.

HISTORICAL OVERVIEW

Long before researchers became interested in the issue of learning styles, it was generally assumed that Native children lacked the innate intelligence to succeed in formal school programs. As late as 1924, one observer of Native education was convinced that the extent to which Native children could succeed in schools depended upon the amount of Anglo blood flowing in their veins (Berry, 1968, p. 320). This assumption was supported, at the time, by findings from an extensive testing program which consistently revealed that Native children achieved less well than non-Native children on tests measuring intelligence and innate ability. It wasn't until researchers began to critically examine the content and bias of these tests that this fallacious assumption was seriously challenged. Researchers suggested that these tests, all of which emphasized verbal reasoning skills, openly discriminated against Native children, many of whom did not understand the English language (Jamieson & Sandford, 1928). Other researchers discredited this assumption by pointing to evidence that indicated that Native children scored exceedingly well on intelligence tests which used visual material such as the Goodenough Draw-A-Man Test (Goodenough, 1926; Telford, 1932; Anderson & Eels, 1935).

The findings of these Draw-A-Man testing programs have had important implications for Native education. Not only did the programs help shatter the ethnocentric assumption that Indian and Inuit children were uneducable, but the findings provided researchers with the first empirical evidence, albeit indirect, that Native children were better able to respond to visually loaded test items than they were to tests which emphasized verbal and auditory skills.

Two researchers (McCartin & Schill, 1977), after reviewing the evidence from several Draw-A-Man testing programs, speculated on the instructional implications of the findings. They wrote, "If performance on tests is any indication, it appears that the American-Indian child has greater facility in learning when visual methods of instruction are used and performs less well when tasks are saturated with verbal content" (p. 15).

RECENT FINDINGS

The hypothesis that Native children learn best from visual stimulation and are less efficient in processing auditory information has been more recently substantiated through a series of test programs designed to delve into the issue of learning styles among Native children. The Illinois Test of Psycholinguistic Abilities (ITPA), a test designed to measure the psycholinguistic abilities and disabilities of children, has been used extensively by researchers to identify the perceptual channels through which Native children appear to learn most effectively (Garber, 1968; Kuske, 1969; Lombardi, 1969; Taylor & Skanes, 1975). The ITPA is comprised of a series of subtests, each designed to reveal pertinent information about specific auditory and visual abilities thought to be basic to the process of learning. The ITPA subtests probe the receptive, associative, and expressive processes (both auditory and visual) used by each learner.

Garber (1968) administered the ITPA to 110 Navajo and Pueblo first-grade children. The findings of this testing program revealed that these children were particularly adept at processing visual information. They were able to remember visual symbols, manipulate pictures and designs, and understand relationships which involved visual associations much better than they could handle the subtests keyed to auditory skills.

These findings are consistent with those obtained from a study conducted among Papago Indian children. Lombardi (1970) administered the ITPA to 80 first and third-grade Papago children from both integrated and segregated schools. He noticed that the Papago children, like the Navajo and Pueblo children studied by Garber, possessed unusual visual channel strength. Both the integrated and segregated groups far exceeded normative standards in subtests measuring visual sequencing memory. However, the children scored significantly below normative standards on tests measuring auditory reception ability to derive meaning from material presented verbally), auditory association (a verbal analogies test) and grammatic closure (ability to respond automatically to verbal expressions of standard English usage). Lombardi attributed the Papago's unusual ability to handle visual information to cultural factors. He wrote, "Papagos still actively engage in activities such as basket weaving, a process which requires considerable visual motor sequencing abilities. It would appear the Papago children have emulated their parents' model" (p. 487).

Results similar to those recorded by Garber and Lombardi were obtained from ITPA testing programs among other Native groups including Sioux children (Kuske, 1969) and children from the Flathead Reserve in Western Montana (Downey, 1977). Yet, of particular interest in northern educators is an ITPA testing program conducted in Northern Canada. Careful to control for the skewing efforts that environmental influences may have upon the ITPA test results, Taylor and Skanes (1975) administered the ITPA to Inuit and white children, all from isolated communities in Labrador. The psycholinguistic differences between these two groups of children were particularly revealing. The authors of the study summarized the results:

> These children (Inuit) score the lowest on the following subtests: auditory association, verbal expression, grammatic closure, auditory closure and sound blending and particularly poorly on three of these. All of the subtests are heavily loaded on a verbal factor. The (Inuit) children score better than the typical Labrador white subjects . . . on visual reception, visual sequential memory, visual association and visual closure (p. 37).

Cautious Interpretation

The results of these ITPA testing programs must be cautiously and carefully interpreted. Indeed a superficial analysis of the findings, considered as a whole would clearly indicate that Native children, in general, possess specific areas of perceptual strengths and weaknesses. All of the studies point to the fact that both Indian and Inuit children are most successful at processing visual information and have the most difficulty performing well on tasks saturated with verbal content. We must remember, however, that many of the ITPA subtests measuring auditory abilities are verbally loaded and, as such, are more a measure of one's receptive and expressive knowledge of the English language rather than one's ability to handle auditory information. Although it is fair to assume that a child lacking receptive and expressive knowledge of English would likely experience difficulty in formal school programs where English is the language of instruction, it is too premature to imply from these results alone that Native children are deficit in their ability to conceptualize through language. Only a testing program conducted in the child's Native language would yield valid information about the child's auditory perceptual ability. Nevertheless, the findings from these ITPA testing programs do clearly indicate that Native children are able to efficiently and effectively process and retain information presented through visual formats.

One Explanation

Numerous explanations, offered by anthropologists, educators and psychologists, have been advanced to account for the Native child's propensity towards a more visually oriented learning style. Berry (1966) has conducted experiments among the Canadian Inuit which has provided the basis for one explanation. He administered a battery of tests designed to measure certain visual perceptual abilities and spatial skills to Inuit subjects from Baffin Island and to a comparison group from Sierra Leone, Africa. The results indicated that the Inuit subjects far surpassed the comparison group on all measures of visual discrimination ability and spatial skills [field independence]. Berry suggested that certain ecological factors such as the nature of the environment and cultural activities to which the Inuit are exposed, may have led to the development of highly acute visual and spatial skills among the Inuit subjects. He elaborated on the nature of these skills:

> It is evident that the (Inuit) must develop certain perceptual skills, merely to survive in their situation . . . He must first of all in order to hunt effectively develop the ability to isolate slight variations in visual stimulation from a rather featureless array; he must learn to be aware of minute detail. Secondly, in order to navigate effectively in this environment he must learn to organize these small details into a spatial awareness, an awareness of his present location in relation to objects around him. (p. 212)

Kleinfeld's (1970) analysis of the perceptual abilities of the Alaskan Inuit has added new insight to Berry's contention that ecological demands are determining factors in the development of certain perceptual skills. She reviewed rich sources of historical and ethnographic research and found that there is constant reference, in this literature, to the highly acute visual skills of the Inuit. Not only could the Inuit navigate across seemingly featureless terrain, but they were able to draw accurate maps and comprehend images regardless of spatial orientation.

In the same study, Kleinfeld reported the results of a research project in which she compared the image memory abilities of village Inuit and urban white children. Image memory, or the ability to recall complex visual patterns, was selected for analysis because such a perceptual task is closely related to the demands made by hunting in an arctic environment" (p. 11). Kleinfeld speculated that the test would favor the Inuit subjects because of their close proximity to the environment and their exposure to a hunting tradition. Indeed, at the conclusion of the testing program, the results indicated that in all age categories the Inuit children outperformed the urban white children in their ability to recall the complex patterns.

It appears, then, based on Berry's (1966) and Kleinfeld's (1970) research and analyses, that the ecological demands placed upon a society help to define and facilitate the development of certain perceptual skills among its members. This may account for the fact that many Native children exposed as they are to an active hunting and trapping tradition, may possess highly refined visual perceptual skills. Yet, there remain many more Native children, unexposed to the harsh realities of hunting, trapping, and a subsistence way of life, who have still the developed the acute perceptual abilities, similar to their more traditional counterparts. Indeed, Berry (1971), in a subsequent study to his first, noted that Inuit subjects from an urban center outperformed Inuit subjects from a more traditional community on specific tests measuring visual discrimination even though the hunting activity of the urban group had diminished considerably. There must remain, then, factors other than ecological ones which have spurred the development of sophisticated visual perceptual skills among Native children. Researchers are now beginning to study the culturally distinct activities associated with child rearing and there is mounting evidence that child-rearing traits, irrespective of a society's orientation toward traditional or nontraditional activities, may account for the distinctly visual style of learning among Native children.

In all societies, the patterns and practices of child rearing generally function to provide each child with the prerequisite social, linguistic, and technological skills necessary for successful immersion within that society. However, history has shown us that in times of rapid and unexpected changes to the economic and cultural fabric of a society, child-rearing practices remain almost as a constant, lagging far behind such developments. Such is the case in many Native communities in which rapid changes to their economy and culture have not as yet profoundly affected the methods of raising children. Irrespective of a community's present orientation toward traditional or nontraditional activities, child-rearing practices among many Native families are much the same as they were a generation ago.

True, the infusion of elements from the white society into the Native culture have changed the materials used in child rearing (milk bottles, toys, etc.), but the practices of child rearing and, in particular, the methods of interaction between infant and parent, have remained relatively constant. The by-product of such practices were and still are visually acute perceptual skills among its young. The literature on both past and present Indian and Inuit societies is replete with suggestions that child-rearing practices have nurtured and reinforced such skills (Hilger, 1951; Cazden & John, 1969; Kleinberg, 1970; Rohner, 1965).

Throughout this rich ethnographic research, constant reference is made to the fact that Native children learn by observing and imitating the actions of their parents, elders and older siblings. Basically, in most Native societies, the child is a revered member of the family unit and, as such, is a welcomed spectator and participant to all types of family and community affairs. Indeed, it is not uncommon to see young Native children accompanying their parents (or siblings) to bingos, community meetings, church, or even to their places of employment. This constant and close proximity to the actions of others provides the child with a valuable opportunity to intimately familiarize himself with a multitude of tasks. These tasks may range from simple domestic duties such as sweeping the floor, carrying water or cooking to highly sophisticated and complex activities such as carving, beading, or making a parka.

Spurred on by a natural curiosity and a desire to become an integral and useful member of the family unit, the maturing child will, in time, attempt to imitate the actions and activities of those he has observed for so long. Often the child will manipulate real tools and equipment during these imitative play sessions and, by so doing, slowly learn the real-life skills necessary to ensure his acceptance within the community.

Cazden and John (1968) characterized this style of learning as "learning through looking." Others labelled it observational learning and learning by doing. Whatever the label, child-rearing practices dictate that young Native children use the tools of observation and playful imitation to learn from their parents, siblings, and elders.

This style of learning has had a profound effect upon the development of certain skills within the perceptual repertoire of Native children. Stimulated, as they are, to observe accurately, these children have acquired the ability to organize their observations and form concepts from them. The children have, in other words, learned to learn through visual means.

In many ways, the patterns of child rearing used in many Native societies resemble those prevalent in all societies. All children, regardless of skin color or culture are encouraged to learn through observing and imitating the actions of others. Indeed, careful observation and imitative play are tools of learning which are universal and are not bound by culture, color, or class. Yet, there remains an important and distinct difference between the child rearing practices used in most Native societies and those employed by adult members of the white culture—the use of verbal instruction.

Much of the informal learning that takes place in native societies is nonverbal in nature. The children learn the customs and skills of their society by sharing directly in the activities of others. In such situations, verbal instruction is neither offered nor required because the child's close proximity to the observable action makes instruction-giving quite redundant. One observer of Inuit society noted that in those infrequent instances where verbal instruction is used, the Inuit adult generally calls attention to the observable aspects of the situation (Kroeber, 1970).

In addition to this, much of the information that a young Native child is exposed to and expected to learn is best exchanged through the act of observation rather than verbalization. Consider, for example, these comments by Scribner and Cole (1973):

> Compare the many rich sources of information available to the child who learns to weave by watching and doing; he sees particular bits of material varying in width and flexibility, feels their tension and resistance, compares his physical movements to those of the modeler and integrates all these inputs from different sense modalities into his cognitive schema of what weaving is all about. Learning to weave by hearing a discourse on it is quite a different situation. (p. 556)

This style of learning, observational rather than verbal, contrasts sharply with the learning styles fostered through child-rearing practices prevalent in the dominant white society. Here, the conditions in which observation is the essential tool of learning, are often absent due, in large part, to the fact that white children do not often share directly in the activities of their parents or siblings as do Native children. Within a white community, a child's older siblings may belong to a peer group that excludes the membership of younger brothers and sisters. Likewise, the parent of the child may be absent from the home for extended periods of time each day as they pursue career goals. In such instances, the child is often entrusted to the care of a babysitter or enrolled in a day care center. Even in social terms, young white children are seldom taken to dances, movies, bingos, meetings, or other gatherings of adults.

This situation adds up to one in which the contextual referents around which learning may take place are not always shared by the members of the family group. As such, language, vis-a-vis question asking and verbal interaction become almost the exclusive means of exchanging information within the family unit.

Evidence to attest to this fact is slowly being accumulated by researchers interested in the topic of culturally dictated communicative styles. Lasoa (1977), for instance, analyzed the type and quality of verbal interaction between adults and children in the homes of white, middle-class, American families. He found that within this cultural group, questioning was the dominant interactive strategy used to solicit and exchange information. Laosa also noted that in comparison to other cultural groups, there was much more verbal interaction between mother and child in the Anglo-American household.

Complementary research has just recently been completed by Scollon and Scollon (1979). In their analysis of the style of communication prevalent among members of a small Native community in Northern

Canada, they noted that the Native children considered question-asking as an interactive strategy found in and reserved for schools. Question-asking was generally not a verbal strategy employed by the Native people in their day-to-day speech habits.

Although far from conclusive, there is a growing body of research to suggest that distinctively different child-rearing practices—one stressing observational learning and another emphasizing learning through verbalization—has fostered the development of very different styles of learning among Native and white children. Whereas many white children, by virtue of their upbringing and their linguistic exposure, are oriented towards using language as a vehicle for learning, Native children have developed a learning style characterized by observation and imitation.

Such differences in learning styles have far-reaching consequences in the formal education of Native students, particularly in view of the fact that the formal educative process almost always favors those who are highly verbal. Much to the detriment of Native children, "observation is a very limited (learning) technique in the overwhelmingly linguistic environment of the school" (Scribner & Cole, 1973, p. 556).

It would appear, then that many Native children, by virtue of their predisposition to a visual style of learning, may be handicapped in their ability to succeed in school because schools and teaching methods tend to cater to the auditory learner. In light of this, there is a definite need to critically examine the methods, programs, and materials we now use in Native schools and test for their effectiveness. The basic question that we must now ask ourselves is—are there better ways?

INSTRUCTIONAL IMPLICATIONS

Several instructional implications naturally emerge from the research and discussion presented in this article. Given the assumption that Native children are visual learners and they have the capacity and perceptual ability to ream details and concepts from visual information, teachers must first attempt to develop instructional materials which appeal to and stimulate the perceptual potential of these children. Such devices as films, diagrams, photographs, pictures, and concrete materials can all be used to supplement regular classroom instruction. Likewise, such visual materials as graphs, Venn diagrams, abstract line drawings, and flow charts may be useful in teaching conceptual relationships and English language abstractions to students in the upper elementary grades.

Second, teachers must work toward developing the methodology that taps and utilizes the perceptual strengths of Native children. Research has shown that visual instructional methods are far more effective in teaching concepts to most Native students than are methods which are oriented towards the verbal factor (Erickson, 1972; McCartin & Schill, 1977). Such methods as diagram supplemented lessons and demonstration-type lessons may both be well suited to the teaching of concepts in the content areas. Likewise, providing the children with illustrated procedures in subjects such as art, mathematics, science and physical education may assist them in learning concepts and following direction.

Third, teachers must critically examine the focus of some of their basic programs and in particular their reading program. If we can imply from the research presented here that visual methods of instruction promise the most success in Native education, then we must question the effectiveness of phonetic based reading programs, both in English and in the child's Native language. Perhaps a more visual approach to reading (i.e., Language Experience, Whole Word Method) would be more appropriate. Indeed, one researcher, in comparing visual and auditory methods of teaching reading to Native children, noted that the low-readiness group of children responded best to the visual method (Shears, 1970).

It should be added, however, that a visually-oriented reading program, to be truly effective, must be accompanied by a program designed to expand the child's conceptual understanding of the world in which he lives. Successful reading involves a process whereby the child interacts with the text and attaches meaning to the words and statements contained within. Any reading program offered to Native children must focus on meaning as its end goal.

Fourth, the entire issue of computer-assisted learning must be examined in regards to its application in Native education. The computer, as a teaching tool, promises to be an effective visual means of presenting and reviewing information. The best educational programs make superb use of visual aids to help the learner understand even abstract concepts. To date, few studies have been completed which have examined the effectiveness of computer-assisted learning in Native education (see Wells & Bell, 1980), but is my guess that the computer, because of its capabilities, may become the single most effective teaching and learning instrument in Native education. Obviously, there is a need for much more research, both in terms of identifying the personalized learning styles of students and developing programs to match those styles, but much of the ground-work has been completed and the potential is very exciting.

Finally, we must also realize that the research that points to the perceptual strengths of the Native students also reveals certain perceptual weaknesses which affect their ability to learn in schools. Minimally speaking, the research indicates that many Native children have difficulty comprehending and conceptualizing through the English language. Although there is an inarguable need to provide instruction wherever possible in the child's language, this research also indicates the need for effective ESL (English as a Second Language) or ESD (English as a Second Dialect) instruction. Therefore, any changes in methodology, materials, or programs to better accommodate the perceptual abilities of the Native child, must also be accompanied by the implementation of a strong ESL–ESD program. Native students must emerge from our school with sophisticated linguistic skills, both in terms of English and their Native language, if they are to succeed in or contend with the new society that is so quickly forming around them. Power lies in language.

To conclude, then, high drop-out rates and school failure among Native children is pressing all educators to examine their approaches to Native education. All too often educational systems respond to statistics of failure with restricted, basic skill approaches to learning. Perhaps, in light of the need for educational reform in Native schools, we must focus our energies towards adapting the method and materials of instruction to better suit the learning styles of Native children. Effective teaching leads to effective learning. Effective learning leads to success in school.

REFERENCES

1. Anderson, R. C. et al.: *Schemata as Scaffolding for the Representation of Information in Connected Discourse* (Technical Report No. 24). Urbana, Center for the Study of Reading, 1977.
2. Berry, B.: *The Education of American Indians*. Washington, D.C., U. S. Department of Health, Education and Welfare, 1968.
3. Berry, J.: Temne and Eskimo perceptual skills. *International Journal of Psychology, 1:*207–229, 1966.
4. Berry, J.: Ecological and cultural factors in spatial perceptual development. *Canadian Journal of Behavioral Science, 3:*324–336, 1971.
5. Cazden, C., & John V.: Learning in American Indian children. In Bureau of Indian Affairs (Ed.), *Styles of Learning Among American Indians: An Outline for Research*. Washington, D.C., Bureau of Indian Affairs, 1–18, 1969.

6. Downey, M.: A profile of psycholinguistic abilities of grades one, two and three students of the Flathead Reservation. Unpublished doctoral dissertation, University of Montana.

7. Erickson, D.: Verbal and diagram supplemented instructional strategies and achievement for Eskimo students. Unpublished qualifying paper, Harvard University, 1972.

8. Garber, M.: Ethnicity and measures of educability. Unpublished doctoral dissertation, University of Southern California.

9. Goodenough, F. L.: Racial differences in the intelligence of school children. *Journal of Experimental Psychology, 9:*388–395, 1926.

10. Havinghurst, R.: Goals of Indian education. The education of Indian children and youth: Summary report and recommendations. *National Study of American Indian Education, IV,* 1970.

11. Hilger, M. I.: *Chippewa Child Life and Its Cultural Background.* Washington, D.C., Government Printing Service, 1951.

12. Jamieson, E., & Sandiford, P.: The mental capacity of Southern Ontario Indians. *Journal of Educational Psychology, 19:*313–328; 536–551, 1928.

13. Kleinfeld, J.: *Cognitive Strength of Eskimos and Implications for Education.* Institute of Social, Economic and Government Research, University of Alaska, 1970.

14. Kuske, I.: *Psycholinguistic Abilities of Sioux Indian Children.* Unpublished doctoral dissertation, University of South Dakota, 1969.

15. Lasoa, L. M.: Maternal teaching strategies in Mexican-American families. Paper presented at the annual meeting of the American Educational Research Association, New York City, April, 1977.

16. Lombardi, T.: *Psycholinguistic Abilities of Papogo Indian School Children.* Unpublished doctoral dissertation, University of South Dakota, 1969.

17. McCartin, R., & Schill, W.: Three modes of instruction. *Journal of American Indian Education,* 14–20, 1977.

18. Rohner, E. P.: Factors influencing the academic performance of Kwakiutl children in Canada. *Comparative Education Review, 9:*331–340, 1965.

19. Scollon, R., & Scollon, S.: The literate two-year old: The fictionalization of self. Unpublished paper, 1979.

20. Scribner, S., & Cole, M.: Cognitive consequences of formal and informal education. *Science, 182:*553–559, 1973.

21. Shears, B. T.: Aptitude, content and method of teaching word recognition with young American Indian children. Unpublished doctoral dissertation, University of Minnesota.

22. Taylor, L., & Skanes, G.: Psycholinguistic abilities of children in isolated communities in Labrador. *Canadian Journal of Behavioral Science, 7:*30–39, 1975.

23. Telford, C. W.: Test performance of full and mixed blood North Dakota Indians. *Journal of Comparative Psychology, 14:*145–157, 1932.

Chapter 10

HMONG CULTURE AND COGNITIVE STYLE

JOAN THROWER TIMM AND BERTTRAM CHIANG

Because the history of the Hmong in the United States is not generally well-known, a brief overview of their history and traditional culture are included in this chapter in addition to the predominant cognitive style of Hmong students and its relationship to Hmong culture. Suggestions for classroom procedures for teachers working with Hmong students are discussed in a later chapter.

Hmong relocation in the United States, following political upheaval in Laos after the end of the Vietnam War, offered promise of a new life for Hmong refugees but created unforeseen difficulties as well. Since the mid 1970s until the present day, well-meaning sponsors, educators and social workers have worked to help the Hmong find their way in American society, but ignorance of American cultural values has confused the Hmong while ignorance of Hmong cultural values has confused those who work with them.

Historical Background

The Hmong trace their origins over four thousand years to central Asia from where they migrated to south central China (Moore, 1989). In the early nineteenth century they began settling in the highlands of what is now Thailand, Vietnam, and Laos. In the twentieth century Hmong experience has been dramatically affected by political events in Southeast Asia. The reasons for Hmong relocation to the United States and elsewhere are the result of events preceding, during, and following the Vietnam War (Livo & Cha, 1991; Moore, 1989; Puthiyottil, 1991; Takaki, 1990; Yang, 1993). In 1954, the French protectorate in Indo-China ended after sixty-one years. When the French withdrew from the region, Vietnam, Cambodia, and Laos became recognized as independent states by the Geneva Accords. In Laos, a struggle for power ensued between the Royal

Lao government, formerly aligned with the French and supported by the United States, and the Pathet Lao who were communists. For a time in the 1960s, some Hmong joined these Laotian Communists in defending Laos against incursions by the Vietnamese (Mattison, Lo, & Scarseth, 1994). When the Laotian communists joined with the Viet Minh (the north Vietnamese communists), the Hmong did not join their alliance with North Vietnam.

Between 1955 and 1975, areas including Hmong lands passed back and forth between the Pathet Lao and the Royal Lao. During the 1960s the U. S. CIA increased secret military operations in Laos and recruited the Hmong, living in villages in the northwestern highlands, to support these operations. Under the leadership of General Vang Pao, they were given three responsibilities: (a) to sabotage North Vietnamese convoys along the Ho Chi Minh Trail; (b) to rescue American pilots shot down in aerial combat; and (c) to protect the radar system located on the Pathee Plateau (Podeschi and Xiong, 1992). In exchange, the United States promised to protect them in the future, regardless of the outcome of the war. When the U. S. withdrew from the Vietnam War in 1975, American support in Laos ceased (Mattison, Lo, & Scarseth, 1994) and the Constitutional Monarchy in Laos collapsed (Dunnigan, 1986). The Pathet Lao gained control of the country and began a bloody campaign to exterminate the Hmong, in retribution for their support of both the Royal Lao and the United States. The Pathet Lao bombed Hmong villages, murdered men, women, and children of all ages and deported some residents to "reeducation camps." The Hmong were forced to flee from Laos in order to survive. It has been estimated that only one third of Hmong refugees succeeded in their attempted escape (Puthiyottil, 1991). These refugees were basically comprised of three different groups. The first group consisted of former CIA-recruited soldiers, anti-communist government officials, and members of their families who fled in 1975 and '76 immediately after the end of the Vietnam war. The second group included soldiers and others who had served the CIA but who had a more limited education than the first group. These fled during 1977 and 1978. The last group was composed of farmers and civilians who fled between 1978 and 1981 (Podeschi & Xiong, 1992). The refugees were interred in relocation camps in Thailand. In the late 1970s, American military personnel assisted those who had served the U. S. in their relocation to America. Many family relatives followed these early arrivals, but some remained in the camps (Goldfarb, 1982). Hmong immigration peaked to over

25,000 in 1980, but subsequently dropped to less than 5,000 per year in the early 1980s. In 1987, it rose to over 5,000 annually and has basically remained near that figure since (Bulk, 1995). An estimated 50,000 remained in relocation camps in 1995. Those who remain face enforced repatriation to Laos because of U. S. immigration restrictions and a Thai policy which forbids their settling in Thailand. Most refugees in America intend to remain, although older Hmong speak nostalgically of returning to Laos someday.

Traditional Hmong Culture

In Laos, the majority of Hmong lived in agricultural farming villages. Occasionally the population of whole villages moved when their custom of slash-and-burn cultivation rendered the land infertile, but this relocation was generally within a two-day walk from the old site (Bulk, 1995). Hunting and fishing were common. Homes had no central heating or indoor water facilities. Single-wall construction was adequate in the mild climate.

Hmong society was organized around patrilinial clans, tracing descent through the father, with a profound respect for elders and ancestral ties. This clan organization was at the core of family and political experience and shaped attitudes about society and one's place in it. Between families, business arrangements or disputes were referred to clan leaders for settlement. The clan defined roles and role relationships, including clearly delineated gender roles. Within families, even adults deferred to their father and clan leaders in making personal decisions. Hmong village leaders could also be clan leaders but they were distinct in their ability to obtain help when villagers needed it. This tradition remains among community leaders in America.

Approximately half of the Hmong refugees were Christians, reflecting the influence of French missionaries in the area (Dunnigan, 1986) but ancestor worship was also practiced in accordance with clan lines. It is important to note here that ancestor worship does not imply a belief that ancestors were divine but rather that they were spirits in communication with the spirit world. Animism was also a part of Hmong spiritual beliefs. Shamans conducted elaborate rituals which continue to be practiced in the United States. Rituals in regard to religious, medical, and funeral rites have been described in detail elsewhere (Mattison, Lo, & Scarseth, 1994). The belief in a relationship between spiritual concerns and health reflected a conviction that people must live in harmony with each other and the spirit world. In addition to shamanistic ceremonies, a form of folk herbal medicine was also practiced (Thao, 1986).

The culture was primarily an oral one whereby knowledge of past events was handed down from generation to generation. In the 1950's missionaries gave the Hmong language a written form. Some Hmong elders refer to an older written language similar to Chinese, which for the most part has been lost.

Formal education was rare. Few Hmong villages had a school. It has been estimated that seventy percent of Hmong refugees were nonliterate when they emigrated from Laos and that even the concept of using a written language was one of the profound difficulties which they faced in their relocation to literate societies including the United States (Takaki, 1990). Puthiyottil (1991) reported that in 1984 the average education for Hmong in the United States over the age of eighteen was 1.3 years. In Laos, one or two sons may have been selected in a family to attend a school in a neighboring village or as far away as a day's walk, where they boarded. It was not uncommon for a student to take a supply of food and remain until that supply ran out, go home for more, and then return to school (personal interviews). Education of girls was not valued but there were some exceptions. A Hmong woman living in Wisconsin reported to us that she was sent to a missionary boarding school because there were no boys in her family and her mother insisted on her attending school. Another woman reported that she attended school because her father, a high ranking military official, did not share the traditional views restricting education for women.

Following an exogamous clan rule, marriages were often arranged between families of different clans. Sometimes considerable bargaining was involved with the help of matchmakers (Merideth & Rowe, 1986). Although the choice of a bride was known, the marriage itself occurred by "capturing" the bride. Traditionally the groom and his male relatives took the bride to his father's house, whereupon the groom's father and/or clan leader notified the bride's family. A "bride price" was agreed upon and paid by the groom's family to that of the bride. This bride price was viewed as a promise that the girl would be well treated in her marriage and should not be interpreted as purchasing a wife. A ceremony then followed and the bride moved permanently into her husband's home. Most marriages occurred early. The ideal age for a bride was considered to be between twelve and fifteen and the ideal age for a groom was between fourteen and sixteen or seventeen. In the United States, this view is changing. Many now believe it is better for a woman to wait to marry until she is eighteen (Merideth & Rowe, 1986). To be considered a "good wife" a bride was expected to listen to her husband, fulfill her obligations to him, his family, and his clan, and to follow the instructions of her husband's mother regarding household responsibilities (personal interviews).

Children were viewed as belonging to their father, or in the case of his death, to his father, brothers, and clan. His widow often married one of his brothers and remained with his clan. This custom was viewed as the continuation of the deceased husband's clan support for his wife and his children. This practice sometimes resulted in there being more than one wife in the household. Children were expected to help with household duties. Adults provided assistance to clan members and cared for parents in their old age.

The Hmong in the United States

Since 1975, when the Laotian Hmong first began arriving in the United States, demographic data indicate a pattern of secondary migration, subsequent to initial settlement. Reasons for this relocation include better employment possibilities, access to language and job training programs, access to short-term welfare support, avoidance of large metropolitan areas, and clan or family reunification (Bulk, 1995). The availability of training programs is important, but these programs have generally been more accessible to male heads of household. Access to these programs for women has not been equitable (Mason, 1986). Family reunification reflects the strong clan responsibilities in traditional Hmong culture. In 1995, 89 percent of Hmong refugees were located in three states: California, Wisconsin, and Minnesota, with the majority of the remaining 11 percent in Michigan, North Carolina, Rhode Island, and Washington (state). Smaller numbers remain scattered throughout the U. S. (Bulk, 1995).

A field based study of Hmong cultural values conducted by one of us (Timm, 1994), examined a variety of issues identified by Hmong as being important in their culture. These issues included marriage customs, child-rearing practices, family and clan relationships, gender roles, linguistic issues, education, spiritual values, and the impact of mainstream American culture on traditional Hmong culture. (For further details, see Timm, 1994).

This earlier study revealed that many Hmong values are similar to American values. The Hmong value their history and cultural traditions. They value family and children, fidelity and loyalty. They value personal honor and responsibility, honesty and good citizenship. They value religion and the spiritual life. They value hard work and recognize the necessity of a good education as the means to economic success in the United States. The study, however, also indicated that the clan continues to have a major influence on Hmong social values and that the primary ideological conflict between Hmong culture and American culture is a focus on the family as compared with an emphasis on individual freedom. This issue of the family vis-a-vis the individual is impacting decision making, personal activities, marriage choices, traditional women's roles, and the attitudes of Hmong youth. The contrast between a focus on family and on individual freedom is at the heart of the Hmong dilemma in the United States and is causing problems within families, across generations, and in the Hmong community.

Basically, those over age thirty-five reported concerns about keeping Hmong values and traditions as they existed "back in Laos" which included clearly proscribed roles within the family. They were particularly concerned about the possibility of losing the Hmong language and the (acculturating) impact of American education on Hmong traditions. Those between age twenty and thirty-five also expressed concerns about keeping important traditions but at the same time recognized a need for changes and flexibility in their new cultural situation, particularly in regard to women's roles and education. Those under age twenty reported feeling torn between remaining loyal to Hmong values and having more freedom over personal decisions (Timm, 1994). Moore (1990) has reported that, although there are differences among Hmong youth, they all feel this inter-cultural pressure. Rick and Forward (1992) have further reported that as students adapt to U. S. values, their perceptions of intergenerational differences with their parents increased and that these perceived intergenerational differences depended on the number of years in American schools. A clan leader summarized this intergenerational and intercultural problem:

> They (the children) misunderstand the word 'freedom' and they say 'Well, this country is free and we have the right to do what we want. We can go to this place and that place' because they learn from school that their friends do this and that. They do not always respect their parents and the parents feel bad.

They would like to see their children grow up and respect the Hmong culture and the American culture—to respect everything.

Cultural Factors and Hmong Students' Cognitive Style

The relationship between cultural experience and cognitive style has been well-documented for diverse groups. Indeed, the various chapters in this volume attest to the importance of cultural experience in students' learning. In the remaining portion of this chapter we report the results of our study on Hmong students' cognitive style and consider some cultural factors in relation to their approach to learning.

There are several ways in which culture influences cognitive style (Worthley, 1987). Among these are the type of socialization, tightness of the culture, ecological adaptation, and language. Jahoda (1980) has pointed out that the primary mode of socialization is an important factor in learning style. Permissive practices result in wider differentiation of style, whereas strict practices include pressure for conformity. An emphasis on obedience is conducive to a cognitive style known as field-dependency (Nedd & Gruenfeld, 1976). Tight cultures also include pressure for conformity. Ecological adaptation describes the type of practices within the culture (Berry, 1976). For example, agriculture and animal husbandry focus on careful routines and use traditional knowledge for survival. Socialization emphasizes responsibility, conformity, obedience, and adherence to traditional ways. On the other hand, a culture which is primarily focused on hunting and fishing for survival requires more individual initiative. Socialization tends to foster self-reliance.

Literate societies emphasize symbolization, while learning in preliterate (oral) societies is enactive and iconic, focusing on observation and role modeling (Hvitfeldt, 1985). In other words, learning is situational and contextually-based, rather than categorical and abstract, as in more literate societies.

Hmong culture traditionally has followed strict socialization practices, with an emphasis on conformity and following situation-specific traditional customs or practices. The primary economy was agricultural. Lee (1986) reported that Hmong children participated in work at a very young age. Hmong culture was also preliterate, with limited access to schooling for all but a few members. Thus, Hmong culture was conducive to a field-dependent approach to learning.

Evidence of a field-independent or field-dependent learning style has been reported among students from diverse cultural backgrounds. Witkin and his associates (1959, 1973, 1977, 1979, 1981) first identified a field-independent and field-dependent learning style by means of The Embedded Figures Test. (Recently the term field-sensitive has been used rather than field-dependent.) This test assessed students' ability to identify geometric shapes hidden within complex spatial patterns. Subsequent to the original test, The Group Embedded Figures Test and The Children's Embedded Figures Test were also developed (Witkin, 1971). It is important to emphasize here that field-independence/dependence are *value free* designates.

Witkin and his associates described the characteristics of these two learning styles. Perception is not strongly influenced by surrounding elements in field-independence but is influenced by these elements in field-dependence. Chickering (1976) further described field-independence and dependence as differences in ability to distinguish figure from ground and a construct from surrounding context.

The characteristics of a field-independent style are: (a) an inclination to work independently; (b) motivation from within (intrinsic motivation) with a lower need for external support and reinforcement; and (c) a preference for personal recognition. More recently, Heppner and Krauskopf (1987) reported that field-independent learners perform well in situations conducive to intrinsic motivation, persevere longer, and are more self-directive in their learning. The characteristics of a field-sensitive style are: (a) a preference to work with others; (b) a need for external encouragement and guidance (extrinsic motivation); and (c) an orientation toward social cues and a sensitivity to others. Heppner and Krauskopf have also reported that field-dependent or field-sensitive learners adapt to new situations more easily.

Two previous studies have reported findings of a Hmong cognitive style (Hvitfeldt, 1986; Worthley, 1987). Hvitfeldt reported findings of perceptual style and classroom behavior among nontraditional Hmong students enrolled in a second language and literacy class for nonliterate and low literate Hmong adults ranging from twenty to sixty-five years in age. Her results indicated behaviors characteristic of a field-dependent style, including consistent interpersonal interactions among the students, a reliance on external or contextual referents, and a personal relationship with the instructor. Worthley administered the Embedded Figures Test to 42 Hmong male students ranging in age from seventeen and thirty-five. Of these participants, 15 were enrolled in high school, and 27 were enrolled in college; vocational, technical, and community colleges. Results indicated that 28 were field-dependent and 14 were field-independent. Worthley further reported that interviews with these participants revealed that in taking The Embedded Figures Test, 21 of the 28 field-dependent students used global strategies but all of the 14 field-independent students used analytic strategies.

We administered the Group Embedded Figures Test (GEFT), following the guidelines in the test manual (Witkin, 1971), to 90 Hmong students enrolled in seven English Second Language (ESL) classes in the fifth through the ninth grade in two Wisconsin communities. Participants included 48 males and 42 females who ranged in age from ten to seventeen years. A Hmong ESL coordinator reported that the 8 sixteen and seventeen year olds had chosen to remain in the ninth grade until they felt more secure with their English proficiency. (In other words, they had not been identified as having learning disabilities.) Seventeen of the participants had been living in the U. S. less than two years. Only four were identified as having special needs. The Hmong ESL teacher in each class was present during all testing sessions. These teachers repeated the instructions in Hmong after we had presented them in English. They also answered any questions that the students had in Hmong after they had been answered in English. All seven of the ESL teachers assisting us were confident that the students understood the procedure.

Six independent or antecedent variables were identified. These were gender, school level, age, grade, the length of time the students had been living in the United States, and whether or not they had been identified as having learning disabilities. The two dependent variables were students' scores on The Group Embedded Figures Test and the quartile of the students' scores. Split half reliability was determined by the correlation of scores for the two sections of the test (r = .72). Validity data is reported in the test manual.

Out of a possible total score of eighteen, the overall GEFT mean score clearly indicated that an overwhelming majority of these students were field dependent (M = 4.91, SD = 4.15). In fact, 83 of the 90 participants (92.2%) obtained GEFT scores indicating a field-sensitive style. Only 7 students' scores indicated a field-independent, cognitive style. We remind the reader here that these scores indicate only a difference in style and are value free designates.

In addition to the test scores, the characteristics of a field-dependent or sensitive style were clearly evident among the students in their behavior during the administration of the GEFT. Interestingly, the student with the highest score (indicating a field-independent style) approached the problem very independently—even competitively—and told a friend who tried to ask him a question during the test to "be quiet" and leave him alone. This eighth grade student took great pride in being the first to complete the test in a class of 35 students. He waved the test booklet in the air and we had to motion to him to put it on his desk and wait until the time was up. His independence was the most noticeable, but the other students whose scores indicated a field-independent style also worked with extreme concentration and paid no attention to their classmates.

In contrast, we constantly had to prevent other students from trying to collaborate. One student tried to lend a pencil to another student when that student's pencil broke. Because the test is timed, we insisted that the students adhere to the test guidelines of working independently. Some students said after the test that they were very unhappy when they could not talk about it with their neighbor.

In addition to an overall field-sensitive cognitive style among the students, a significant difference in scores was found for gender. All seven (7) of the students whose scores indicated a field-independent style were boys. When we discussed these results with the Hmong ESL coordinator in one of our school districts, she reported that she was not surprised by the significant differences between the males and the females, but that the degree of difference did surprise her. She went on to describe some cultural factors which she believed could account for these differences.

She reported that learning in Hmong culture was different for boys and girls and that boys are encouraged to watch, analyze, and then act in accordance with their observations. Girls, on the other hand, are often shown what to do. In addition, boys learn to participate in shamanistic and other ceremonies during which they are instructed to observe and learn. Thus, even though both boys and girls are taught through demonstration, the boys are more encouraged to observe before they act while girls are encouraged to follow the directions that are presented to them. We should point out here, however, that both methods are conducive to a field-sensitive style and that 41 of the 48 boys' test scores indicated a field-dependent or field-sensitive style. Apparently, the socialization practices and demonstrated instruction in Hmong homes set the stage for a field-sensitive, observational, and algorithmic learning style over a problem-solving and heuristic approach for the majority of Hmong boys as well as girls.

No significant differences were found for those students identified as having learning disabilities, (but N = 4 in this group). No significant differences were found for age, grade, school level, or length of time the students had been living in the United States. Scores on the GEFT did not significantly increase with age, grade, school level, or length of time they have been in American schools. We had predicted that the older students would become more field independent over time, but apparently classroom procedures were not influencing the development of a more individually-oriented, cognitive style. This finding is interesting in conjunction with the finding cited above by Rick and Forward (1992) that perceived intergenerational differences between Hmong youth and their parents were associated with the number of years the students had spent in American schools. We interpret these results to suggest that *acculturation of values are occurring more rapidly than changes in learning style.* In other words, specific value differences may be more easily learned than different approaches to learning situations.

REFLECTIONS FOR THE FUTURE

In many ways, the story of the Hmong in America reflects that of many others before them. In their efforts to learn a new language, adapt to new cultural expectations, and maintain their time-honored customs, they are following in the path of countless other immigrants and refugees, but the degree of their preliterate traditional culture in contrast with that of mainstream America resulted in extreme culture shock for many people. Their adaptation to American ways has involved a profound reorientation and integration of discrepant knowledge, technologies, and values. When we consider the circumstances under which the Hmong were forced to leave their homeland, their courage and determination command our profound respect. When we consider the needs of Hmong students, acculturation has resulted not only in intergenerational differences in knowledge and values but in learning situations as well. We turn to their educational needs in another chapter.

REFERENCES

1. Berry, J. W.: *Human Ecology and Cognitive Style: Comparative Studies in Cultural and Psychological Adaptation.* New York, John Wiley, 1976.

2. Bulk, J. D.: *American Hmong on the move: An explanation of very distinctive secondary migration patterns.* Paper presented at The First Annual Hmong National Education Conference, St. Paul, MN, 1995.

3. Chickering, A. W.: Commentary: The double bind of field dependence-independence in program alternatives for educational development. In Messick, S. (Ed.): *Individuality in Learning.* San Francisco, Jossey-Bass, 1976.

4. Dunnigan, T.: Processes of identity maintenance in Hmong society. In Hendricks, G. L., Downing, B. T., & Deinard, A. S. (Eds.): *The Hmong in Transition.* Staten Island, NY: Center for Migration Studies.

5. Goldfarb, M.: *Fighters, Refugees, Immigrants: A Story of the Hmong.* Minneapolis, Carolrhoda Books, Inc., 1982.

6. Heppner, P., & Krauskopf, C.: An information processing approach to personal problem solving. *Counseling Psychologist,* 15:371–447, 1987.

7. Hvitfeldt, C.: Picture perception and interpretation among preliterate adults. *Passage: A Journal of Refugee Education,* 1:27–30, 1985.

8. Hvitfeldt, C.: Traditional culture, perceptual style, and learning: The classroom behavior of Hmong adults. *Adult Education Quarterly,* 36:65–77, 1986.

9. Jahoda, G.: Theoretical and systematic approaches in cross-cultural psychology. In Triandis, H. C., & Lambert, W. W. (Eds.), *Handbook of Cross-Cultural Psychology: Perspectives, Volume I.* Boston, Allyn & Bacon, 1980.

10. Lee, G. Y.: Culture and adaptation: Hmong refugees in Australia. In Hendricks, G. L., Downing, B. T., & Deinard, A. S. (Eds.), *The Hmong in Transition.* Staten Island, NY, Center for Migration Studies, 1986.

11. Livo, N. J., & Cha, D.: *Folkstories of the Hmong: Peoples of Laos, Thailand and Vietnam.* Englework, CO, Libraries Unlimited, 1991.

12. Mason, S. R.: Training Hmong women: For marginal work or entry into the mainstream. In Hendricks, G. L., Downing, B. T., & Deinard, A. S. (Eds.): *The Hmong in Transition.* Staten Island, NY, Center for Migration Studies, 1986.

13. Mattison, W., Lo, L., & Scarseth, T.: *Hmong Lives: From Laos to La Crosse.* La Crosse, WI, The Pump House, 1994.

14. Merideth, W. H., & Rowe, G. P.: Changes in Hmong refugee marital attitudes in America. In Hendricks, G. L., Downing, B. T., & Deinard, A. S. (Eds.), *The Hmong in Transition.* Staten Island, NY, Center for Migration Studies, 1986.

15. Moore, D. L.: Between cultures: Oral history of Hmong teenagers in Minneapolis. *Vietnam Generation,* 2:38–52, 1990.

16. Moore, D. L.: *Dark Sky, Dark Land: Stories of the Hmong Boy Scouts of Troop 100.* Eden Prairie, MN, Tessera Publishing, Inc., 1989.

17. Nedd, A. N., & Gruenfeld, L. W.: Field dependence-independence and social

traditionalism: A comparison of ethnic subcultures of Trinidad. *International Journal of Psychology,* 11:23–41, 1976.

18. Podeschi, R., & Xiong, V.: *The Hmong and American Education: The 1990s.* Milwaukee, WI, University of Wisconsin-Milwaukee, 1992.
19. Puthiyottil, C. C.: *Welcoming Strangers to a New Land: A Model for Successful Refugee Sponsorship.* Minneapolis, Augsburg Press, 1991.
20. Rick, K., & Forward, J.: Acculturation and perceived intergenerational differences among Hmong youth. *Journal of Cross-Cultural Psychology,* 23:85–94, 1992.
21. Takaki, R.: *Strangers From A Different Shore.* Boston, MA, Little, Brown & Company, 1989.
22. Thao, X.: Hmong perceptions of illness and traditional ways of healing. In Hendricks, G. L., Downing, B. T., & Deinard, A. S. (Eds.), *The Hmong in Transition.* Staten Island, NY, Center for Migration Studies, 1986.
23. Timm, J. T.: Hmong values and American education. *Equity and Excellence in Education,* 27:36–44, 1994.
24. Witkin, H. A.: The perception of the upright. In Coopersmith, S., *Frontiers of Psychological Research: Readings from Scientific American.* San Francisco, CA, W. H. Freeman & Company, 1966 (1959).
25. Witkin, H. A., Oltman, P. K., Raskin, E., & Karp, S. A.: *A Manual for the Embedded Figures Tests.* Palo Alto, CA, Consulting Psychologists Press.
26. Witkin, H. A., Oltman, P. K., Cox, P. W., Ehrlichman, E., Hamm, R. M., & Ringler, R. W.: *Field-dependence-independence and psychological differentiation: A Bibliography.* Princeton, NJ, Educational Testing Service, 1973.
27. Witkin, H. A., Moore, C. A., Goodenough, D. R., & Cox, P. W.: Field dependent and field independent cognitive styles and their educational implications. *Review of Educational Research,* 47:1–64, 1977.
28. Witkin, H. A.: Socialization, culture and ecology in the development of group and sex differences in cognitive style. *Human Development,* 22:358–372, 1979.
29. Witkin, H. A., & Goodenough, D. R.: *Cognitive Styles: Essence and Origins, Field Dependence and Field Independence.* New York: International Universities Press.
30. Worthley, K. M. E.: *Learning style factor of field dependence-independence and problem solving strategies of Hmong refugee students.* Masters Thesis. Menomonie, WI, University of Wisconsin-Stout, 1987.
31. Yang, D.: *Hmong at the Turning Point.* Minneapolis, World Bridge Associates, Ltd., 1993.

Chapter 11

CULTURAL DIFFERENCES IN THE COGNITIVE STYLE OF MEXICAN-AMERICAN STUDENTS*

OLIVIA N. SARACHO

M any researchers (e.g., Saracho, 1983; Ramirez, 1982; Kagan, and Buriel, 1977) have found a significant relationship between cognitive styles and the Mexican-American culture. Ramirez (1982) describes students of minority groups to be, on the average, less competitive, less sensitive to spatial incursions by others, less comfortable in trial and error circumstances, and less interested in fine details of concepts, materials, or tasks that are nonsocial. Such behaviors indicate that minority students are more field-dependent. If these behaviors really describe Mexican-American students (See Fig. 10-1), they have a field-dependent orientation. Unfortunately, the cognitive style of Mexican-American individuals is one which has been easily oversimplified, misunderstood, and misinterpreted. Many have assumed that the process of environmental incidents depend on the interaction of experiences and the cognitive activities such as thinking, learning, language, and cultural transmission. Two popular books have focused on this process. They were written by Holtzman, Diaz-Guerrero, and Swartz (1975) and Ramirez and Castaneda (1974). The authors affirm that traditional, sedentary, and agricultural cultures have socialization practices which focus on strong family ties and respect for obedience to elders, practices that characterize field-dependent persons. On the other hand, modern mobile urban industrialized societies have socialization practices which focus on individuality and autonomous functioning, practices that describe field-independent individuals. A large number of studies have found that Mexican-American students are field-dependent as compared to Anglo-American students (Ramirez & Castaneda, 1974; Buriel, 1975; Sanders, Scholz, & Kagan,

---

*From Saracho, Olivia N. Cultural differences in the cognitive style of Mexican American Students. *Journal of the Association for the Study of Perception, 18:*3–10, 1983. Reprinted with permission.

1976; Ramirez, 1973; Ramirez & Price-Williams, 1976; Canavan, cited in Kagan & Buriel, 1977; Kagan & Zahan, 1975). Dyk and Witkin (1965) attributed the results of these studies to the traditional child rearing practices of the Mexican-American families which emphasize close family ties. On the other hand, the child-rearing practices of the middle-class, Anglo-American culture promote assertiveness, autonomy, and a more individualistic sense of self-identity. The different socialization practices influence the cognitive styles of the Mexican-American and Anglo-American children (Ramirez & Castaneda, 1974). Members of the traditional communities who have Mexican cultural values and social practices have field-dependent features (Ramirez, Castaneda, & Herold, 1974). The studies indicate that since Mexican-American parents stress social integrative values, their children are more socially-oriented. The assumption that a generally prosocial orientation of Mexican-American children is related to their field-dependence has been formulated. Some research contradicts this assumption. Survey of studies where parent beliefs toward socialization practices were assessed along with their children's cognitive style do not support such a conceptualization (Holtzman, Diaz-Guerrero & Swartz, 1975; Sanders, Scholz, & Kagan, 1976).

The Community's Ethnic Orientation

Studies have been conducted to examine the relationship between the ethnic orientation of a community and its members' cognitive styles. Mexican-American families of first-, second-, and third-generation immigrants from Mexico were investigated. The researcher found that while first- and second-generation subjects had cognitive styles similar to the traditional communities, the third-generation subjects did not (Buriel, 1975). The results of the study suggest that the subjects' contact with the Mexican culture was related to their cognitive style: the first- and second-generation subjects had the most direct contact with the Mexican culture, while the third-generation subjects had the least direct contact. Ramirez, Castaneda, and Herold (1974) studied Mexican-American children and their mothers in three types of communities: (1) traditional communities where the members were mainly Mexican-American and displayed a culture bias on Mexican sociocultural premises; (2) dualistic communities where the members were Mexican-American and had a mixture of both the Mexican and Mexican-American cultures; and (3) traditional communities where the members were Mexican-American and had manifested values and standards from the Anglo-American culture. The results indicated that the traditional community members were the most field-independent and the dualistic community members were intermediate between both extremes.

Some recent studies were conducted in which cognitive styles among Mexican-American people in traditional and dualistic communities were found to be relatively field-dependent, while those in the dualistic community were found to be relatively field-independent (Laosa & DeAvila, 1979).

These studies show that Mexican-American children are more field-dependent than Anglo-American children, although the degree of field-dependence varies. The degree of traditionalism in the child-rearing community as well as the children's generational distance from their migration to the United States affect the variance in cognitive style. According to these studies, the more field-dependent individuals are closer to the traditional Mexican (rural) culture. However, the field-dependence-independence dimension is evaluated in relative rather than absolute terms. In addition, a recent study (Saracho, 1983) indicated that five-year-old, Mexican-American children were field-dependent. The results also showed that the children increased in relation to field-independence as the children matured in age. Therefore, this study indicated that Mexican-American children can be field-independent even at an early age. Another investigation (Saracho, 1983) on ethnicity provided similar results. Since the outcomes differ in the above studies, it is not possible to generalize that the social orientation of Mexican-American students causes field-dependence. Extensive research with a wide range of variables needs to be conducted before formulating any type of generalizations.

Interactional Styles*

Cognitive style and culture affect the individual's behavior in educational settings. A variety of interactions between students and teachers occurs in a classroom setting. Educators have advocated an optimum match between the students' characteristics and the educational setting, including the personal characteristics of the pupils and teachers (Hunt, 1970). The match of students and teachers provides the pupils with an appropriate educational setting, because it promotes a positive interper-

---

*Editors Note: An individual's interactional style is the social dimension of their cognitive style rather than the perceptual dimension usually measured by the field-independence-dependence construct.

sonal relationship, whereas a mismatch does not. The "match" in cognitive style fosters a better interpersonal relationship between individuals because of similar interests, interpersonal characteristics, and communication modes (Witkin, 1976).

Researchers of cognitive style have examined the match and mismatch of students' and teachers' cognitive styles to understand the educational implications and the outcomes of these interactions (Saracho & Spodek, 1981; Saracho, 1984). They did not support the match in educational settings. The results of most studies indicated that the match and mismatch did not make a difference. However, the cognitive style of the teachers influenced their students' academic achievement (Saracho & Dayton, 1980). The changes during the school year on students' achievement scores suggested that students be grouped in the following order:

- Field-independent students with field-independent teachers
- Field-dependent students with field-independent teachers
- Field-independent students with field-dependent teachers
- Field-dependent students with field-dependent teachers

(Saracho and Spodek, 1981)

Saracho and Spodek (1981) further suggest that if the teachers' cognitive styles have a significant impact on their students' learning outcomes, then the selection and education of teachers need to consider the teachers' personal characteristics. Such characteristics should relate to the program's educational goals. An educational program which emphasizes social goals could select and educate field-dependent teachers, while an educational program which focuses on academic goals might select and education field-independent teachers. Ramirez (1973), whose studies indicate that Mexican-American children are more field-dependent, was concerned that field-independent teachers may be insensitive to the field-dependent children's needs.

The matching of students and teachers on cognitive styles to raise the pupil's academic achievement is an unresolved issue. There are two studies in which the results show that Mexican-American pupils have greater academic achievement with field-independent teachers. Sanders and Scholz (cited in Kagan & Buriel, 1977) compared the relationship between the match in cognitive style and school achievement in mathematics of Mexican-American and Anglo-American children as a result of student characteristics and the interaction of these variables. They assumed that the match of cognitive styles would increase the student's mathematics achievement gains. Their outcomes contradicted this assumption. All students with field-independent teachers gained more than one grade equivalent while those with field-dependent teachers gained less than a grade equivalent. It was apparent that field-dependent pupils benefited from cognitive style mismatch. This finding contradicts the researchers' expectation on cognitive style. The results also show that the students rated the field-independent teachers significantly warmer, more rewarding, and more giving of responsibility than their field-dependent teachers. These outcomes also do not support the assumption that field-dependent individuals have better interpersonal skills. The relationship between field-independent teachers' warmth and the mathematics achievement gains was significant for Mexican-American children and for field-dependent children but not for Anglo-American children nor for field-independent children.

Saracho and Spodek (1981) suggest several characteristics to differentiate between field-dependent and field-independent individuals. Field-dependent individuals:

- rely on the surrounding perceptual field;
- experience their environment in a relatively global fashion by conforming to the effects of the prevailing field or context;
- depend on authority;
- search for facial cues in those around them as a source of information;
- are strongly interested in people;
- get closer to the person with whom they are interacting;
- have a sensitivity to others which helps them to acquire social skills;
- prefer occupations which require involvement with others.

In contrast, *field independent* individuals:

- perceive objects as separate from the field;
- can abstract an item from the surrounding field and solve problems that are presented and reorganized in different contexts;
- experience an independence from authority which leads them to depend on their own standards and values;
- are oriented toward active striving;
- appear to be cold and distant;
- are socially detached but have analytic skills;
- prefer occupations that allow them to work by themselves (pg. 154)

Figure 11-1.

A study conducted by Saracho (1983) is consistent with these results. The relationship between the teachers' cognitive styles and/or ethnicity and the students' standardized achievement scores was examined. The results show that no relationship was found between teachers' cognitive styles (field-dependent or field-independent) and the Mexican-American students' standardized achievement scores. However, there was a significant difference in students' achievement related to the teachers' ethnicity. All of the students (i.e., both field-dependent and field-independent students) with the Mexican-American teachers achieved higher gains in a standardized achievement test.

This study indicates that the teachers' ethnicity may make a difference in students' learning. The match of ethnicity between students and teacher may decrease the students' fear of school and school learning as well as increase the students' competence in communication skills. The students with the Mexican-American teachers may be perceiving an acceptance and may be experiencing in the classroom many of their cultural values. For instance, the teacher may provide an atmosphere where the family relationship is valued, personal loyalty to friends is encouraged, and where sensitivity to praise and criticism to their pupils is adopted. The Mexican-American teachers' educational program could have included culturally diverse skills such as reinforcing the culture of the home, adapting curriculum materials to make them more relevant to the children's cultural needs, building curriculum based on the life and language experiences, and involving the parents in the educational experience (Saracho, 1983).

SUMMARY

Cognitive style characterizes the individual's preferences relating to their modes of communication and modes of cognitive processing. Some studies indicate a relationship between ethnicity and cognitive style. The cognitive style of Mexican-American children was assumed to be influenced by the degree to which individuals have adopted Mexican rural values, Anglo, middle-class values or a combination of the two value systems.

Educators have advocated the use of individual differences to plan instructional programs. They have usually suggested several alternatives [but] . . . such alternatives do not take into account the students' or teachers' functioning mode, and their cultural background. A better understanding of the concept of cognitive style and its relationship to culture (particularly with the Mexican-American culture) is essential to develop new ways of meeting individual differences in education.

REFERENCES

1. Buriel, R.: Cognitive styles among three generations of Mexican-American children. *Journal of Cross-Cultural Psychology, 6:*417–429, 1975.
2. Dyk, R. B., & Witkin, H. A.: Family experiences related to the development of differentiation in children. *Child Development, 36:*21–25, 1965.
3. Holtzman, W. H., Diaz-Guerrero, R., & Swartz, J. D.: *Personality in Two Cultures.* Austin, University of Texas Press, 1975.
4. Hunt, D. E.: Conceptual level matching model for coordinating learner characteristics with educational approaches. *Interchange, 1:*68–82, 1970.
5. Kagan, S., & Buriel, R.: Field dependence-independence and Mexican American culture and education. In J. L. Martinez (Ed.): *Chicano Psychology.* New York, Academic Press, 1977.
6. Kagan, S., & Buriel, R.: Field dependence-independence and school achievement gap between Anglo-American and Mexican American children. *Journal of Educational Psychology, 67:*643–650, 1975.
7. Laosa, L. M., & DeAvila, E. A.: Development of cognitive styles among Chicanos in traditional and dualistic communities. *International Journal of Psychology, 14:*91–98, 1979.
8. Ramirez, M.: Cognitive styles and cultural democracy in education. *Social Science Quarterly, 53:*895–904, 1973.
9. Ramirez, M., & Price-Williams, D. R.: Cognitive styles of children of three ethnic groups in the United States. *Journal of Cross-Cultural Psychology, 7:*451–461, 1976.
10. Ramirez, M.: Cognitive styles and cultural diversity. Annual Conference of the American Educational Research Association, New York, 1982.
11. Ramirez, M., & Castaneda, A.: *Cultural Democracy, Bicognitive Development and Education.* New York, Academic Press, 1974.
12. Ramirez, M., Castaneda, A., & Herold, P. L.: The relationship of acculturation to cognitive style among Mexican Americans. *Journal of Cross-Cultural Psychology, 5:*425–433, 1974.
13. Sanders, M., Scholz, J. P., & Kagan, S.: Three social motives and field-independence/dependence in Anglo-American and Mexican-American children. *Journal of Cross-Cultural Psychology, 7:*
14. Saracho, O. N.: Cognitive style and Mexican-American children's perceptions of reading. In Escobedo, T. (Ed.): *Early Childhood Education: A bilingual perspective.* New York, Academic Press, 1984.
15. Saracho, O. N., & Dayton, C. M.: Relationship of teachers' cognitive styles to pupils' academic achievement gains. *Journal of Educational Psychology, 72:* 544–549, 1980.
16. Saracho, O. N.: The relationship of teachers' cognitive style and ethnicity to predictions of academic success and achievement of Mexican American and Anglo-American students. In Garcia, E., & Sam-Vargas, M. (Eds.): *The Mexican-American Child: Language, Cognitive and Social Development.* Tempe, Arizona University Press, 1983.

17. Saracho, O. N., & Spodek, B.: Teachers' cognitive styles: Educational implications. *The Educational Forum, 45:* 153–159, 1981.
18. Witkin, H. A.: Cognitive style in academic performance and the teacher-student relations. In Messick, S., & Associates (Ed.): *Individuality in Learning.* San Francisco, Jossey-Bass, 1976.

THE EDUCATIVE PROCESS:
Teaching to Cultural Learning Styles

Chapter 12

TEACHING STUDENTS AS THEY WOULD BE TAUGHT: THE IMPORTANCE OF CULTURAL PERSPECTIVE*

CHRISTINE BENNETT

The three schools you are about to visit are real. Although the names have been changed, the teachers and students you will meet are actual people, and the incidents have recently taken place. There is nothing unique or unusual about these classrooms, except to those of us who have been in one of the schools and become involved with the people described.

It is 2 p.m., beginning of the sixth-period class, and Warren Benson, a young teacher, looks around the room. Eight students are present out of 30.

"Where is everybody?" he demands. "They don't like your class," a girl volunteers. Three girls saunter in. Cora, who is playing a cassette recorder, bumps over to her desk in tune with the music. She lowers the volume. "Don't mark us down late," she shouts. "We was right here, you mother f——."

Benson, a first-year teacher who spent four years in the Navy between high school and college, had requested this school. Here you find students from poverty homes, students who can't read, students who hate school and teachers, students with drug problems, students waiting to drop out. Almost one-third of the students come from homes where one or both parents speak only Spanish.

For years, Warren's dream was to teach on an Indian reservation. He believed this school would be good preparation. Now after two months in the classroom, he has real doubts. Doubts about these kids. Doubts about himself.

*From Bennett, Christine. Teaching students as they would be taught: The importance of cultural perspective. *Educational Leadership, 37*:259–268, 1979. Reprinted with permission of the Association for Supervision and Curriculum Development. Copyright © by ASCD. All rights reserved.

Benson tells everyone to take out today's vocabulary words. "Aw, come on man, give us a break," a student named Spark moans. Cora turns up the volume and croons, "Hey-ey-ey, bay-bee . . . ah wants to know-o-o- . . . " Then, lowering the volume, she asks, "Mr. Benson, you got a pencil?" Another straggler walks in. "You late, boy," one student says. "So what, boy," the straggler answers. Benson asks for a definition of the first word, "tariff." No response. "Richard?" "What?" Ricardo asks, tuning in briefly. A few students busily leaf through the text, trying to locate the glossary.

Spark tells some nearby students his ancestors are Aztec Indians. "You an Indian?" Ricardo asks. "You got a tomahawk and all?" Benson defines tariff for Ricardo, who listens for a second, then throws a paper airplane across the room and hits a girl in the neck. "Ouch!" Benson continues. "Number two is Treaty of Guadalupe. Who can tell us what the Treaty of Guadalupe is?"

"Mr. Benson," Cora interrupts, "I got to go to the bathroom." Benson tells her, "No." "Goddammit, I got to go to the bathroom," she yells. "I'll give you a pass today," says Benson, "but this is the last time."

Benson tries to get back into the lesson. "Who can tell us what the Treaty of Guadalupe is?" "Ain't no word Treaty of Ha-wa-da-loop in here," shouts Spark. A blonde student sits silently in a corner chair, everyone else is talking. Cora returns to the classroom. She grabs Benson's hand and pats it. "You ain't mad, is you?" Benson ignores her. Then he shouts to make himself heard about the din of conversation. "Get quiet!" Benson slams his fist on the lectern. Then he glares at the students until he has their attention. "Okay. It is obvious that you haven't learned these words. Everybody take out a paper. I'm going to give you a vocabulary test."

Comments

Warren Benson's class typifies one of the most difficult and challenging teaching situations. Benson faces poorly skilled students, high absenteeism, and unruly classes—problems faced by teachers throughout the nation's schools.

Can anyone handle classes like Warren Benson's? We can begin by teaching others as they would be taught rather than as we would have others teach us. This means we must be able to cue into those characteristics that strongly affect the way a person learns. Some of these characteristics are accurately labeled individual differences, others are cultural differences or, preferably, cultural alternatives.

The case of Kevin Armstrong illustrates that it is often difficult to distinguish between individual and cultural characteristics unless a teacher knows what to look for.

It is September 10, 2:15 p.m. The phone rings in the Armstrong home.

"Hello, Mrs. Armstrong?" a voice inquires. "This is Mrs. Dixon over at Wildwood Elementary School. Kevin's teacher. I . . . "

Mrs. Armstrong interrupts, "What's wrong?"

"Nothing is *wrong,*" answers Mrs. Dixon. "I'm just calling to let you know that we've decided to put Kevin back in second grade. He just isn't ready for third-grade work."

Mrs. Armstrong is stunned. Prior to their move from Denver to a midwestern university town, Kevin had done superior work in a desegregated school that was considered good. Over half of the students were white. "What do you mean he isn't ready for third grade?" she asks coldly. "Teacher last year didn't say nothing about him having problems."

"Mrs. Armstrong," the voice tries to be reassuring, "what I'm suggesting is for Kevin's own good. He's way behind the other children in my class. He'll feel like a failure if he stays."

"How you think he'll feel if you put him back?" the mother snaps. "He been looking to third grade all summer long."

"I hoped you would understand that we want to do what's best for Kevin," responds Mrs. Dixon. "Would you like to come to the school and talk this over with the principal?"

"Comin'," answers Mrs. Armstrong. She hangs up and turns to face her husband.

Wildwood is considered by many to be the best elementary school in town. Standardized achievement tests are among the highest in the state, and the school boasts of many innovative academic programs. Except for a few who, like Kevin, live in a string of apartment buildings bordering the school district, most of the children come from wealthy homes. The parents are mostly professionals. A handful of black and Latino children attend the school, most of whom have been adopted by Anglo parents.

Mr. Peters, the principal explains to Mr. and Mrs. Armstrong why he and Mrs. Dixon believe that Kevin would be better off in second grade. Mrs. Dixon, also present, remains silent.

"Kevin is too immature for third grade. Mrs. Dixon picked this up immediately. Physically he is small for his age, and his attention span is very short. During music class he is unable to sit still. He wiggles all over. In class, he can't wait for his turn to speak and in general he hasn't learned to control himself the way our other third graders do. And, of course, his reading, writing, and math skills are way below grade level."

"Can't you give him a chance? This is just the second day of school. Can't we get him some tutoring or something?" Mrs. Armstrong asks. "I read somewhere about some special programs for kids in the district who have problems."

"Some schools in the city do, but not us. We don't have enough students here who need them to justify the expense. If we keep Kevin in third grade, he'll be isolated from his classmates, working off by himself. That doesn't seem fair to Kevin."

"But still that's better than putting him back," counters Mrs. Armstrong. "We'll be going back to Denver in a year and a half."

Stating that it is against their best judgment, Mrs. Dixon and Mr. Peters agree to keep Kevin in the third-grade class on a trial basis.

Comments

Mrs. Dixon's conclusion that Kevin was not capable of third-grade work after less than two days of observation deserves questioning. She was aware of his geographical move. The adjustment to a new home, new school, and new friends can be difficult for any child. The additional adjustments a black child must make to a setting such as Wildwood can be traumatic. According to black educator, Geneva Gay (1975), many children like Kevin are raised in a cultural environment that is significantly different from what predominates at school. For these black children so much energy is used up adjusting to the school's expectations of appropriate behavior that there is very little energy left for the business of learning.

Anglo middle-class children, too, can find it difficult to adjust to new schools. Thrust into a desegregated setting, they often misinterpret and are misunderstood, and they are sometimes fearful and vulnerable.

Marcia Patton is the twelve-year-old daughter of Mavis and Lew Patton, two politically active lawyers in a large midwestern city. Marcia is one of a first group of white children to attend Jefferson Junior High School, traditionally a school for inner-city blacks. Although most of the children in her neighborhood attend a high-powered prep school, Marcia's parents are sending her to Jefferson as a matter of principle.

Today is her second day at Jefferson. She clutches her books tightly to her chest as she enters Mrs. Samson's language arts class. Mrs. Samson, a black woman in her mid-forties, neatly dressed in a rose-colored suit, smiles as she greets Marcia. Then she steps into the hall to speak with several noisy students who are scrambling around the drinking fountain.

At that moment a group of five classmates burst into the room. They slam their books down on the desk and crowd in around Marcia.

"You got pretty hair," offers Rheba as she handles one of Marcia's blond braids. Marcia is tight-faced, her blue eyes unusually wide.

"You like it here?" quizzes Jackson, a big muscular twelve-year-old who sits on Marcia's desk top.

"Yes, I—I guess so," whispers Marcia, her voice barely audible.

"C'mon, Rheba, let her hair alone," Jackson shouts as he swats the braid out of Rheba's hand and shoves her away from Marcia.

"Keep you hands offa me," yells Rheba, eyes flashing.

Marcia is pale and sitting erect. Her fingers press into the seat of her desk. Mrs. Samson reenters, and the students find their places.

"Me and Marie, we take you to the cafeteria today at lunch," offers Rheba as she sits down next to Marcia.

That evening, in the secrecy of her bedroom, Marcia writes a letter to Miss Bryant, her teacher last year.

"When I first walked in, I saw all these dark faces and for the first time I felt so white. There was nothing but laughing, noisy, dark-skinned faces. My heart was beating so fast I thought I would drop dead for sure. I guess a lot of them won't like me. Still most of the kids are real nice to me. But even so, I'm scared. Everyone is so loud and sometimes they get so close I can hardly breathe.

"The teachers are real nice to me, but I wish Mrs. Samson wouldn't call on me so much. We use the book we used in your class last year, but lots of the kids can't read it. . . .

"I've been there over a week now and was feeling better until today. A horrible thing happened and I can't tell anybody but you. I went to the bathroom after lunch, and two girls I don't know told me to give them all my money or they would hurt me. I gave them twelve dollars, all I had. They said they'd slash my face if I told anybody. I'm afraid to go back."

Comments

Marcia's situation, that of being one of a few white students in a predominantly black school is a reversal of what many black, Latino,

Asian, and native American children often face. Her situation is complicated by the fact that her parents are using her to act in accordance with their belief in school desegregation. "Liberal" white parents are frequently criticized for not sending their children to inner-city schools.

Students like Marcia need a good deal of emotional support. Marcia is afraid of disappointing her parents; she confuses her fears and anxieties about her classmates with being "racist" and thus, is unable to confide in her parents.

While most of the black students are willing to accept Marcia and try to make her feel welcome, there are some who will use her to take out their anger and frustration. As a symbol of "white oppression," Marcia's safety may be endangered.

These classroom examples illustrate that teachers' efforts to respond to the individual and cultural characteristics of learners must be broad in scope. We are not concerned only with inner-city schools or settings where the deck is stacked against racial and ethnic minorities. We are concerned about any classroom where students are not achieving because of personal and/or cultural characteristics that conflict with what predominates in a school or classroom. Is there a classroom in existence that does not merit this concern? The following may clarify what is happening in classrooms similar to those just described.

THE IMPORTANCE OF WORLDVIEW

Worldview refers to the way a cultural group perceives people and events. While individual idiosyncrasies do exist, it is also true that the people who share common dialects and primary experiences learn to see "reality" in the same ways. They develop similar styles of cognition; similar processes of perceiving, recognizing, conceiving, judging, and reasoning; as well as similar values, assumptions, ideas, beliefs, and modes of thought (Kraemer, 1973). What we see as good or bad depends on whether or not it supports our view of reality.

The worldview concept was illustrated by an Anglo-American student of speech and communications who related the following two experiences, one with a Hopi Indian, the other with Trukee islanders (Bennett, 1977).

"Look at those clouds!" I exclaimed one afternoon. "We'll probably have rain later today."

"What clouds?" my Hopi companion asked.

"Right there!" I responded in amazement, pointing to obvious puffs of white and gray.

"All I see is the sky."

"You mean you really don't see those clouds?"

"There's nothing there but sky."

Several months later, this same student was in the opposite situation with a group of Trukee fishermen.

"I thought we were lost. There had been no sign of land for hours. My companions tried to reassure me that we weren't lost at all. They read the wave patterns like I'd use a map. All I could see were waves. Even when they pointed to specific signs, I couldn't see anything. Here we were looking at the same body of water. It felt strange to know that I simply could not perceive what they actually saw. (Bennett, 1977).

In the words of Tulsi Saral (1976):

"It is thus apparent that there is not absolute reality, nor is there a universally valid way of perceiving, cognizing, and/or thinking. Each world view has different underlying assumptions. Our normal state of consciousness is not something natural or given, nor is it universal across cultures. It is simply a specialized tool, a complex structure for coping with our environment.

The definition of worldview used here is roughly equivalent to Triandis' meaning in "subjective culture." Triandis defines "culture" as the human made part of the environment, while "subjective culture" refers to the way a cultural group perceives its environment including stereotypes, role perceptions, norms, attitudes, values, and perceived relationships between events and behaviors (Triandis, 1975).

Different worldviews or cultural orientations often lead to mutual misperceptions, hostility, or conflict. For example, the American professor and his wife, visiting Thailand for the first time, were greeted with inquiries about their weights and salaries. The Japanese businessman terminated dealings with an insensitive American because the American, not wishing to waste time or pry, initiated business discussions without the customary inquiries about family and other personal matters.

Evidence indicates that the same process of misperception that operates between members of different nations who are unaware of each other's worldview also operates in many of our schools and classrooms. The "Panther Prowl," an annual homecoming assembly at a high school in central Florida, illustrates this misperception and cultural conflict. Two different musical groups had been hired to perform at the assembly, one black and one white. When the black musicians began to perform, blacks in the audience responded by clapping, stomping, singing, and dancing. The black performers kept cool, interacted with the black audience, and were clearly enjoying it. White students became very upset, demanded quiet, and many finally walked out. Black students, in turn, felt the whites were being purposefully rude and unresponsive to the black performers. Later that evening, several interracial fights broke out on the campus.

According to anthropologist Roger Abrahams, what happened at the Panther Prowl is an example of the different performance traditions in black and Anglo cultures. The Anglo-European tradition places a virtuoso performer "on a pedestal." The audience is a passive recipient, and appreciation is expressed with applause at acceptable times. For many black Americans, however, the essence of the performance is an active interchange between performer and audience. Great performers, including public speakers and ministers, are those who keep their "cool" while getting their audience "hot."

Student' Cultural Alternatives

Often we are unaware of, or fearful of recognizing, our students' cultural alternatives. Yet even the most sensitive and dedicated teachers can be frustrated in their attempts to reach individual learners if they are unaware of how their own cultural orientations cause learning difficulties for some children. For example, by treating Kevin the same as his classmates, Mrs. Dixon is probably stacking the deck against him. Mrs. Dixon is fearful of probing into Kevin's blackness and dismisses that fact as irrelevant. She is unable to recognize Kevin's special needs because she fears this may be racist.

Obviously it is impossible for us to fully understand the cultural orientations of all the students we will find in our classrooms. Nevertheless, there are at least two common components of any cultural orientation that we can cue into: preferred mode of communication (both verbal and nonverbal) and preferred mode of participation.

The greater the differences between the worldview of teacher and students, the more likely it is that students' and teachers' preferred ways of communicating and participating are different. Those teachers who are unaware of their pupils' needs and preferences force the learner to do most of the adjusting. Those pupils who can't make the adjustment can't learn much in the classroom.

Studies examining the core values of Spanish-speaking communities and native Americans of the Southwest have identified areas of cultural conflict with the Anglo-American worldview. These include priorities such as:

1. Harmony with nature rather than "controlling" or "harnessing" nature;
2. Sharing rather than "saving" the basic necessities of life (also sharing praise and blame);
3. Present time orientation rather than future time orientation. (Time is a continuum. It is important to live each day as it comes. There is no strong orientation to "tomorrow." Patience rather than "action" is stressed, and there is a lack of concern for time schedules);
4. Nonscientific rather than scientific explanations;
5. Noncompetitive behavior rather than aggressive competition;
6. Group identity rather than individuality

(Young, 1968)

In the cases of Anglo-Americans, Latinos, and Native Americans, the existence of different languages makes the coexistence of distinct cultures within our boundaries apparent. The many similarities between Anglo and black culture, though, often prevent the recognition and acceptance of some distinct cultural characteristics. For instance, black English is often perceived as "slang" or poor quality standard English. Thus, when we examine how alternative worldviews result in classroom conflict, it seems appropriate to focus on blacks and mainstream whites.

PARTICIPATION AND COMMUNICATION IN THE CLASSROOM: BLACK AND WHITE PREFERENCES

1. **Cooperation and Competition.** Most academic activities are based upon competition and individual achievement. Therefore, many Anglo middle-class children learn best working on their own, sometimes with the help of an adult. Most learn to expect and accept, and some to need and thrive on this competitive structure. Tests in school are nearly always individual rather than group exercises. Whole systems of instruction are individualized (programmed texts, learning labs, computer-assisted instruction, and independent study projects). We motivate students with classroom games modeled after competitive sports and quiz shows (for example, baseball and Jeopardy). We reward individual achievement with gold stars, "happy face" stamps, and privileges.

Within the black worldview, these preferences are reversed: competition and individual excellence in play and cooperation in work situations.

Gay and Abrahams suggest that the preference for cooperation in work may develop, "because so much of the transmission of knowledge and the customs of street culture takes place within peer groups [and thus] the black student is prone to seek the aid and assistance of his classmates at least as frequently as he does the teacher's" (Gay & Abrahams, 1976). What is nearly always interpreted by teachers as cheating, copying, or frivolous socializing may in fact be the child's natural inclination to seek help from a peer (borrowing a pencil or talking after a test has begun).

2. **The Speaker-Listener Relationship.** The typical mainstream mode is for the teacher to talk and students to listen. Students are passive recipients. And indeed, research indicates that teachers do over 75 percent of the talking in classrooms. The cardinal rule is that students must raise their hands and may not speak until given permission. One must never interrupt another who is speaking, especially the teacher.

This may sound like good classroom management, and often it is, especially for middle-class children. In many middle-class homes, adult questioning of children is common practice. Parents enjoy that kind of interaction and often use it to develop the child's ability to speak. Thus, the child is not confused when adults in school continue the process. For many black children, however, question and answer elicitation may be wrongly interpreted as hostile, because it occurs most frequently in black homes when the adult is angry at the child.

What about students who learn best in a more informal setting that encourages an active interchange between the speaker and the audience? Think back to the Panther Prowl and the different participation styles of blacks and whites in the audience. Communication expert Jack Daniels (1972) shows how for many blacks communication and participation involve the whole self in a simultaneous interaction of intellect, intuition, and sensuality. Since communication and participation are central to learning, it appears that children coming to school with the black worldview learn best in settings encouraging a simultaneous response of thought, feeling, and movement. Silence and "sitting still" are often a sign that the black child is bored.

In the mainstream culture, on the other hand, intellectual, emotional, and physical responses are easily separated. Messages become distinct from people in the form of memos, and ideas are analyzed in their written form only. Individuals such as lawyers sometimes argue viewpoints they do not believe. In some cultures, these are impossibilities

(Bennett, 1977). Children of this world view can be comfortable in the classroom role of passive recipient. They can learn to be "rational" and to remove emotions and feelings from decisions. Many are unable to concentrate in a more active "noisy" environment.

3. **Written Versus Oral/Aural Tradition.** Mainstream culture emphasizes visual learning through the written word. In Euro-American tradition, "seeing is believing," and it is commonly accepted that the highest levels of thinking are possible only for humans who can reflect upon thoughts recorded on the written page. No equivalent to the African griots, those living/singing encyclopedias, exist in mainstream culture.

Many blacks, as well as other microcultural people, have grown up in an oral tradition. Herskovits claims this orientation is a carry-over from Africa. For example, traditional Africa boasted of elaborate communication systems using drums, singing, and dance rituals. From the time blacks first arrived in this country, music and the spoken word have been at the heart of the black experience (Herskovits, 1969; Kiel, 1966; Jones, 1963). Their oral/aural tradition thrives in the New World. The classroom implications of the oral/aural tradition are easily illustrated. A geography teacher in California discovered that her students, mostly black or Latino males labeled remedial, scored considerably higher on tests when she read the questions provided in written form. Another teacher, working with black and Latino eighth graders in Texas, found that their comprehension of a U.S. history text was better if they listened to a tape of the text while reading it. Her Anglo pupils preferred to read without hearing the tape.

4. **The Uses of Words: Communication Versus Manipulation.** Both blacks and whites use words to communicate *and* to manipulate or gain power over others. The mainstream mode is usually to find meaning in the words themselves. How accurately a message is interpreted depends upon the similarity of the meanings senders and receivers attach to the words. Among blacks, however, words often become power devices, and the style of delivery is as important as the words expressed.

Within both cultures, whether one becomes a leader or a follower depends upon the ability to influence and control others. Control and influence in the white community usually accompany wealth. Among blacks, for whom wealth is more difficult to obtain, adeptness with words and skill at "performance" lead to power and influence. Abrahams and Gay (1976) have clearly identified some critical classroom implications:

Language in the largest sense plays a fundamental role in the process of survival in ghetto neighborhoods, in addition to being the basis of acquiring leadership, status, and success. The popularly held belief that it takes brute physical strength to survive in the ghetto is a myth. It may help one endure temporarily, but fists alone are not the answer to survival. Survival is based on one's versatility and adeptness in the use of words. The man-of-words is the one who becomes the hero to ghetto youth. Consider the current conditions and compile a profile of spokesmen of ghetto action groups. These persons in the spotlight are dynamic speakers whose jobs are frequently dependent on the effective use of words, such as lawyers and ministers. Verbal ability can make the difference between having or not having food to eat, a place to live, clothes to wear, being accepted or rejected by one's peers, and being personally and emotionally secure or risking a complete loss of ego. . . . Teachers make their mistakes by looking at individual words or phrases as proof that the children are limited in their verbal abilities. For example, they fail to understand that what they choose to call profanity and coarse four letter words may be used as tools to indicate importance and emphasis. Street people are not inclined to use words for the mere sake of using them. They are used for their performance qualities.

To understand the relationship that exists between herself and her students, and the students' classroom behavior, the middle-class teacher needs to realize that her older black students use a variety of verbal techniques, and that they use these techniques to discover her strengths and weaknesses, to find out where she stands on issues ranging from how "hip" she is to racial attitudes, and to locate her breaking point. Once these are discovered they help the student to exert some control over the situation.

Because street culture is an oral culture, and is dependent largely upon the spoken word for its perpetuation and transmission, its language is very colorful, creative, and adaptive. It is in a constant state of flux and new words are always being invented. Further, new slang words are constantly created as a way of maintaining an in-group relationship and of excluding outsiders. Thus, there merges something of a secret code that only in-group members completely understand. It is used by students and others in street culture to convey messages to each other about the "enemy," even in his presence. Of course, some of these terms have been picked up by white "hipsters," but often the meaning is changed because of the different cultural perspective.

5. **Standard English.** The almost exclusive use of standard English in our nation's schools is a blatant example of mainstream orientation. We are not debating whether or not we accept the position that all school children should develop enough skill in standard English to make its use a functional option. We are examining the cultural conflict many children experience in schools that ignore or repress the language they have lived with since birth. According to Benitez (1973).

All the pre-primers available on the market assume a level of development in oral languages that the Mexican American child has not reached at the beginning of first grade. Phonologically speaking, he neither hears nor discriminates certain sounds. Accustomed as he is to hearing Spanish mostly at home, he hears Spanish in the classroom instead of English and tries to decode accordingly. The result is frustration and awareness that he is failing at something [while] the other children are succeeding (page 7).

The truth of Benitez's remarks is usually accepted when referring to Latino, Native American, and Asian American children—children whose first language is not English. Rarely, however, is it recognized that standard English may create similar learning problems for black children.

A group of elementary teachers in a rural school in central Florida noted that, as early as first grade, they could see white students moving ahead of blacks in reading. Until they listened to tapes of the black students speaking, they were oblivious to the distinct black dialect. They then realized that asking these children to learn to read available materials was like asking whites to begin reading Old English.

Teaching others as they would be taught becomes more difficult to achieve when teachers and students have alternative worldviews. It's a challenge to find out "how learners would be taught" when we don't understand their language, when we misinterpret their behavior, when our "tried and true" methods of diagnosing and motivating don't work.

REFERENCES

1. Abrahams, R. D.: Cultural conflict in the classroom. Symposium sponsored by the Alachna County Teacher Center, Gainsville, Florida, January 30, 1975 (Videotape).
2. Abrahams, R. D., & Gay, G.: Talking black in the classroom. In Roger D. Abrahams and Rudolph C. Troike, (Eds.): *Language and Cultural Diversity in American Education.* Englewood Cliffs, Prentice-Hall, 1976.
3. Benitez, Mario: A blueprint for the education of the Mexican American. ERIC ED076294, March, 1973.
4. Bennett, Milton: Culture and changing realities. Society of Intercultural Training and Research (SIETAR) Pre-conference workshop. Third Annual SIETAR Conference, Chicago, February 24, 1977.
5. Daniels, J., et al: Teaching Afro-American Communication. ERIC ED 082247, November, 1972.
6. Gay, G.: Cultural conflict in the classroom (Videotape). Symposium sponsored by the Alachna County Teacher Center, Gainsville, Florida, January 30, 1975.

7. Gay, G., & Abrahams, R. D.: Black culture in the classroom. In Abrahams, R., & Troike, R. C. (Eds.): *Language and Cultural Diversity in American Education.* Englewood Cliffs, Prentice-Hall, 1976.
8. Herskovits, M. I.: *The Myth of the Negro Past.* Boston, Beacon Press, 1969.
9. Jones, L.: *Blues People.* New York, William Morrow, 1963.
10. Kiel, C.: *Urban Blues.* Chicago, The University of Chicago Press, 1966.
11. Kraemer, A. J.: A cultural self-awareness approach to improving intercultural communication skills. ERIC ED079213, April 1973.
12. Saral, T. B.: Consciousness theory and intercultural communication. Paper presented at the International Communication Association, Portland, Oregon, April 14–17, 1976.
13. Triandis, H. C.: Cultural training, cognitive complexity and interpersonal attitudes." In Brislin, R. W., Bachner, S., & Bonner, W. J. (Eds.): *Cross Cultural Perspectives on Learning.* New York, John Wiley & Sons, 1975.
14. Young, R. W.: *English as a Second Language for Navajos.* Albuquerque, New Mexico. Albuquerque Area Office — Navajo Area Office Division of Education, 1968.

Chapter 13

TEACHING TO AN AFRICAN-AMERICAN COGNITIVE STYLE

Barbara J. Shade

In a recent conversation with an administrator of an urban school, I heard this story:

"A young African-American boy around age 9 went up to his teacher's desk to ask a question. The teacher answered his question then she said: 'Go directly back to your seat.' Upon hearing this directive, the young man proceeded to return to his seat, but instead of going in a direct line from the teacher's desk, he walked around the room, touching his friends on the shoulder to say hello and then sat down. His line to his seat was that of a right angle while the teacher determined the correct response should have been a linear one. The teacher considered this difference in perception of such magnitude that it should require a conversation with the principal. Thus, the student was sent to the principal's office. From the young boy's perspective, he had done nothing wrong and could not understand why he was being punished. He reported to the principal that the teacher obviously didn't like him."

This difference in the interpretation of the word "directly" by the teacher and student created a classroom behavior problem and probably ended a student-teacher relationship needed to enhance learning. The teacher assumed that the student was deliberately defying her authority and, thus, was unworthy of being present to receive instruction; while the student decided the teacher had a personal dislike for him and was not interested in teaching him.

This type of conflict is common in urban schools. It is a sample of the differences in perception of appropriate behavior which has generated the opinion that African-American children are difficult to teach. More important, it is this type of variation in interpretation which causes many children to conceive schools as places to be avoided, ignored, or merely tolerated because they have difficulty deciphering behavioral and communicative expectations (McDermott, 1977).

The teaching-learning interaction in urban schools can be rewarding, stimulating and productive for both teacher or student if certain orientations and rules are applied which make the classroom more compatible with student styles of thinking, perceiving, and interacting. It requires teachers to connect with students at the point of their orientations toward life in order to establish a relationship which can foster success in the educative process. Here are some suggestions:

1. *Begin by creating a culturally compatible classroom.*

As Purkey and Novack (1984) indicate, children are like flowers which need the sunshine of a warm and inviting environment. For example, principals like Mrs. Opal Taylor of the Charles Lake Public School in Cleveland, Ohio have found that this means establishing a pleasant, warm, and inviting climate throughout the entire school. In her building, bright, attractive, and well-designed bulletin boards which help children focus on educational objectives are found in the office, halls, and every classroom. When you walk into Charles Lake, the entire hall has color, flowers, sparkling floors and a sense of cleanliness and orderliness which transmits the message to all entering—"You are expected. You will do well." Most of all, there is a climate of respect and belonging which is reinforced once a week when all students and teachers wear their special shirts with Charles Lake School printed boldly across the front. The effect of this climate shows in the low rate of discipline and attendance problems and the rising achievement scores.

2. *Concentrate on developing motivation rather than classroom discipline and management techniques.*

Perhaps the greatest conflict which teachers and students have to resolve is the issue of the definition of discipline and classroom management. Too often with African-American children, the definition means conformity to the point of "lockstep" behavior. The result is that students often receive more rewards for behavioral conformity than for academic competence. It is a variance in expectations noted by African-American children. In a study done by Holliday (1985) many African-American children noted that when they were in their neighborhoods, they felt that learning to solve problems and complete cognitive tasks were extremely important behaviors; but when they were in school, they paid more attention to how they were to behave and how to develop interpersonal competence.

If Good and Brophy (1986) are correct in their assessment of effective instructional techniques, teachers who excite students about learning and motivate them to expend their mental energy on tasks and ideas are engaging in the most effective discipline and classroom management techniques available. George Cureton's active discussion approach, and Marva Collin's methods of building bridges between cultural behavior style and the curriculum and teaching-learning process are examples of how children from different cultural orientations can be encouraged and involved in the learning process.

Other suggestions which emanate from the literature include:

a. Develop activities and a classroom which are moderately structured.
b. Arrange the classroom so that the teacher is in close proximity to the students.
c. Present self as a warm, encouraging yet authoritative figure.
d. Use frequent praise to acts of learning rather than negative comments on behavior.
e. Use small groups and cooperative learning rather than expecting students to work alone.
f. Be sensitive to the social and emotional factors in the classroom and use them as positive influences on learning.

Once the school and classroom becomes conducive and inviting, more time can be spent on teaching and learning activities.

3. ***Teach the process of handling material as well as content.***

African-American children can read faces, recognize people and situations, encode and elaborate on nonverbal cues and information, memorize correctly in a short-time the words to every song on the radio which they hear in passing; use colorful and articulate metaphors and analogies to describe behavior and situations; and find creative ways of manipulating people to act in ways which are congruent to their needs. They appear to have what Keating (1978) and Ford and Tisak (1983) have identified as social intelligence. Their people perceptual skills and social cognitive skills are finely tuned abilities. This type of intelligence, however, does little for the abstract and more object-oriented information which is presented by teachers and texts. A successful teacher of African-American children must enter the classroom prepared to teach processes of academic learning as well as content. This requires attention being given to several important information processing areas. Some suggestions which should be considered are:

(a) *Memory Process:* African-American children have excellent memory processes but they need to have more information committed to their long-term memory which can be used to interpret material used in texts. This means teachers must take the responsibility of introducing children and their parents to new experiences and relationships. Suggest to parents and siblings that they explore museums and, what appear to be foreign worlds, right in their own city with their children. More important, teachers should take them to new places and experiences as a part of their teaching activities to ensure that the exposure is active and related to other content being covered in the classroom.

African-American children are more likely to remember ideas and concepts with which they have interacted and touched and discussed rather than through lecturing, notetaking, underlining or other passive activities. As suggested by Sutro et al. and Barbe, include additional modalities in the classroom, particularly the tactile and kinesthetic approaches.

(b) *Elaboration Process:* A significant amount of teaching and testing is designed to foster regurgitation of exactly what the teacher said and interpreted, particularly for African-American youngsters. Yet, this approach does little to improve intellectual development of African-American youth. If true learning is to occur, the material must become a part of their schemata. Ideas which are to be assimilated or accommodated by African-American youth are best done if the students paraphrase, summarize in their own words and find ways to relate it to their environment and personal life. However, it cannot stop there. If concepts and ideas are only related to the African-American community or the particular city, children become ethnocentric and geocentric. Again, this limits their ability to venture out and explore new ideas and people and things which can help them grow and develop. Find ways to extend their knowledge base to other communities, other situations, and other contexts.

(c) *The structuring process:* In the recent issue of *Ebony* magazine, a number of outstanding teachers of African-American children were identified, one of which was Mrs. Dorothy Wilson of Chicago, Illinois. An example of her successful teaching strategies included diagramming ideas out of paragraphs to teach reading. The students pointed out that Ms. Wilson broke the work down into main components so they could work on it and understand it.

Throughout the literature and studies, African-American children have been found to be field-dependent (Shade, 1982). Rather than concentrate on what this means from a personality perspective, the primary information processing attribute this represents is that African-American youth are perceptually diffuse and have trouble dissecting tasks. This can be taught and, as demonstrated by Ms. Wilson, facilitating this differentiation is imperative for successful approach to the learning activities for African-American children. But perhaps the most important aspect is to model the thinking which occurs in diagramming and identifying the main components so that African-American children can take responsibility for their own learning.

SOME FINAL COMMENTS

In a recent study by Borkowski and Krause (1983) the findings suggested that the processing of African-American children could be enhanced if their executive system was strengthened. Such suggestions, of course, set off a series of debates as to whether African-American children should change their style of learning or whether or not schools and texts should find ways to accommodate the style used by African-American children. Perhaps the best answer is a bicultural approach, i.e., understanding, allowing, and accommodating the African-American student behavioral and communicating styles while helping them develop cognitive skills which are important to the information requirements in an academic setting. Three processes seem to need particular attention and development: memory, elaboration and structuring content skills.

Teaching African-American children is no more difficult than teaching any child if you believe that learning can occur, make necessary cognitive style accommodations, and accept culturally-different interpretation of the world and behavior. Many individuals have done this and are doing the task very successfully. However, more individuals are needed to accept the challenge to build a bridge between the school and African-American culture as a means of making educational success a reality for more children. It is a task which must be done in every classroom.

REFERENCES

1. Borkowski, J. G., & Krause, A.: Racial differences in intelligence: The importance of the executive system. *Intelligence, 7:*379–395, 1983.

2. Ford, M. E., & Tisak, M. S.: A further search for social intelligence. *Journal of Educational Psychology, 75:*196–206, 1983.

3. Good, T., & Brophy, J. *Educational Psychology.* San Francisco, Longman Press, 1986.

4. Holliday, B. G.: Toward a model of teacher-child transactional processes affecting Black childrens' academic achievement. In Spencer, M., Brookins, G., & Allen, W.: *Beginnings: The Social and Affective Development of Black Children.* Hillsdale, Lawrence Erlbaum Associates, 1985.

5. Keating, D. P.: A search for social intelligence. *Journal of Educational Psychology, 70:*218–233, 1978.

6. McDermott, R. P.: Social relations as contexts for learning in school. *Harvard Educational Review, 47:*198–213, 1977.

7. Purkey, W. W., & Novak, J. M.: *Inviting School Success.* Belmont, Wadsworth, 1984.

8. Shade, B. J.: Afro-American cognitive style: A variable in school success? *Review of Educational Research, 52:*219–244, 1982.

Chapter 14

USING A BLACK LEARNING STYLE*

GEORGE O. CURETON

Is there such a thing as a black learning style? Some argue indefatigably that there is not, while others argue just as vehemently that there is. Before we look more closely at this question, let's be sure what we are talking about. What do we mean by "black learning style?"

Perhaps the term is at fault. What I am talking about is a style of learning for children, primarily in the inner city, primarily members of minority groups, who have traditionally had difficulty with academic school work, especially reading. For a complex of historical, sociological, and economic reasons, a majority of these children are black.

Those who oppose the idea of a distinct "black learning style" feel that to suggest a difference in learning style between blacks and others is to reinforce the insidious myth that innercity children are inferior. Instead, these opponents tell us, what we are really talking about is motivation. The inner-city child does not have the same motivation as do middle-class children.

Yes and no. Motivation is important, in fact necessary. But it will have little effect until the inner-city child's learning style has been established. Moreover, the type of motivation differs from that of the middle-class children, who usually come to school already motivated to a considerable degree. Jackie, our inner-city child, often does not. So it is important that we understand the type of motivation that turns him or her on and off to learning, and that we know how to utilize his or her strengths so that motivation leads to learning. As Reisman (1976) says, "In everybody's style there are certain strengths. And everybody has an Achilles' heel. In developing a significant change in learning, one must control the Achilles' heel and utilize the strengths. This is the central

*From Cureton, George. Using a black learning style. *The Reading Teacher*, 41:751–756. Copyright © International Reading Association. Used with permission.

problem of the strategy of style, especially in its application to the inner-city pupils in our schools."

Inner-city Jackie's battle with reading is his or her Achilles' heel. But this problem may result from overlooking the strengths Jackie brings to school. These strengths are not measurable by readiness tests or other criteria usually used to assess readiness, but they can be determined through cognitive style mapping.

The term cognitive style mapping refers to a process in which the individual is assessed for his or her most comfortable manner of learning, whether visual or auditory, independent or in a group. Evidence from cognitive style mapping indicates that innercity children learn more effectively when physical and oral involvement are present in the learning (Cureton, 1977).

Evidence from teachers confirms this. While the term cognitive style mapping may be new in educational literature, the practice is not. A group of successful primary grade teachers from inner-city schools, for example, use the phrase "when and how." By "when," they mean the time at which to introduce a new skill; by "how," they mean the manner in which the skill is presented. To achieve this knowledge of when and how, they have practiced cognitive style mapping, though not by that name.

Only on Wednesday

To these teachers, the variables of time and day are very significant in getting inner-city Jackie to react positively to learning a new task. Although these teachers lack scientific data, they do have success to substantiate their assumptions. For example, their experience, and it is considerable, tells them that Wednesday is the best day for teaching new skills. They also want their classes tested on Wednesday. One teacher showed me the results of two tests taken by her class. The results from the first test, given early in the week, showed the class to be below grade in reading. However, when the students took another form of the test on a Wednesday, they came out on grade level. Why Wednesday? I questioned these teachers, but they were unable to supply any real explanation.

The "how" for inner-city teachers varies, of course, from class to class. But one "how" that has worked for many combines, as it were, business with pleasure. If you observe these teachers, it is difficult to determine when the game is over and when learning is taking place. They have chosen to use a phonic approach to teach reading because they have found that their students are better able to cope with a program that is heavily based on phonics than with a program that places more emphasis on sight words. With a phonic program, they can provide more action, more fun, in contrast to the quieter setting of the traditional classroom, a setting which is not characteristic of the inner-city child's daily life.

Inner-city children, although used to talking a great deal, often come to school with a poor auditory set. They are not accustomed to listening for long periods. The action approach to learning, which demands continuous participation by the children, also teaches them to listen as they learn, for their participation is in response to questions from the teacher, questions that must be listened to and understood before they can be responded to. That the action approach works, and that acquisition of knowledge takes place, are attested to not only by the teachers' evaluations of their students but also by these children's scores on standardized reading tests.

Putting Sounds Together

Come with me to a first-grade classroom where the action approach is being used. Today the teacher is developing the concept of blending by having the children slide around the room. This is done to demonstrate physically how letters and sounds are blended together into words. This psychomotor technique makes the concept of blending letters meaningful, especially when the teacher says, "Slide the sounds together." To further reinforce the skill of sliding or blending, the teacher has the children "slide" the initial sounds in their names together to produce a word. For example, Mary *muh*, Albert *aah*, Pam *puh*, would produce the word "map." (In sliding sounds, the teacher always leads the children through three steps: the separate sounds—*muh, aah, puh;* the sounds joined together— *muhaahpuh;* and the word with no distortions Oo*map*.)

Another way in which the concept of blending is reinforced is to have children slide objects or pictures of objects together on a table. As they slide *soap, apple,* and *money* together, they blend the initial sound of each to make the word "Sam." Teaching the skill of blending in a concrete manner before applying it to letters brings the concept to life and makes it make sense to the children. The transition from object to letter is a natural progression and far less frustrating than starting with putting letters together to make words.

The last stage of the acquisition of blending skills is seen as the class plays a game. The teacher calls out a series of code words and the students synthesize the sounds these code words stand for into words. For example, the teacher called out, "soap, money, apple show," and the class responds with the word "smash." The game has two main purposes: to help develop listening skills, and to give students a background—a frame of reference—to call upon when they apply the concept of blending to the abstract symbols of the alphabet. This happens later, as the teacher systematically replaces the objects with the letters that represent them. Using this concrete approach to blending eliminates the problem most discussed in teaching with a phonetic approach, getting the children to put the sounds together.

As the children master the concrete representations of the alphabet and of letter combinations, the teacher will play the game again, but this time the students will have to write the letters representing the code. Use of the code not only facilitates the decoding process but also aids those children who have difficulty in hearing the difference between similar sounds, for example, between the short *i* and short *e*. The picture of itching (a girl scratching an itch) which represents the short *i* sound and the picture of another girl names Ethel which represents the short *e* sound makes the difference between the two concrete and unforgettable.

During the teaching of skills, this first grade teacher has everybody in the class participating simultaneously in answering questions. The purpose of this choral response mode is twofold: to keep everyone alert and to build confidence. Children are able to make a wrong response and have it blend in with the correct one—and not be embarrassed; but the response will be right next time. The choral response also gives security to the shy child. Many questions are repeated and responded to several times so that children who are unsure the first time can respond correctly the next.

In this class, both teacher and children stand during the presentation of new skills; the teacher moves around the room, with every eye pinned on her. This strongly teacher-centered approach might be frowned on in some schools as being too authoritarian and uncreative. However, as one teacher put it, "Creativity will become a part of the children's learning styles when they have mastered the basics." Furthermore, it works. The children, far from feeling cramped or frustrated, are eager to learn. The pace and the action of the class, and the accomplishment they feel as they acquire new skills and review earlier ones make them look forward to the reading period.

Can individualized reading programs be successful in inner-city schools, where the learning style of the children favors teacher-centered instruction? The answer will depend somewhat on what is meant by individualized programs. Research by Amidon and Flanders (1963) suggests that achievement level is higher where there is interaction between teacher and student. As one of my students declared after a year using an individualized program, "I need a teacher who will make me learn."

The foregoing paragraphs describe a learning style that results in achievement on the primary level in reading. The next question is how to solve the perplexing problems of maintaining this achievement. Research indicates that by the time most inner city children reach the fourth-grade level, they have lost from a few months to a year in reading. Why?

One reason appears to be the nature of the tests measuring reading achievement. The questions on intermediate grade tests require critical thinking rather than simple recall. Teachers who have been successful in maintaining inner-city children's reading achievement have, therefore, devoted large portions of time to the development of children's interpretive skills.

One such teacher points out that development of comprehension skills with her inner-city children is a persistent search for "why." In this search, oral discussion is essential. The students must give reasons why one answer is better than another and must defend that answer with proof. The proof may come from the story or from his or her experience. In order that the "give up" syndrome does not creep into the children's desire to go after the problem, the teacher never tells a child he or she is wrong. Instead she responds to the student with something like, "Now that's thinking. But is there another answer even closer to the problem?" (Such a discussion does not always have to be the outcome of a reading lesson. It could also result from work on an oral puzzle, which allows for participation of the entire class.) Such teacher interaction with the students may take a great deal of time, but it is time well spent, for it builds a pattern for students' thinking that will stand by them.

Another way to insure participation is to have the students act out the passage read. In this way, emotion and feelings can play a role in comprehension.

Taking Tests

These techniques have been very helpful in building comprehension skills. But many children do not transfer the acquisition of these skills to testing situations. To correct this, we must make students test-conscious and test-wise and point out the "trickery" of some test questions and the ways in which some test authors try to get students to choose wrong answers. Alerting students to these techniques insures careful reading of each test question and also helps to build critical thinking skills. Again, this is done through teacher-student interactions.

Why so much emphasis on oral interaction between student and teacher? Simply because of the student's oral background. As one student pointed out, he could see the causal relationship in the story better when the choice of best answer was thrashed out by the class. The innercity student's learning style depends on oral involvement. The student needs to talk out, with the group, the rationale for a particular choice. This oral exchange of reasons and answers also helps to provide the less apt student with strategies for selecting answers. Most "individualized" programs cannot provide this kind of support.

Computer Assisted Instruction is a case in point. The machine does not help show why a chosen answer is wrong. The cold response "incorrect read again" leads to guessing—and a disdainful attitude toward the computer. To be sure, some self-directed students using the machine enjoy the instruction it offers and seem to profit from its use. But they feel that they work better at the machines when the classroom teacher is in the laboratory to praise their achievement and to record their progress. Even though the machine keeps an accurate account of their answers, the students want the teacher to write the percent of correct responses in a record book.

Interaction between teacher and student plays a particular role in helping students prepare for standardized tests. When you have interacted with the students all through the term before they are tested, they have this action involvement with which to associate in the test-taking situation. As they take the test and choose their answers, they can "hear" the class discussion.

Test taking is something many of us dread, and for the inner-city child it is an especially traumatic experience. An effective way to lessen this fear is to place students in as many testing situations as possible, to give them practice in taking tests. This is particularly needed in the area of reading. In content areas such as mathematics, science, and social studies, students know essentially what the content of the test will be and they can prepare for it. In reading, however, they have no clue as to the content of the passages on which they will be asked questions. This content may be totally unrelated to their daily lives and experience. Thus it seems mandatory to provide ample preparation, again using the teacher-student interaction learning style.

When inner-city students who have been given practice in test-taking situations are given standardized tests, they seem to perform better than students who have not had this kind of practice. Perhaps one more reason for this is that these students have learned to work against time. Inner-city students are often disturbed by the pressure of time. Practice reduced this anxiety.

Is there a black learning style, a learning style especially suited to inner-city students? I believe there is. Use of such a style does not mean lowering standards or expectations, however. It does mean recognizing the students' strengths and utilizing them. Nor are all these students necessarily in the inner city. This learning style has been successful in rural, suburban, and small-city settings with students from many ethnic backgrounds. All of these students, however, share many characteristics of inner-city children.

Teachers must become attuned to the learning style of the many inner-city Jackies so that these students' fullest potential may become visible on standardized tests. This is as true of secondary school and college age as it is of beginners. To develop this learning style, the classroom atmosphere should be that of an "ideal marriage" between teacher and student. This does not mean that similar ethnic background should be the criterion. It does mean that the attitude of teacher toward students and students toward teacher is of vital importance in developing the full potential of our most talked about students.

REFERENCES

1. Amidon, E. J., & Flanders, N. A.: *The Role of the Teacher in the Classroom.* Minneapolis, Amidon & Associates, 1963.
2. Atwood, B. S.: Helping students recognize their own learning style. *Learning, 3:*73–74, 1975.
3. Cureton, G. O.: *Action Reading: The Participatory Approach.* Boston, Allyn & Bacon, 1977.
4. Reissman, F.: *The Inner-City Child.* New York, Harper & Row, 1976.

Chapter 15

THE MATCH: LEARNING STYLES OF AFRICAN-AMERICAN CHILDREN AND MICROCOMPUTER PROGRAMMING*

MARJORIE W. LEE

The primary mission of schools is to provide a quality education for each child. Quality education is provided when learning circumstances (activities or lessons) are in harmony with each child's existing repertoire of experiences and cognitive structure so that information can be accommodatingly modified (Hunt, 1961). When this ideal environment exists, an educational "match" has occurred. As the principal personnel to whom this task is given, teachers have the mandate to solve the "problem of the match." The milieu in which teachers attempt to accomplish an educational match for each student contains many variables that may facilitate or impede the teaching-learning process. Fulfillment of this aim is sometimes not realized for children from white middle-class families, but is often not accomplished for children who are black, regardless of family socioeconomic level.

Achievement in school "depends upon controlling appropriately the match between what environmental circumstances (objects, models, Socratic questions or explanations) the student . . . encounters and the schemata or concepts he has already assimilated" (Hunt, 1961, pg. 268). For the most part, the classroom environment emphasizes the experiences and values of the white, middle-class segment of our society, while it either excludes experiences of minority groups or assigns a demeaning role to those experiences. Likewise, our schools reward the predominant learning style of white children and fail to recognize the predominant learning style of black children.

As if the problems teachers face in achieving an instructional match

*From Lee, Marjorie W. The match: Learning styles of black children and microcomputer programming. *Journal of Negro Education*, 55:78–92, 1986. Used with permission.

156

for each child were not difficult enough, advances in technology have entered the classroom and have become central to good instruction. Computers are so pervasive in all phases of education that teachers not only have more to teach, but they must also demonstrate competence in their teaching with the use of this machine. They must use computers as a medium of instruction and also provide direction about this technology as a curriculum-subject with its own vocabulary, concepts, and skills to be mastered. Therefore, an already difficult task—achievement of a match between a student's learning style and the instruction given—has become more complicated and, concurrently, needed more than ever.

A large proportion of black Americans live in large urban areas of the United States and are educated in public schools. Therefore, it is essential that public school teachers be trained to teach blacks and other minority children in urban areas. Teachers are now faced with a triple quandary: (1) solving the problem of the match, (2) understanding and using new technology, and (3) recognizing the needs of black or other minority students and using the new technology to meet those needs.

Juxtaposed to the variables that affect the teaching-learning process are some school practices that contribute to the school failure of many public school children, most of whom are black. Racism, poverty, poorly trained teachers, or some deficit on the part of the students are offered as influences on these children's failure. Other practices that contribute to the "mismatch" between instruction provided for black children and their school success are: (1) a general lack of knowledge about and appreciation for the importance of ethnic experiences that black children bring to school—consequently, this important information is not usually utilized in the curricula; (2) an emphasis on the eradication of the preferred learning styles of black children, instead of using their strength-learning-style to teach them other styles; and (3) a misplaced focus on the computer as a tutor for black children (if they have computer experiences at all) in place of teaching them also to program this machine, and thus, to generate knowledge. These practices limit the black student's chances at achievement as much as direct racism, poverty, and poorly trained teachers do.

Mass school failure for black students need not occur, as demonstrated by Head Start and Follow-Through studies. These programs have demonstrated that when quality instruction and comprehensive care are provided for black children, achievement of the match is facilitated and these children learn. A review of the literature on these programs shows that student ethnicity is included in the curricula and reinforced through parental involvement. Also, the instructional activities teach the school-valued cognitive style without attempting to eradicate the children's preferred learning style. Rather, attempts are made to instruct through cultural activities, using familiar stimuli. Recently, the High/Scope Demonstration Center in Ypsilanti, Michigan, reported findings from their ongoing longitudinal study of low-income black children that give concrete evidence for this fact. The preliminary findings point out that when computers are used with children as just one part of a high-quality preschool program, this technology can be a powerful learning device that facilitates cognitive (and perhaps emotional) development without harm to young children (Hohmann, 1984). The center's Perry Preschool Project has reported resounding success in teaching low-income black children using computers as tutors and in teaching children to program computers. Findings such as these provide important implications for teaching children, especially those who are minority preschoolers and/or from poor families.

This article examines how changes in the traditional school practices can facilitate achievement of an "educational match" for more black children than customary practices can provide. These changes are recommended for school curricula, in teachers' attitudes toward relational learning styles, and in the ways computers are used with children. Hence, this article emphasizes achieving a "teaching-learning match" for African-American children by: (1) incorporating the African-American experience into existing curricula in ways that are meaningful for children throughout the grades; (2) training teachers to value and foster relational learning styles while they also continue to teach by means of analytical styles; and (3) teaching children, starting in preschool, to use both relational and analytical reasoning as they program and use computers.

LEARNING STYLES AND THE CURRICULUM

There is a relationship between an individual's learning style and his/her cultural or ethnic group membership. Hale stated that a person's behavioral style is usually a cultural framework for how that person views the world, but a person's basic style can be changed when aspects of other styles are taught (Hale, 1982). Successful people use not only their preferred learning style, but they integrate and harmonize different styles within their cognitive structures so that they can function in different settings for various reasons and can complete many diverse kinds of tasks.

The ways in which a person learns are directly related to that person's cognitive style (way of thinking) (Cole et al., 1971). Cole explains that cognition develops in conjunction with the behaviors in which people engage in everyday life. Therefore, if there is a vast difference in the daily experiences of two people (regardless of ethnic group affiliation), it is likely that they will develop different cognitive styles. Within a complex society, social classes and ethnic groups are two major ecological structures that produce diversity in human lifestyles and development (Havighurst, 1976). Combined, these structures both influence a set of behaviors and attitudes that define a person's lifestyle and development and also separate him/her from other groups.

All people have unique cultural experiences that influence their styles of learning. And everyone has a preferred way in which information or skills are concentrated on, absorbed, and retained. This individual way of processing new or difficult information is known as a person's learning style. Stodolsky and Lesser found that different kinds of intellectual skills are fostered or hindered in different environments (Stodolsky & Lesser, 1967). This means that different home and school environments influence how one thinks and what is learned.

If instruction is to match the cognitive styles of all children and thus increase their chances for school achievement, public school curricula must also include the cultural behaviors, values, and cognitive styles children bring to school. It is well documented that American public schools value the analytical learning styles, which emphasize spoken and written language as used by the middle class and emphasize content reflective of the lifestyles of white Protestants. African-American children, on the other hand, usually are proficient in the relational learning styles, which emphasize visual and audio stimuli. Webb points out that relational learners fail in school far more often than analytical learners do (Webb, 1983). Our schools are focused away from large segments of students; this omission is unrecognized for its relationship to school failure and, thus, not addressed in plans for school improvement or increase in achievement (Webb, 1983). In his eight-year study of schools, John Goodlad found that these institutions (schools) are trying to improve themselves when they have not determined "how balanced the curriculum [is] for each student [or] the relevance of school to students' lives" (Schere, 1985). With this lack of vital knowledge, there is no wonder that teachers have difficulty matching their instruction to children's needs, and existing curricula are not meaningfully inclusive of minority cultures.

There is no basis for rewarding one learning style and labeling the other a liability. Webb reported that neither the left brain (which is superior for analytical thinking) nor the right brain (which is superior for relational thinking) is better than the other. Each side of the brain has different functions and both should be used cooperatively. He states that "to be truly competent, independent, effective learners, individuals need to team both . . . hemispheres of the brain," and thus become competent in both learning styles (Webb, 1983).

An implication of Webb's work is that children need to experience different cultures and ways of viewing their environment during their critical learning periods in order to stimulate use of both sides of the brain cooperatively. Research supports the fact that multi-ethnic experiences provide the opportunity for individuals to develop facility in both learning styles, and thus have the opportunity to achieve the most from schooling (Duncan & DeAvila, 1979). Therefore, it is clear that there is no basis for valuing one ethnic group over others. Instead, school instruction must draw from a curriculum that *values and includes the cultures of all children* enrolled in their classrooms.

For black children this means that "traditional curriculum [should] include the study and legitimizing of Africa and African-American culture along with assimilation of skills children will need to survive in the mainstream American culture" (Hale, 1982). This does not mean the exclusion of the dominant cultural experiences or that of other ethnic groups. In fact, all cultures that make up American should be experienced (firsthand or by way of a technological medium) by all children schools through curriculum components such as songs, arithmetic problems, science experiments, arts and crafts activities, social studies, dance forms, reading materials, and media experiences.

CHILDREN'S LEARNING AND COMPUTER PROGRAMMING

Most computer experiences provided for children are of the information/input type. That is, computers are used to tutor children concerning some skill, concept, or content, or to drill them in some skill or facts. Sometimes this machine is used to simulate a real-life situation or event. Again, this use of the tool is to provide children with information.

Information-input type computer experiences require facility with the basic thinking processes; observing, remembering, classifying, interpreting, and the beginning levels of decision making and problem solving. Using computers in these ways helps children acquire large amounts of information, but children do not engage in the higher levels, more abstract thinking processes required in scientific and mathematical fields. These processes utilize an ability to perform mental operations (both analytical and relational) that children have not yet experienced.

Teaching African-American children to program computers at an early age will provide them with opportunities for analytical thinking at the same time that their environment is teaching them to function with relational thinking skills. The computer can help all children learn to be functional in styles that assist them in better integration of, and perhaps knowing more completely, concepts, facts, principles, rules, and approaches needed for school success. In learning to design, write, and debug their own mathematical or logical operations in the form of instructions for the machine, young children learn to engage in the higher level though processes as applied to concrete objects. They learn to infer, hypothesize, predict, analyze, synthesize, and evaluate relative to some firsthand experience or real objects. What may seem like fun is also teaching them content, thinking styles, and behaviors needed to achieve in school, and later, to succeed in the adult world of high technology.

Computer use, along with the ability to program the machine as well as operate it using good programmed packages, can make a difference in the school achievement of African-American children. Individuals who are computer-literate (knowing what a computer can and cannot do, how to operate the machine, programming procedures, and strategies for changing programs) must have high language competencies, and have fluency in sequential, symbolic, analytical, and logical reasoning (analytical skills) as well as be competent in visual-spatial, nonverbal synthetic reasoning (relational skills). Microcomputers provide high visual and audio stimuli while they allow the user to express creativity. This feature makes computers compatible with behaviors fostered in the African-American community, since this environment contains high visual and audio stimuli from the creative and expressive arts (Hale, 1982). As children program computers and use them, they experience familiar stimuli levels while they use relational skills to develop computer activities and use analytical skills in writing their own programs.

Young children who become computer-literate gain facility in both thinking modes during their critical period of cognitive development, value both styles, and function competently in both. With good software programs (a dozen have been identified by the High/Scope Demonstration Center) children can explore concepts reflective of many cultures. Early establishment of these competencies would help all children learn more effectively and, perhaps, achieve better academically in school.

Writing a computer program calls for "hierarchial thinking" (thinking from simple processes such as recall to more complex processes such as analysis). Debugging requires "procedural thinking," i.e., thinking of strategies for doing something to find errors and then using classification and/or organization of the elements to be expressed in new ways. Operating a computer calls for viewing the machine as "friendly," an ability to follow directions, and an orientation to what it takes to make a computer function (use of the keyboard or a joystick).

Preliminary findings of Sheingold and Pea show that programming computers encourages development of problem-solving skills (Sheingold & Pea, 1981). Sheingold explains that microcomputers help children get in touch with the symbolic aspects of what they already know or are learning from other kinds of experiences (Sheingold, 1983). This makes the computer a valuable tool for teachers in incorporating children's culture and at-home experiences into the school curriculum.

Computer programming offers opportunity for virtually unlimited creative expression. The user can think about a real-life experience and produce it as an abstract entity for the computer. Thus, two processes (remembering and interpreting) that are prerequisites to the valued abstract higher levels of thinking are fostered by computer use. As children write programs, they learn to communicate ideas, knowledge, accomplishments, and feelings to others. In fact, Goodman reports that computer programming extends the duration (length) of children's written messages (Goodman & Damarin, 1982).

Goodman also finds that children who use computers are as social as children who do not use them. They collaborate on lessons and interact with peers as they do in other tutoring sessions. Use of this machine helps children receive positive socialization experiences in two ways: while interacting with the machine and while interaction with peers. As children acquire accomplishments, experiences, and feedback regarding these computer activities, their self-concepts are being nurtured. Constructive messages from the environment such as those provided in computer-use build self-esteem, i.e., satisfaction with and respect for oneself. Success in school work is also a contributor to a child's self-esteem (Coopersmith, 1967). There is also wide support for the fact that control over one's environment is another salient component of self-esteem (Brim, 1976). Paisley and Chen point out that all children seem to increase in self-esteem as they master programming the computer (Paisley & Chen, 1982).

TEACHER EDUCATION AND AFRICAN-AMERICAN CHILDREN'S LEARNING

Since teachers must be prepared to teach the diverse ethnic groups of children who come to them for instruction, they must know how to facilitate cognitive, social, emotional, and physical development of both the majority and minority ethnic groups. That is, teachers must have an understanding of how humans (multiethnic groups) grow, develop, and change in order to teach them effectively. The content and methods used in the classrooms must reflect the unique features of each child, if instruction is to match the cognitive styles each child brings to school, and if it is to increase each child's chances for academic achievement. These competencies should be acquired during the preservice period. Thus, teacher education programs must train teachers who can capably instruct all children, i.e., children from different ethnic groups, who live in different aggregate-locations such as urban areas or small towns, and who come from various family income levels.

McKenzie identified three salient characteristics that teacher education programs must develop in teachers from urban schools: a positive attitude, intelligence, and computer skills (McKenzie, 1984). A positive attitude refers to an orientation that includes commitment to education in urban schools and willingness to function in several roles: instruction, counselor, surrogate parent, nurse, custodian, and role model. A positive attitude also suggests being able to identify with children who are struggling to cope with the psychic stress of late twentieth-century pubescence and adolescence, and who are trying to come to terms with the realities of being in the United States of America.

Intelligence is self-explanatory, but in relation to teacher education it should be viewed as a teacher's form of superior interest in the "life of the mind," and as the ability to display this intelligence to students while teaching all subject areas. It should be reflected in the fact that urban teachers are required to have high standards, but even more in their high expectations for the children they teach. These master teachers should also be familiar with black and other ethnic urban cultures, while also knowledgeable about the special considerations these cultures place on teaching urban children.

Today, teaching children skills and information needed to succeed in mainstream America means that teachers must be computer-literate themselves and able to implement curricula that teach children to use this technology. In recognizing the value of computers in teaching all children, especially those who are black and attending urban schools, McKenzie proposes that teacher education programs emphasize mastery of computer usage for prospective teachers prior to graduation. Inclusion of these competencies will require that teacher preparation curricula be expanded and, therefore, that the current four-year training period also be lengthened. Institutions of higher education will certainly have to comply if their graduates are to be competitive for employment in tenure-track positions.

Teachers already in service must learn to use computers. The District of Columbia school system has been a forerunner in requiring all teachers and high school graduates to be computer-literate and in providing inservice training for teachers in order to accomplish this goal.

Although more evidence is needed regarding the relationship between teachers using computers in instruction and increased student learning, some support does exist for this connection, and thus, support exists for training teachers to use this medium in teaching. Black low-income children enrolled in the Perry Preschool Project in Michigan since the late 1970s have learned to accomplish a variety of learning tasks using computers and have shown gains from their preschool experiences (*Washington Post,* 1984). The investigators of this project reported that "high-quality preschool education pays life-time dividends for poor children, from greater success in high school and the job market to lower rates of teenage pregnancy, welfare, and crime." Hohmann (1984) reports that the computer is an effective "vehicle" for inducing certain types of exploration that can help these low-income black children think. The youngsters at the Perry Preschool used the computer to learn such concepts as similarity, difference, matching, grouping, space, and time. They also acquired some basic skills via the computer that should be learned in early childhood, such as basic words and beginning writing. From good computer-based instruction, these children have been able to enter new worlds through images on the screen and to learn from these experiences. This information is presented to children on the screen in interesting, colorful, and challenging formats that allow active participation while it reflects their work pace and adjusts to their skill levels.

The District of Columbia Public Schools System has been a leader in using computers and other electronic developments to improve children's learning. For many years children finishing grades 3, 6, 9, and 11 in the District of Columbia schools have scored above the national norm in several basic skills categories. Students in these grades scored from several months to two and one-half years higher in abilities than the national norm in subjects such as reading, mathematics, language, reference skills, science, and society studies (White, 1984).

While the specific contributions of computer instruction to children's gains are not currently known, it is known that advanced technology used in instruction does hold some very effective new ways of helping children to learn, and thus is one of the variables influencing the children's school success. Further support for using computers in school to teach black children is provided from the investigations of Piestrup (1981) and Hungate (1982). These educators found that children as young as three years of age improved on certain skills after using computer lessons. More investigations, such as the work done by Nida (1984) and Springle and Schaefer (1984) are being conducted to provide additional information about the impact of computer instruction on children. Regardless of the outcome of these studies, we know that before children can benefit from this machine at school, their teachers must acquire techniques, teaching strategies, and competence in teaching children to use this tool and learn from it.

Teacher education programs are in the early stages of incorporating computer-literacy into their curricula so that prospective teachers can obtain methods and practice in using this technology in their teaching. To date, little is known about the effectiveness of teachers' computer training in enabling staff to teach computer skills to children. There is a need to investigate the effectiveness of learning via computers on school success.

CONCLUSIONS

One's level of knowledge is increased when one functions competently in both the relational and analytical thinking styles. Computers can foster proficiency in both of these required thinking styles, and thus facilitate school success of *all children* who use them. Literacy regarding this technology is important since computers are central to the way we process and access information today, and will remain a vital tool for the foreseeable future. While this tool holds benefits for all users, children as well as adults, it has the potential to make a difference in the school success and overall level of achievement of African-American and other minority children. Computers can assist teachers to achieve the elusive educational match for these children. What is needed to attain this benefit is trained, competent teachers who will use this technology as a supportive part of their instructional efforts.

Learning, for African-American children, with the use of a computer (programming it) and from use of it (using a programmed package for computers) is compatible with the culturally-based learning style many black children bring to school. This machine also teaches nonminority children how to increase their level of knowledge with use of the relational style. Thus, computers placed in classrooms for use by children can make a difference in the overall learning and quality of life for all students enrolled.

REFERENCES

1. Brim, O. G.: Lifespan development of the theory of oneself: Implication for child development. In Reece, H. W. (Ed.): *Advances in Child Development,* New York, Academic Press, 1976.
2. Cole, M., & Scribner, S. et al.: *The Cultural Context of Thinking and Learning.* New York, Basic Books, 1971.
3. Coopersmith, S.: *The Antecedents of Self Esteem.* San Francisco, W. H. Freeman, 1967.
4. Duncan, S., & DeAvila, E.: Bilingualism and cognition: Some recent findings. *Journal of the Association for Bilingual Education, 4:*43, 1979.
5. Goodman, F. L.: Computer and the future literacy. Paper presented at the National Computer Conference, Denton, Texas, 1981 cited in Damarin, S. K. The impact of computer technology on children. Paper presented at the Symposium on the Impact of Computer Technology on Children, American Society for Information Scientists, Columbus, Ohio, 1982.
6. Hale, J.: *Black Children — Their Roots, Culture and Learning Styles.* Provo, Brigham Young University Press, 1982.

7. Havighurst, R.: The relative importance of social class and ethnicity in human development. *Human Development, 19:*56–64, 1976.
8. Holmann, C.: Computers and active learning; Are they compatible? *High Scope Resources, 3:*2–3, 1984.
9. Hunt, J. McV.: *Intelligence and Experience.* New York, Ronald Press, 1961.
10. Hungate, H.: Computers in kindergarten. *The Computing Teacher, 10:*15–18, 1982.
11. McKenzie, F. D.: Education, not excuses. *Journal of Negro Education, 53:*97–105, 1984.
12. Nida, R. E. et al.: Introducing a microcomputer to a preschool classroom: The effects on children's social interaction. Greensboro, North Carolina University, Family Research Center, 1984.
13. Paisley, W. J., & Chen, M.: Children and electronic text: Challenges and opportunities of the new literacy. A research report prepared at the Institute for Communication Research, Stanford University, 1982.
14. Piestrup, A. M.: Preschool children use Apple II to test reading skills programs. ERIC Document Reproduction Service ED 202 476, 1981.
15. Preschool pays off, study says. *Washington Post,* September 14: A-10, 1984.
16. Schere, M.: John Goodlad talks to *Instructor* readers: How do we improve a place called school? In *Early Childhood Education 85/86,* Guilford, Dushkin Publishing Group, 1985.
17. Sheingold, K.: Young children in our technological environment: The impact of microcomputers. Paper presented at the University of Maryland, March 9, 1983.
18. Sheingold, K., & Pea, R. D.: *The Impact of a Classroom Computer Experiences on Children's Problem Solving, Planning, and Peer Collaboration,* New York Bank Street College of Education, 1981.
19. Springle, J. E., & Schaefer, L.: Age, gender and spatial knowledge influences on preschoolers' computer programming ability. *Early Child Development and Care, 14:*243–250, 1984.
20. Stodolsky, S., & Lesser, G. S.: Learning patterns in the disadvantaged. *Harvard Educational Review, 37:*546–93, 1967.
21. Webb, G. M.: Left/right brains, teammates in learning. *Exceptional Children, 49:*500–515, 1983.
22. White, R. D.: 8th, 9th grades in D. C. improve scores on tests. *Washington Post,* July 13, A1–A28, 1984.

Chapter 16

SOCIAL AND CULTURAL EFFECTS ON INDIAN LEARNING STYLE: CLASSROOM IMPLICATIONS*

Floy C. Pepper and Steven Henry

In this era of technological advancement and excellence in education, new approaches to learning are being introduced. There are many different approaches to learning styles including the Jungian approach, the right brain/left brain concept, the field dependent/independent concept of cognitive style, the locus of control concept and Dunn's (1983) work on learning styles which includes environmental, emotion, sociological, physical, and psychological elements of cognitive, affective, and physiological styles.

However, after more than a decade of continuing research, it seems that one reason for the variety of theories concerned with how students achieve academically is that each theorist contributes only partial insight into the learning process and that none provides a complete explanation of how individuals gain and retain knowledge. Neither theories of how one functions nor those concerned with how we develop account for the total phenomenon of learning style. Needed is an integration of such theories with concepts of the individual's relationship with the environment. This includes such things as the conditions under which learning repeatedly takes place and the opportunities and directions in which learning may be expressed. Such conditions and opportunities are often structured by the cultural and social environment of the individual. Most useful would be a theory which presents a holistic view of the individual as a developing organism through the interaction of innate

*From Pepper, Floy C. and Henry, Steven. Social and culture effects on Indian learning style: Classroom implications. *Canadian Journal of Native Education,* 13:54–61, 1986. Reprinted with permission of the Canadian Journal of Native Education. All rights reserved.

equipment and developmental processes with the individual's social/ cultural influences. The theory of Alfred Adler offers such an approach.

Adler (1930) suggests we are who we are by virtue of observing things around us and making choices and reaching conclusions as to what are effective and constructive ways to get along in the world as we see it. Adler believed that the child has an inner and outer environment. The child's inner environment is his/her hereditary endowment. There are three factors in the child's outer environment:

> 1. *Family atmosphere.* This is the family's cultural setting. The attitudes and values of the parents, their character traits, the general quality of their marital relationship, as well as the influences of their parents and relatives, all of which have an impact upon the family atmosphere;
>
> 2. *Family constellation.* That is the characteristic relationship of each member of the family to each other. Each family has its own distinctive pattern. In the interaction of responses and influences with each other, the role a family member plays will have an effect upon the whole family and the personality of each member;
>
> 3. *Child rearing practices.* [This includes the types of rewards given, the type of tasks determined to represent competence, and the various practices which influence various stages of development.]

As the child interprets his/her experiences with the inner and outer environments, he/she draws conclusions about effective approaches toward social living, and develops an attitude toward life in general which constitutes his/her pattern of life (Dreikurs, Grunwald, & Pepper, 1982).

The basic influences as presented by Adler seem to offer learning contexts or vehicles which account for the phenomenon of ethnic development presented by Longstreet (1983). Ethnic development is "behavior learned . . . as a result of direct contact with people and immediate environment" (p. 63). Such learning, she feels, contributes to behavior patterns associated with an ethnic learning style. The behavior patterns include such things as the areas of learning a student is disposed to feel are relevant and preferred modes of learning (e.g., visual).

Ethnicity of a child's learning style undergoes modification through exposure of the child to his or her broader culture. The child's uniquely intimate ethnic learning experiences are the basis of, but sometimes blended into, the child's culturally-related learning style (e.g., reserve Cree versus "Indian"). Let us consider these broader cultural effects on learning.

CULTURE AND CHILD-REARING
PATTERNS AFFECTING LEARNING

The activity patterns to which many Indian children are exposed are rooted in a number of important values. These include such things as generosity and sharing, cooperation and group harmony, placidity and patience, behavioral expression, different concepts of time, different values of ownership and property. These values are generally learned in an informal manner and unconsciously applied.

Traditional Indian child-rearing practices have been labeled by some as "permissive" in comparison to European-American society standards. This misunderstanding usually occurs because Indian child-rearing is self-exploratory rather than restrictive. In this way, self-discipline is learned by an Indian child as a natural result of child rearing practices whereas the European-American child has to be taught self-discipline later in life. Many Indian children are trained to be self-directed and self-reliant by having the freedom to make many of their own choices and decisions.

For some European-Americans, childhood is bootcamp and children are in training to become "good adults." For these youngsters, discipline becomes largely a matter of obedience and then we have a "discipline problem" every time a child doesn't do what he/she is told. For most Indian people, childhood is a time for figuring out the world and for giving a full rein to curiosity by experimenting and testing, by questioning the old and trying to invent the new. For Indian people, discipline doesn't mean something as simple and narrow as obedience. It is a process powerfully connected to an Indian child's emergence of self-discipline.

Another outgrowth of this self-exploratory approach is that many Indian children come to regard absolute noninterference as normal. Respect for individual dignity and personal autonomy are valued and youngsters are taught not to interfere in the affairs of others. European-Americans usually do not understand the concept of non-interference and sometimes appear to Indians to be attempting to pry, to give advice, or to involve themselves in Indian business. A conflict sometimes occurs when Indians resist and resent the involvement of outsiders in their affairs. This has some real implications in the classroom where European-American adults are doing what seems to them normal teaching activities, which may be perceived as "butting into" the business of the Indian student. The student may resent the involvement of outsiders in what they perceive as their affairs—that is, their learning tasks.

In most Indian families, the child is a revered member of the family unit, and as such, is a welcomed spectator and participant to all types of family and community affairs. Indeed, it is not uncommon to see young Indian children accompanying their parents (or siblings) to bingos, community meetings, church, or even to their places of employment. This constant and close proximity to the actions of others provides the Indian child with a valuable opportunity to intimately familiarize him/herself with a multitude of tasks. These tasks may range from simple domestic duties such as sweeping the floor, carrying water or cooking, to highly sophisticated and complex activities such as carving, beading, or making a basket.

This style of learning, observational rather than verbal, contrasts sharply with the learning styles fostered through child-rearing practices prevalent in the European-American society. Here, the conditions in which observation is the essential tool of learning are often absent, due in large part to the fact that European-American children do not often share as directly or consistently in the activities of their parents or siblings as do Indian children. Within a European-American community, the child's older siblings may belong to a peer group that excludes the membership of younger brothers and sisters. Likewise, the parent of the child may be absent from the home for extended periods of time each day as they pursue career goals. In such instances, the child is often entrusted to the care of a babysitter, or enrolled in a day-care center. Even in social terms, young European-American children are seldom taken to dances, movies, bingos, meetings or other gatherings of adults.

This situation adds up to one in which the contextual referents around which learning may take place are not always shared by the members of the European-American family group. As such, language, vis-à-vis question-asking and verbal interaction, become almost the exclusive means of exchanging information within the European-American family unit (Kaulback, 1984, p. 34). It has been noted that Indian children consider question-asking as an interactive strategy found in and reserved for schools. Question-asking generally is not a verbal strategy employed by the Indian people in their day-to-day speech habits.

Basically, careful observation and imitative play are tools of learning which are universal and are not bound by culture, color, or class. Yet there remains an important and distinct difference between the child-rearing practices used in most Indian families as compared to those employed by adult members of the European-American culture—the use of verbal instruction (Kaulback, 1984). Much of the informal learning that takes place in Indian families is nonverbal in nature. The children learn the customs and skills of their society by sharing directly in the activities of others. In such situations, verbal instruction is neither offered nor required because the child's close proximity to the observable action makes instruction-giving quite redundant. Philips (1983) states that it is not that Indian children are nonverbal or are unable to use the verbal channel, but rather that the interaction systems in different cultures allocate the use of the verbal plus the visual systems differently.

Although far from conclusive, there is a growing body of research to suggest that the distinctively different child-rearing practices—one stressing observational learning and another emphasizing learning through verbalization—has fostered the development of very different styles of learning among Indian and European-American children. Many European-American children, by virtue of their upbringing and their linguistic exposure, are oriented towards using language as a vehicle for learning. Indian children have developed a learning style characterized by observation and imitation. Such differences in learning styles have far-reaching consequences in the formal education of Indian students, particularly in view of the fact that the formal educative process almost favors those who are highly verbal. Much to the detriment of Indian children, "observation is a very limited (learning) technique in the overwhelmingly linguistic environment of the school" (Scribner & Cole, 1973, p. 556).

The result of an upbringing with such a cultural background is that Indian children attending the characteristically highly-verbal school may find themselves in a culturally incoherent situation with an effect approximating culture shock. An analysis of these incongruencies was done by Arbess (1981). He looked at a number of factors with the discovery that the kind of expectations held by an Indian child were almost directly opposite to those of the school setting. For example, the Indian child may have been expecting freedom of movement, but discovered restrictive movement; where visual-spatial kinesthetic learning was the mode, the verbal dimension is stressed; where direct experience had been the route for learning, now most experience is indirect, and so on.

Cultural incongruence is a matter of degree, depending upon the stage of acculturation of the child's family, where one member of a family may be more or less acculturated than others. The family atmosphere (parental relationship) and family constellation (interactional influences of siblings) involve the people most powerful in the child's early learning opportunities. Through these contacts, ethnicity and subsequently culturality serve as the basis of learning style through which the child acquires attributes, values, and beliefs. Such factors affect a child's congruency within the school setting. The teacher needs to decide where the incongruencies occur and can then include some considerations in planning.

It would appear, then that many Indian children, by virtue of their predisposition to a visual style of learning, may be handicapped in their ability to succeed in school because schools and teaching methods tend to cater to the auditory learner. Also, some beginning Indian readers may have difficulty due to "cognitive confusion" (Dowing, 1977). Some Indian children do not seem to understand why a certain succession of printed letters should correspond to certain phonetic sounds in words. Sometimes their concepts of the communicative functions of writing are unclear and they may not understand the purpose of reading. In light of this, there is a definite need to critically examine the methods, programs and materials we now use with Indian students and test for their effectiveness. The basic question that we must now ask ourselves is: "Are there better ways?"

The determination that an Indian behavioral learning style exists may be harmful due to the danger of stereotyping. There is no *absolute* Indian behavioral learning style, however, a wide variety of individual difference have been identified. The individual differences and the information discussed here can be viewed as tendencies or learning style inclinations. When looked at from this perspective, an Indian student behavioral learning style may look like the following:

1. They are skilled in nonverbal communication;

2. They are less skilled and have a low frequency in verbal coding;

3. They are skilled and have a high frequency in processing visual and spatial information;

4. They are skilled and have a high frequency in holistic processing on both verbal and nonverbal tasks (More, 1984, pg. 9) (i.e., are able to see the whole versus the parts).

5. They have relative strength and high frequency in imaginal coding (More, 1984, pg. 9).

6. They use a "community learning style" (Wyatt, 1978) i.e., the child observes carefully over a long period of time followed by practice of the process (direct experience), with a minimum of verbal preparation or interchange (takes longer).

7. They are group-oriented and prefer to work in small groups.

8. They prefer an informal setting with freedom of movement.

CLASSROOM IMPLICATIONS OF THE INDIAN BEHAVIORAL LEARNING STYLE

Educational literature contains a number of references to the process of teaching to the student's learning strengths. Applied here, it means fitting the instruction to the real nature of the Indian learning, rather than to make the Indian learning fit a preconceived curricular structure. The approach, often referred to as aptitude-treatment interaction (ATI), opens the door to recognizing individual differences and behavioral learning styles, and providing more tailored teaching strategies. Recognition and understanding of a student's unique learning needs allows us to pick and choose from a range of teaching techniques to meet those learning needs.

As a rule, Indian students frequently learn faster when the teaching style uses the concrete approach and moves to the abstract—from practice to theory—but most schools follow the European-American model from theory to practice. The best learning and study approach for most Indian children is to see and do, or to observe and imitate a practical application. [Teaching strategies which may prove helpful in addressing these particular behavioral learning style tendencies are noted in Figure 1.] . . . Indian children do not like being involved in questioning sorts of strategies. Students, especially those in the secondary schools, like the values discussions. Individuals' assignments, when effectively used, are most liked and most successful. The most effective strategies are group problem solving at the elementary level and individual assignments at the secondary level (Leith & Slentz, 1984).

If one is aware of different learning styles, planning lesson delivery and classroom learning activities to accommodate learning styles will, research suggests, help students achieve more. [However,] perhaps there is another danger hidden in the exclusive use of such strategies. Could it be that the exclusive use of an ATI approach may actually contribute to forcing our Indian students into another stereotypic posture (i.e.,

"Indians are nonverbal and visual, so don't expect anything from them verbally.")? Perhaps it would be more effective to do something like the following:

TEACHING STRATEGIES WHICH MIGHT ASSIST WITH INDIAN LEARNING STYLE

1. Use cooperative learning groups rather than traditional grouping;
2. Provide a high percentage of group projects and a low percentage of oral questions and answers;
3. Incorporate manipulative devices and activities which allow a student to "feel and touch;"
4. Provide a variety of informal classroom settings with freedom of movement—studying on the floor, sitting at a table or desks arranged in small groups, etc.;
5. Present the whole picture of things before isolating skills into small segments;
6. Provide activities which are experience based;
7. Provide a high rate of encouragement;
8. Provide mobility through scheduled activities;
9. Provide values clarification activities;
10. Use peer tutoring and cross-age teaching;
11. Provide artwork illustrating people and animals; cartoons, wood carving, model building, miniature displays, map-making;
12. Use role-playing and creative dramatics;
13. Organize learning center materials to address all the needs of all learners in the classroom;
14. Encourage opinionated expression of viewpoints in social studies and other subjects where controversy can be found;
15. Present new and difficult material in a visual/spatial mode rather than a verbal mode;
16. Use metaphors, images, analogies and symbols rather than dictionary type definitions;
17. Use parades and productions such as "Classroom 20/20" or "News In Review;"
18. Use brainstorming and open-ended activities;
19. Schedule sports and play days;
20. Use instructional games; and
21. Student-designed games are particularly effective.

Figure 16-1.

1. Teach to their learning styles when presenting new concepts.

2. When new concepts are learned and students are comfortable with the concept, present it in a different learning style.

3. Present lessons in the Indian child's learning style at least 65 percent of the time.

4. Present lessons in different learning styles at least 25 to 35 percent of the time so that the Indian student will not only learn but continues to grow and stretch.

5. Present learning activities and tests in the preferred learning style and in a different learning style.

6. Have a repertoire of different teaching strategies for different subject areas.

By building on their strengths, a variety such as this encourages students to engage in activities that are not so preferred and gives students opportunities to explore and strengthen behaviors and activities they might otherwise avoid.

For the Indian student, there is life outside and after the classroom. It is our responsibility to prepare our students to be able to cope in various situations. It has been observed that, too often, Indian students make normal or above normal academic gains while attending a "sheltered" school setting (typically a tribal and/or elementary classroom) only to fail once they leave that situation. Could this be due to our narrow perspective of teaching only to the Indian student's learning style? All students usually have skills in other learning styles, and these need to be encouraged to keep from locking our Indian students into a certain mold. The caution is not to fall into the trap that "this way is the only way" but to remain flexible in our approach. By so doing, we can prepare Indian students for success wherever they find themselves. This can be helpful in teaching students to live in a bicultural world with bicultural successes (Pepper, 1985).

When learning style differences are understood and accepted, the classroom changes to a place where individual differences among students become an incentive for teachers to provide a rich variety of lessons, teaching strategies, learning activities, and testing challenges. This variety not only enhances the equity of the instructional setting, but enriches the thought processes and behavior learning styles of all students.

REFERENCES

1. Adler, A.: *The Science of Living.* London, England, Lorne & Brydone, 1930.
2. Arbess, S.: *New Strategies in Indian Education.* Province of British Columbia, Ministry of Education, 1981.
3. Dowing, J.: Concepts of language in children from differing socioeconomic backgrounds. *Journal of Educational Research, 5:*277–281, 1977.
4. Dreikurs, R., Grunwald, R., & Pepper, F. C.: *Maintaining Sanity in the Classroom.* New York, Harper & Row, 1982.
5. Dunn, R.: Learning style and its relation to exceptionality at both ends of the spectrum. *Exceptional Children, 49:*1983.
6. Kaulback, B.: Styles of learning among native children: A review of the research. *Canadian Journal of Native Education, 11:*27–37, 1984.
7. Leith, S., & Slentz, K.: Successful teaching strategies in selected Northern Manitoba schools. *Canadian Journal of Native Education,* 11, 1984.
8. Longstreet, W. S.: Learning and diversity: The ethnic factor. *Educational Research Quarterly, 2:*60–73, 1983.
9. Moore, A. J.: Indian students and their learning styles: Research and results and classroom applications [Prepublication draft], 1984.

10. Pepper, F. C.: Effective Practices in Indian Education: A teacher's monograph. Portland, Northwest Regional Educational Laboratory, Research and Development for Indian Education, 1985.
11. Philips, S. U.: *The Invisible Culture: Communication in Classroom and Community on the Warm Springs Indian Reservation.* New York, Longman, 1983.
12. Scribner, S., & Cole, M.: Cognitive consequences of formal and informal education. *Science Magazine, 182:* 533–559, 1973.
13. Wyatt, J. D.: Native involvement in curriculum development: The cultural broker. *Interchange, 9:* 17, 1978.

Chapter 17

CULTURALLY RESPONSIVE TEACHING STRATEGIES FOR AMERICAN INDIAN STUDENTS

MAUREEN E. SMITH AND BARBARA J. SHADE

Learning styles refer to the way Native students confront a learning task. Pipes and her colleagues indicate that the approach that an individual takes to learning and the demonstration of learning is culturally determined by the child's early socialization experiences (Pipes, Westby, & Inglebret, 1993). If children are to be comfortable in school and perform successfully, their culturally preferred approaches to the world must be considered an inherent part of the teaching-learning process. Here are some key points of concern for American Indian children.

Classroom Management

Most American Indian homes and communities stress cooperation which leads Native children to understand that the group good is paramount. Within this framework, American Indian children often are not used to authoritarian rule. Instead, they are accustomed to having input in decisions, and having their opinions respected. More important, they have autonomy in their lives, a privilege not easily given up by many. Allowing students to develop their own set of rules and class decisions respects the Native child's sense of autonomy.

Because Native students are familiar with the extended family concept, teachers can easily help a class develop a community ethos by utilizing this particular value and tradition. Stressing this value of group cohesion can be a powerful tool in the classroom particularly as it helps maintain order. This can be accomplished by using peers to help monitor behavior and building a group-based positive reward system in which the teacher praises those groups working well. Ignoring bad behavior once having set clear expectations for behavior articulated by

178

the teacher is in keeping with Native tradition (Little Soldier, 1992; Slavin, 1995). Most important, teachers should not embarrass children by singling them out for good or bad behavior. It is critical that students are respected. Within the Native community, children are treated as equals in their home communities and are a part of a home environment which is loving and accepting. Strict discipline is seldom seen in traditional homes. Therefore, the teacher must establish a warm, accepting environment for the Indian student to feel comfortable and safe enough to learn (Little Soldier, 1992). To correct a child, the teacher will be more effective by speaking quietly and privately to the child without hurting his or her pride. Generally speaking, in most American Indian communities, once the punishment is over all resentments are gone. Therefore, once the child has served the punishment, the expectation is that whatever misbehavior occurred is now forgotten (Gilliland, 1995).

Conflict resolution is a critical skill for Native people to develop as a part of their ability to participate harmoniously within the tribal community. This skill allows Native students to practice a cherished Native value: thinking before acting; perceiving that the world is neither good nor bad, or that people must either win or lose, and that two states of existence can happen simultaneously. Inasmuch as the concept of paradoxes is a central belief in the world view of Native Americans, they are able to function in situational ambiguity. The skill of problem solving, an integral part of conflict resolution, is a highly prized value of most tribes in reaching true consensus (Teolis, 1996) and can be used effectively by the teacher. It is also important to encourage active listening and allow each student the opportunity to express his/her feelings without interruption which is a technique used in traditional Native talking circles.

American Indian children are traditionally taught that to share is far superior to acquiring. Therefore, reward systems that reward only certain students probably will not be successful. Traditional Native children who are successful in receiving the reward from the teacher will undoubtedly share it with their less successful friends. With this knowledge, teachers can develop a system of rewards that assures that all students receive some kind of recognition and frequently use group reward and praise.

Cognitive Style

Although American Indians are field-independent within their natural physical environment, they appear to be field-sensitive or field-dependent when in a school setting (Shade, 1990). To address the learning style of Native children, then requires the adaptation of both field-independent as well as field-dependent approaches.

As field-independent learners, Native American students prefer visual approaches to information such as demonstrations and illustrations. Subsequently, they may not be as academically successful if the teacher uses a predominately auditory mode of information transmission. In learning new concepts, Native children have a decided preference for images to assist in thinking and remembering. Because it is apparent that a large majority of American Indian students are relatively stronger in visual-spatial abilities than in verbal skills, it is imperative that verbal lessons are enhanced with visual material. To this strength, teachers can draw models and diagrams which demonstrate how elements of a process relate to one another. Concept mapping, the use of pictures, videos, photographs and art can be useful techniques for demonstrating the main ideas and the interconnections of ideas and concepts (Kleinfeld & Nelson, 1991; Slavin, 1991).

A study conducted by Sawyer and Rodriguez (1992) indicated respondents had "an overwhelming preference for some variation of a 'watch-then-do' approach" when learning a new task or skill. The Native learner needs to carefully, quietly and individually watch the skill or process to be learned before feeling comfortable enough to perform. Therefore, teachers must allow students to have many opportunities to observe and practice the expected skill before production is required.

As field-sensitive or field-dependent learners, many Native students approach new ideas and concepts from a global or holistic perspective which suggests that the whole is more important than the parts. While it is critical for teachers to teach discrete concepts or facts, it is helpful for Native children if the ideas have a contextual base in order to perceive how the facts exist in the real world or in relationship to each other. The use of advance organizers can be an excellent tool for helping students see the overall point of the topic and why it is to be studied. Also, the use of mapping and diagrams which show the whole, as well as the relationship to the parts, can help students better understand the concept. Examination has shown that when Native students engage in simultaneous and global processing they are much more successful in learning and retention.

Many Native cultures stress cooperation, not competition, so cooperative learning activities are often very successful in Native classrooms. Setting up activities for students to help one another also enable Native students to better work together, share their knowledge, and utilize traditional belief patterns. As Lee Little Soldier (1992) points out, teachers of Native children should capitalize on the propensities of the pupils to share and cooperate. Successful instruction will stress group interaction that is consistent with the students' cultural models (Kleinfeld & Nelson, 1991; Pipes, et al., 1993; Sawyer & Rodriguez, 1992). Competition should not be avoided, it should be used only when it is a natural outgrowth of the situation such as in games and sports.

Curriculum

Pedagogy and content cannot be separated. Therefore, it is insufficient for teachers to adjust only their strategies of teaching. The curriculum must also be a critical area of concern for teachers.

Traditionally in Native cultures, curricular materials were tied to real-life problems. The lessons were student generated so students often chose their own curriculum based on what was important to them (Hankes, 1995). Historically, Native children have often found no relevance or an accurate portrayal of themselves in the content or materials used in the traditional classroom. If students do not see themselves in the curriculum materials, they feel as if they do not exist, are not important or do not matter to other people. Such a feeling of a lack of significance or existence can lead a student to lower their sense of self-worth. Therefore, it is recommended that teachers use culturally appropriate curricular materials to assist students in developing positive self-esteem (Sawyer & Rodriguez, 1992). Teachers must find ways to make common course subjects culturally relevant. The following suggestions can assist teachers in accomplishing this task.

Conventional science can pose a problem. Because many traditional Native students learn that one must co-exist with nature, not master it, some science experiments run counter to their belief system. As Little Soldier (1992) points out, belief in the supernatural, mythology, and nonscientific explanations of natural phenomena continues. Therefore, the teacher should be sensitive to the view of nature and the supernatural when planning science lessons and celebrating holidays. Matthews and Smith (1994) reported that using science curriculum that was culturally relevant to American Indians increased their achievement levels significantly and their attitude toward science improved profoundly. Teachers can assist student involvement in this discipline by comparing the Native traditional explanation of things with "scientific" explanations and verify that each is valid scientific thinking. Teachers can further help students process scientific data more effectively if hands-on or manipulatives are used and the interconnectedness of ideas and the natural flow of things is clearly demonstrated (Butterfield, 1994; Greer, 1992).

Native students are able to perceive the relevance of mathematics when real world problems are used, particularly when the problems involve Native American culturally relevant concepts and traditions. However, changing the content is not enough. Teachers can help American Indian students deal with math anxiety and improve their attitudes toward math by approaching the teaching of mathematics in a nonremedial approach. When students work together, the stronger students will work with the less talented to learn math and performance will be improved (Anderson & Stein, 1992; Garcia, 1984; Hadfeel, Martin, Wooden, 1992).

When considering reading curriculum, it is important to select materials that depict the Native student's home and background. As such, it may be necessary for the teacher to find or develop appropriate reading materials that bridge home and school, particularly in the area of social studies and literature and language arts where material from the history and culture of the community can be used as conduits for teaching skills of reading, writing, listening and speaking (Reyhner & Garcia, 1989) as well as providing a contextual basis for the study of history and geography. According to Kasten (1992), teaching using the whole language approach is in complete alliance with Native cultural beliefs. Whole language classrooms function in a communal fashion, in an oral tradition using stories, and teaches the whole as well as the parts. The instruction is far less teacher directed and, in fact, is usually student initiated (Kasten, 1992; Sawyer & Rodriguez, 1992).

It should also be noted that teaching Native children requires the use of a bilingual approach as their ancestral languages differ significantly from English. Again, Little Soldier (1992) notes in his review of the educational implications for the Navajo, that the Navajo language differs considerably in sounds and structure from English which led to it being used as a military code during World War II. This tonal language has a

22-letter alphabet with no *p, q, f, v, u, w,* or *r* nor consonant clusters such as *kl* and *gl* (Fedder & Gabaldon, 1970; Cook & Sharp, 1966). Therefore, it is important for Navajo pupils to be assisted in their production of English sounds and sound clusters through such activities as using mirrors or through tactile or kinesthetic cues. Like the African-American Black English Vernacular, there is a tendency to use present tense of verbs and omit verb endings. Subject/verb agreements in English are also difficult as is the use of he/she or his/hers since Navajo language does not have a gender distinction. Similar observations have been made about other tribal languages which suggests that particular attention should be given to teaching English as a second language to Native children (Leap, 1992). Opportunities to learn English informally through songs, games, stories, rhymes and whole language activities is encouraged.

Assessment

The area of assessment and American Indian students has been a well-documented, albeit controversial subject. Standardized, quantitative assessment can be inaccurate in assessing Native students; therefore, alternative methods of assessment may be required and the testing situations may require modifications. One cause of problems in assessment is the world view of many Indian people. Indians tend to be very pragmatic and tests often are not. Native students often perceive that tests seem to conjecture, deal with the abstract, and are far too theoretical. From their perspective, questions as asked on traditional tests cause Indian people to speculate about the possible trickery of the test writers (Plas & Bellet, 1983).

Decision-making is another factor which impacts negatively on Indians and test-taking. Most intelligence (aptitude or achievement) tests are multiple-choice, timed tests which are scored favorably in the direction of individuals who respond quickly. Many Indian children are taught to be very deliberate, thoughtful and to consider all alternatives before responding. Such thoughtful deliberations cost test takers precious time and points on a multiple-choice timed test (Deyhle, 1985). In addition, many Native students are taught to answer questions as directly and to the point as possible. This can be detrimental on a test that asks for elaboration. Assessments that ask for specific, allegedly "right" answers can also fail to correctly assess what the student has actually learned. It is far more beneficial if the child can explain his/her answer (Deyhle, 1985).

The nature of standardized multiple-choice tests present problems due to the learning style propensity of many Indian students. It has been stated that Indians tend to learn more holistically, are more intuitive and feeling, and deal much better with concrete information and experiences. Often test questions are very particularistic, theoretical and analytical and this leads many American Indian students to view them as absurd and meaningless. Feelings and intuition, highly prized in the Native community, when used can lead to incorrect responses (Deyhle, 1985; Plas & Bellet, 1983). In addition, the testing period should be longer to allow time for reflection and a longer incubation period to allow processing of information.

Authentic assessment could be a potentially helpful means of assessment, especially if it is combined with teacher conferences with the student allowing them to explain why he or she did what they did. Allowing students to pick for themselves their best work to include in a portfolio allows Native students an opportunity to utilize their sense of autonomy. Authentic assessment also stresses process over product, a traditional value in Native communities. Traditionally, task mastery was demonstrated through performance (Hankes, 1995).

CONCLUSION

Teachers should use a variety of approaches to teaching. Too often teachers teach as they were taught. Therefore it is critical that educators examine their method of instruction and use a multiplicity of modalities. They should not rely solely on verbal communication, but also use visual aids. They should use and teach using all learning approaches and allow students to practice different learning methods in a safe environment. To be academically successful, Native students need to increase their capabilities in logical, sequential, and verbal learning skills. It is through practice that such capabilities are enhanced.

Responsive teachers who understand the needs of the Native children will find ways to teach which better fit their students' experiences (Reyhner & Garcia, 1989); will become "cognitively flexible" and tailor the teaching style to the strengths of the child; and the instruction, curriculum and pedagogy will be child-centered. The teacher who can be flexible and open to sharing his/her classroom with students will be much more successful in working with American Indian children. The task is difficult for it requires a great deal: sensitivity, a caring nature, an open mind, imagination, reflection, feelings, vulnerability and love. If the teacher can open his/her heart and mind to the Native students and their families, they may find a rich resource that will gladly assist and clarify cultural blind spots and allow them to provide Native students a chance to compete in the 21st century while celebrating their race, ethnicity, traditions and learning styles.

REFERENCES

1. Anderson, L., & Stein, W.: Making math relevant. *Tribal College Journal of American Indian Higher Education. 2:*13–19, 1992.
2. Butterfield, Robin: *Blueprints for Indian Education: Improving Mainstream Schooling.* Ann Arbor, MI, Eric Document ED372898, 1994.
3. Cook, M. J., & Sharp, M. A.: Problems of Navajo speakers in learning English. *Language Learning,* 16:21–29, 1966.
4. Deyhle, D.: Testing among Navajo and Anglo students: Another consideration of cultural bias. *Journal of Educational Equity and Leadership. 5:*119–131, 1985.
5. Fedder, R., & Gabaldon, J. *No Longer Deprived.* New York, Teachers College Press, 1970.
6. Garcia, R.: Countering classroom discrimination, *Theory Into Practice, 23:*104–109, 1984.
7. Gilliland, H. *Teaching the Native American.* Dubuque, IA, Kendall/Hunt Publishers, 1995.
8. Hadfeel, O., Martin, J., & Wooden, S.: Mathematics, anxiety and learning style of the Navajo middle school student. *School Science and Mathematics,* 92:171–176, 1992.
9. Hankes, J.: *Native American Pedagogy and Cognitive-Based Mathematics Instruction.* Madison, WI, University of Wisconsin-Madison, unpublished doctoral dissertation.
10. Kasten, W.: Bridging the horizon: American Indian beliefs and whole language learning. *Anthropology and Education Quarterly, 23:*108–119, 1992.
11. Kleinfeld, J., & Nelson, P.: Adapting instruction to Native Americans' learning styles: An iconoclastic view. *Journal of Cross-Cultural Psychology,* 22:272–283, 1991.
12. Leap, W. I.: American Indian English. In Reyhner, J. *Teaching American Indian Students.* Norman, OK, University of Oklahoma Press, 1992.
13. Little Soldier, L.: Building optimum learning environments for Navajo students. *Childhood Education,* 68:145–148, 1992.
14. Matthews, C., & Smith, W.: Native American related materials in elementary science instruction. *Journal of Research in Science Teaching,* 31:363–380.
15. Pipes, M., Westby, C., & Inglebret, E.: Profile of Native American students. In Clark, L. (Ed.): *Faculty and Student Challenges in Facing Cultural and Linguistic Diversity.* Springfield, Ill: Charles C Thomas, Publisher, 1993.

16. Plas, J., & Bellet, W.: Assessment of value-attitude orientations of American Indian children, *Journal of School Psychology,* 21:57–64, 1983.
17. Reyhner, J., & Garcia, R.: Helping minorities read better: Problems and promises. *Reading Research and Instruction,* 28:84–91, 1989.
18. Sawyer, D., & Rodriguez, C.: How Native Canadians view literacy: A summary of findings, *Journal of Reading,* 36:284–293, 1992.
19. Slavin, R.: *Cooperative Learning,* Boston, Allyn & Bacon, 1995.
20. Shade, B. J.: The influence of perceptual development on cognitive styles: Cross-ethnic comparisons. In Saracho, O. (Ed.), *Cognitive Styles in Early Childhood.* London: Harwood Academics, 1990.
21. Teolis, B.: *Ready to Use Self-Esteem and Conflict-Solving Activities.* West Nyack, New York, The Center for Applied Research, 1996.

Chapter 18

ENGLISH LITERACY ACQUISITION: FROM CULTURAL TRAUMA TO LEARNING DISABILITIES IN MINORITY STUDENTS*

HENRY T. TRUEBA

The democratic fabric of American society is intimately related to its ethnically diverse and dynamic population (Spindler, 1977; Spindler & Spindler, 1983, 1987a, 1987b). Waves of immigrants and refugees enter this country joining other minorities in their quest for a better life. Their overall adjustment, and ultimate success or failure in mainstreaming, is determined both by people's prearrival experiences and by their ability to handle cultural conflict and change (Trueba, 1983, 1987a, 1987b; Trueba & Delgado-Gaitan, in press).

Literacy in English plays a crucial role in the adjustment of immigrant, refugee, and other minority children. The school is often viewed as the primary social institution responsible for mainstreaming minorities. Yet, some schools are overwhelmed by the rapid and unexpected increase in minority populations to be served. To complicate matters, school administrators, teachers, psychologists, and educational researchers have typically paid little attention to cultural factors in determining the differential school achievement and long-term psychological adjustment of minority students (Goldman & Trueba, 1987; Trueba, 1987a).

Failure to acquire literacy in English by speakers of other languages has become a key factor in the classification (or misclassification) of learning disabled students, as well as a key factor for dropping out of school (Rueda, 1987). Ethnographic studies in English literacy acquisition have shown that there is a significant relationship between cultural congruency in instructional practice (both in method and content) and

*From Trueba, Henry T. English literacy acquisition: From cultural trauma to learning disabilities in minority students. *Linguistics and Education, 1:*125–152, 1988. Copyright Ablex Publishing Company. Used with permission.

187

children's progress (Au & Jordan, 1981; Diaz, Moll, & Mehan, 1986; Duran, 1983; Erickson, 1986; Tharp & Gallimore, in press). However, there are many instances in which persistently low literacy levels cannot be explained exclusively by cultural incongruencies or language differences, or even by family socialization patterns. There seem to be structural factors in society, which are rooted in cultural value differences, which accentuate the differential response (including academic performance) in cross-cultural encounters (Ogbu, 1974, 1978, 1981, 1982, 1987; Ogbu & Matute-Bianchi, 1986; Suarez-Orozco, in press). Perhaps the nature of children's cultural conflict, and their experience of cultural discontinuities in this country, affect their response to school demands in some specific instructional contexts in which they feel disenfranchised. Thus, at the heart of literacy problems there may be serious and unresolved cultural conflicts and discontinuities in the transition from the home to the school culture (Spindler, 1974, 1982; Spindler & Spindler, 1983, 1987a, 1987b). Illiteracy in English, particularly as it affects the future educational level and productivity of large numbers of minority students (Trueba, 1987a, 1987b, in press) is a critical issue.

It is expected that linguistic minority enrollment in the public school will increase significantly in the next 15 years. While in 1970 there were 85 percent white students, this majority population in the schools decreased to 72 percent in 1980. It is expected that by the year 2000 white students will make up only 57 percent, and that one out of three students will be a minority (Dunn, 1987, pg. 13).

The 1980 Census of Population (U.S. Bureau of the Census, 1984) reports the presence of about 35 million linguistic minority persons in this country. Of them, 10.5 million are under the age of 17 and 19.5 million are not fluent in English. Almost half of this linguistic minority population, that is, 15.5 million (45%) is Hispanic. This census further indicates that two-thirds of the Hispanic population which constitutes 8 percent of the total U.S. population, resides in California, New York, and Texas.

The overall academic attainment of Hispanics is extremely low in the nation: 18 percent of documented Hispanic adults aged 25 and over are illiterate in English (as compared with 10% blacks and 3% whites), and half of those Hispanic adults have completed fewer than 11 years of schooling. . . . The importance placed on educational attainment by these groups is stressed by recent Rand Reports (McCarthy & Burciago-Valdez, 1985, 1986), which did find progress and upper mobility within Hispanic groups, and specifically discovered better education, higher levels of English proficiency, and better jobs among second- and third-generation Hispanics (McCarthy & Burciaga Valdez, 1986, pp. 60–65).

... Our study focused on 12 minority children considered to be the most educationally needy cases among 40 students classified as "learning disabled" in the La Playa Elementary School (pseudonym) in west central California. The purpose of the study was to understand the nature of reading and writing problems faced by children with diverse cultural and linguistic backgrounds. We focused on English literacy issues which appeared to be theoretically and pragmatically significant across disciplines. In this article I report and discuss part of the corpus of data collected through systematic observations, interviews, and tape recordings conducted over 18 months (September, 1984 to March, 1986).

The concern of this study was to explore the implications of the English-Only policy at the local school level, in an elementary school with over 50 percent Limited English Proficient [students] and with 25 different languages represented in the student body. The school was atypical in many respects, but its ethnic and linguistic diversity brought into perspective important aspects of the English-Only policy and its implications for at least some LEP (Limited English Proficiency) children. In a sense, the La Playa School represents an extreme case. It was used because it forces reflection about English-Only as a policy within the constraints of enormous ethnic and linguistic diversity.

One of the basic questions raised in our study: What is the impact of the English-Only policy on refugee students (particularly Indochinese) and on low-status immigrant children (particularly Hispanic)? Specifically:

1. Did this policy increase stress and trauma levels in some students to the point of jeopardizing their participation in academic and social activities as well as their overall development?
2. Did this policy hinder the transfer of cognitive skills and slow the acquisition of English literacy?
3. Did this policy lead to social and psychological isolation of LEP children, thus hindering their overall long-term cultural adjustment and academic achievement?

The La Playa Elementary School is located within walking distance of a university and next to a beach community composed largely of students, transients, and low income and some mainstream families. The school attracts children of married students as well as of recent refugee populations. In 1986 La Playa served 591 students, half of whom spoke as a first language one of the following twenty-five languages: Spanish (101), Hmong (77), Lao (31), Vietnamese (28), Chinese (12), Portuguese (7), Japanese (6), Hebrew (6), Arabic (5), Korean (5) and [thirteen other languages represented by a small number of students.] Our main concern was with the first four groups, not only because they were the most numerous, . . . but also because they represented the most acute adjustment and achievement problems. A general examination of the files, along with the recommendations of school personnel, led us to observations of some children both in main classroom activities and in ESL classes or special education groups. . . . Following methodological approaches used in previous studies (Trueba, 1983), members of the research team each selected specific students to be studied in class and at home. After becoming familiar with the student file, the initial efforts concentrated on systematically assessing the degree and nature of student participation in academic tasks, both in the general classroom activities as well as in small groups for specific tasks. Interviews with the student, the student's teacher, the school psychologist, the principal, and the student's parents followed. The research team would reconvene to discuss observed patterns of participation, information gathered from interviews, and any materials gathered, such as student compositions and samples of homework. The fundamental assumption was that participation structures would reveal the degree of meaningful and active engagement in learning activities on the part of the student.

Findings

For some of the 40 children identified as learning disabled or lowest achievers, their inadequate performance in school seemed to increase from year to year. For the twelve children of this study, their learning problems were manifested in three forms: (a) lack of overall participation in whole class activities, (b) lack of academic productivity in school and at home, and (c) the presence of vague and pervasive stress, fear, confusion, and other signs of ongoing emotional turmoil. For example, from our field notes we have the following observations:

> Rosita, a 10-year-old quiet girl, sits quietly at the back of the class, rests her head on her hands and stays that way for the entire period. Once in a while she responds in Spanish to friends who tell her, "mira, Rosita" ("Look, Rosita") pointing at a drawing, by saying, "Que?" ("What?").
>
> Douan, an 11-year-old Laotian girl reading at the second grade level, is placed in 5th grade (The ESL teacher had warned me that Douan rarely talks,

and "When pushed, Douan talked in some complete sentences, but her expressive language is still very weak"). The 5th grade classroom teacher had said, "Her attitude and attentiveness are good. I felt she was trying, but don't really know, because I don't remember her speaking at all!" One morning, in a group of four children, the teacher presents a list of words needed for the reading lesson: "fuss, snooze, separate, rock garden, marigold, and zinnia." Children are then asked to silently read the first paragraph. The teacher asks, "Is there anybody who did not finish?" The teacher quickly reads the passage and begins to discuss vocabulary. Douan avoids eye contact and persists in keeping her eyes down. Teacher: "Douan, what is 'snooze?'" Douan does not move. After a short wait, the teacher gives the answer: "Like when you take a nap, you know, a sleep." The lesson goes on like that. Douan continuously moves her feet and shakes all over. She looks terrified of being asked another question. Similar incidents go on as the teacher gets to the other parts of the lesson. At the end, Douan stands up, not having said a single word, runs to the side of another Laotian girl who is more fluent in English and whispers a brief comment. The math lesson is very similar but less stressful, partially because the teacher knows better and does not ask Douan to answer in public, but rather approaches Douan's bench and asks her, "Do you know how to divide these fractions?"

Robert is an 11-year-old Sudanese who speaks perfect English with a British accent, the son of a doctoral student working for the diplomatic service in his country. Robert's mother, the first wife of Robert's father, was left in Sudan, while his stepmother (a younger black woman) came to the U.S. with the family. The reading lesson starts. Robert seems alert and aggressive. He pushes a kid who is crowding him. The lesson is about American rivers. The teacher has read a paragraph, two Israeli children have answered questions about the reading promptly and correctly. It is Robert's turn. Teacher: "Where is the Mississippi?" Robert delays his answer for a while, and then, just about when the teacher is going to give the answer, Robert: "It is the largest American river, but I know the Nile, and it is enormous." Robert surprises the whole group with his knowledge, but essentially is not interested in American rivers. The next day, in the context of a question related to some news about the President of the U.S., Robert recites by heart several names of presidents and explains who Tip O'Neill is. Yet, his tests and his regular participation are very limited. In math, he refuses to do some operations on the groups that the method is wrong. He says, "Is not that way; you do it this way." Over the academic year his participation in class decreases. His father comes to the teacher and says, "If you don't want to hit him, I will."

Oudin is a 12-year-old Laotian boy who came to school two-and-a-half years ago. He is sociable but has a volatile temper. He is constantly moving his feet, hands, and eyes. His restlessness increases during reading lessons, which require reading in front of the entire class. The teacher no longer asks him if he will try to read a brief sentence because he refuses and kicks the bench. He says he likes school, but that he does not like his teacher or the English

Table 18-1. LEP Children with Learning Difficulties by Language, Group, Sex and Grade

Sex, Pseudonym, Birth Date/Place		Grade in 1985–1986	WISC–R I.Q.	Referral and Comments
Hispanic				
M 5-7-76	Carlos Ca. USA	3	75	Unmotivated; living with disabled father. Slow English language development. "Language impaired" 2nd grade. Deterioration of skills.
F 1-10-75	Rosita Mexico	4	—	Low reading comprehension and low math. Slow English language development.
M 9-1-76	Emilio Mexico	3	—	Overall low academic performance. Slow English language development.
M 8-27-77	David Ca. USA	3	115	Anglo mother, divorced. Difficulties in completing work and reading. Bright! Maladjusted!
Laotian				
M 3-2-73(?)	Oudin Laos	4	86*	Came to U.S. 9-15-82. Large family, angry, poor reader, UNHAPPY. Low performance and self concept. Cognitive skills deteriorated.
F 2-21-79	Narath Laos	1	—	Sister of above. Artistic talent. Physical disability? Complications at birth. Father was in prison, mother under stress, poor. Slow English development.
F 12-4-73(?)	Douan Laos	5	92*	Slow progress. Quiet. Paralyzed with fear in large groups. Reading comprehension 2.5. Tries hard. Health problems.
Hmong				
M 7-18-76	Chou Thailand	3	104*	Retained in Kindergarten. Reading level 1.8. Oral fluency in English. Unmotivated, distracted! Thought by teachers as retarded!
M 6-21-75	Pao Laos	3	87	Reading comprehension and auditory processing problem. In this country since 1970. Retained in Kindergarten.
M 10-7-76	Tou Thailand	3	111*	Bright. In the U.S. since 1970. Reading and writing problems in ESL class. Fluent bilingual English oral proficiency.
Vietnamese				
M 11-27-77	Bou Vietnam	2		Speaking difficulties. In the U.S. since 1984. Speech therapy. Problems with English syntax and vocabulary. Affectionate!
Sudanese				
M 10-31-74	Robert Sudan	5		Fluent speaker of English and 4.9 math level! Angry. Black. Father PhD student. Socially and culturally maladjusted. Also speaks Arabic and Dinka.

language. The teacher notes in her report that Oudin is very low in math, "even counting beans and trading for 10 sticks is hard for him. Little visible progress in math. He learns words by rote, has no consonants or other phonic skills." Oudin's friends say that he has older siblings who yell at him and hit him often. His reading teacher writes in the monthly report, "Poor Oudin, he didn't have a clue . . . , but he tried so hard with the less difficult materials I gave him; it was sad. . . . Excellent artist and superior motor skills, but something is not attached right."

This perception of Oudin is in contrast with that of his ESL teacher who finds him smart and willing to learn. From the field notes taken during the ESL classes, the following will give the reader a feeling for the different learning environment in this class:

> Oudin had great anxiety today about his homework assignment. He tries to read it and cannot understand it. The teacher keeps trying to explain. He is bored. Does not pay attention to directions any more. The teacher comes to talk to him, and he says, "I want to be in Laos. No. I don't want to be anywhere." Then he tells Richard (a child in the same class) "fuck you," and gets into an argument. His face is red and the veins are clearly protruding. He cannot talk out of anger. Goes out of class and comes back shortly. He apologizes to Richard, and says to the teacher, "We're friends now," then goes back to the theme, "I don't want to be here," and adds "I had many animals in Laos—ten horses and many chickens."

His writings show the turmoil and difficulties he was facing at the time. From my observations in the large classroom, however, I found him restrained and tense. Once, after a movie on Vietnam, he walked out angry, screaming something nobody understood. It was a clear case of insensitivity on the part of the teacher. She was asking the children to write about their fears "like being scared, with bombs," she said. Many students, including Oudin, had written nothing and were refusing to deal with such a composition. She decided to show them a picture on Vietnam. I will never forget some of the faces of Indochinese children in that class (perhaps as many as half of the group).

The above examples illustrate the differential (often minimal) participation patterns, but conceptually these patterns can be reduced to three, as I have argued elsewhere (Trueba, 1983): (a) hypoparticipation to the extreme of making efforts to be inconspicuous; (b) hyper-participation, often superficial and unproductive (as I will argue below); and (c) hostile/selective participation as in the example of Oudin and Robert given above.

Carlos was born in the central west coast to a Mexican couple, and at the time of the study he was 11 years old, in 3rd grade and the only child living at home. His father, a divorced and disabled ex-policeman, had a history of emotional problems. His older brother, now living elsewhere, had been classified as "communicatively handicapped," as was Carlos himself during preschool. This classification was removed at the request of his father in the 2nd grade. He was placed in a bilingual 2nd grade classroom and did very well. Then he was transferred to all English 3rd grade and both his attendance and his achievement went down. For several months he missed 50 percent of the school days. A new teacher referral for special education classes came with the teacher statement: "Cannot follow oral directions. Needs a great deal of help. Is easily distracted. He is depressed." My observations showed that Carlos could not concentrate on a task for more than a few seconds. I collected his work for a month and discovered that he was doing exercises from the year before, and that his writing (in content, productivity, and structure) was superior the year before. For example, he was repeating 3rd grade, and the year before had produced a composition about three pictures describing spacecraft on the surface of the earth. The first year he wrote:

The earth was going to is explod the world. And they made a spceship. And they had all ready gone to the other planet. They land already. The planted flowers and trees. And the trees grow with food and they build a hose [a house]. And they went back to see oh [?] the plant is but it was not thir [there] so they went back home and it was already night so they all went buck [back] to sleep. And it was moring [morning] now und [and] it was breakfast now. And they ate organes and cornflakes and they drank orang [orange] juice and grape and mil. And they all played a game called steal the bake.

The same composition a year later was turned back empty. He said he did not know what to write. I called him and asked him to look at his work from the year before and he looked surprised. There were serious family and personal problems which may explain Carlos's behavior, but the overall productivity was clearly down. In the interview with his father (which I found extremely difficult, because he pretended not to understand English first, and when I talked to him in Spanish pretended not to understand Spanish) revealed that the father would justify keeping Carlos at home "just in case I need some water or something." The man was physically able to walk two miles every day, and he seemed to intimidate the child with veiled threats. There were some suspicions of child abuse. But even in the previous year's composition, there was some fragmentation, and Carlos's composition was not as good as that of his peers.

The compositions from Douan show determination to succeed, regardless of the serious problems she was facing in school, as we saw above. November 19, 1985, she wrote:

> when I am 18 I plan to get an car I am going to ride to school I will learn more I think I would go to college or UCSB I will learn and if I learn college I will graduate. when I am 22 I will found a work to do or learn more english again or I will ask my brother to found me some work to do.

These students described classroom activities and talks with the teacher as too fast and too difficult, and their homework as confusing and boring. Robert would sit, yawn, and say quietly: "I don't want to do it." Carlos would just smile, look around, get up and, if the teacher or I were looking at him, pretend to write. Then, when asked how the task was progressing, he'd say, "I don't know what to write." Douan would say nothing and often copy from the book words or sentences that were not part of the assignment.

Douan's performance deteriorated in two ways during the research period: (a) the written exercises she had done were more fragmented and less meaningful, and (b) her actual attempts to participate in academic tasks were reduced with the increase of fear to perform in public. Between September and December of 1985 she wrote a number of compositions which showed syntactic cohesiveness and ability to communicate. Toward the end of the year, after much work, she wrote in almost illegible writing:

> Today I was drawing a cat picture. My firend [friend] told me to ware dress. I eat orange yesterday. My bother [brother] have [has] a big map. Yesterday my mother make a sandwish [sandwich]. Las night I call my firent [friend]. I was sit [sitting] on a big rock. Yesterday I see [saw] many star [starts].

A few months later, Douan wrote the following composition:

> At my house we have 13 people in the house and we have three bed room [bedroom] my brother my brothe [brother's] wife sleep in one bed room [bedroom] my brother have a lot of cloth and my bed room [bedroom] is environment [spacious] because we have 7 people in my bedroom and we have lot of both to and other bed room have 4 people sleep in my house is enviorment.

After this period, between January and March of 1986 she started writing very short compositions and withdrawing more from classroom activities. She said, "Mrs. X [the math teacher] never speaks to me. I have lots of time with nothing to do." One day she came and said, "I don't want to be nothing when I grow up. . . . I loved my horses in Laos. We had a brown and a white one. Love my animals." From that time to the end of the academic year, Douan just sat, copied simple sentences, and turned in assignments with the same errors, sometimes 15 to 20.

Oudin was emphatic saying, "I don't want to be anywhere but in Laos." He wrote a composition on Halloween:

> I Buy A pumpkin and I Drow [draw] my punkin [pumpkin] face is gross: One boy came and trick or treat at my hous [house] and the punkin [pumpkin] (is took)[?]. The boy ran and throw the candy and the punpkin [pumpkin] laugh. They boy cry and go homes and tell his mother. Boy come [The boy came] trick or treat, can you give some candy and the pumpking said no and I will give the boy candy to you. The boy wan. . . . [?]

While talking with these children about their compositions it became apparent that the content of many compositions (as well as of reading lessons), for example, stories about holidays such as Halloween and other traditions, was at times meaningless, but the level of difficulty was not as great as in the study of taxonomic structures, for example in the flora and fauna peculiar to the U.S. This was the case with Oudin, Douan, and Robert, as well as with the Hmong children. Many objects and many taxonomic concepts about the organization of these objects were culturally foreign to them.

The three Hmong children studied here had problems with those taxonomies. The Hmong have no written language, and since they had practiced slash-and-burn agriculture in China, Laos, and Vietnam, they had no reason to be concerned with plant classification. The exposure to English that their parents had during their stay in settlement camps in Thailand helped these children.

Chou, a 9-year-old Hmong boy, is the son of an educated Hmong who is fluent in English and works in a print shop as the manager. Chou's family is considered by other Hmong to be the best educated and most affluent of all the Hmong in La Playa. Chou is alert and competent in school, but somewhat confused about his background, home culture, and his place in school. He is always distracted, daydreaming, and absorbed with the beautiful drawings he makes. His drawings are well known in the Hmong community. Some families come to his home just to admire them. Our classroom observations indicate that he is uninvolved and not very concerned about school work. He tells the teacher he forgot to do his homework, but tells researchers he had planned to stay up late watching TV and uses an excuse he learned from his Anglo friends the next day, "I forgot."

To Pao and Tou the language of instruction, English, was extremely difficult, and their families did not have a literacy tradition. Text was viewed by their parents as something generated by white Americans for other Americans. The content of the textbooks easily reinforced this belief.

There was quantitative evidence of less academic productivity on the part of the twelve children under study (in contrast with their peers), in the form of classroom tasks and homework assignments completed. Also the quality of the structure and penmanship...was much lower in comparison with mainstream and high-achieving minority children. This fact, however, needs to be qualified. While all children classified as "learning disabled" (the 40 children from which we selected our 12) were perceived to be unable to read or write at the same level or with the same skill as other children, Chou, Tou, David, and Robert often surprised their main teachers with unexpected amounts of text produced during ESL or special education classes, on subjects selected by the students themselves. And even the least involved students from our sample, Douan, Rosita, Narath, and Emilio, would sometimes bring pages of text and lists of words copied verbatim from books, dictionaries, and other sources without much regard for their meaning. We asked them why they did that while they had not completed the mandated homework, they answered that their parents forced them to do so. That exercise seemed to the researchers to be a rather mechanical exercise related to the physical production of text without processing it. This was the case with Douan.

From the 40 children who were originally identified as having some learning difficulties, those who had been in this country for four or five years and were at the bottom of the achievement ladder (this includes most of the 12 children in the study) tended to be relatively passive during classroom activities and to produce homework or other text in a typically fragmented fashion, with grammatical problems of the type shown above. In many instances, the observer could find evidence that they were grasping the central meaning, or at times even the intended purpose of the task. Worse still, sometimes there was no participation whatsoever. Chou, for example, would keep his head down on the bench the entire class period, and Rosita would do likewise, but to a lesser extent they just sat quietly, daydreaming as if they had given up entirely any attempts to make sense of the world around them. This was less frequently the case with Carlos, Oudin, Douan, and Robert in our study. There was one important exception to this lack of participation and lack of productivity. During small group sessions with tutors, or in ESL and special education sessions when children were encouraged individually to select the content of the task and were given assistance step by step, Oudin, Carlos, Douan, and Pao produced imaginative text (albeit full of error) describing experiences (real or fictitious) in their home countries.

From the long interviews with main classroom teachers, we realized that these teachers rarely saw the sample children as being actively involved in learning activities. In fact, their comments about Oudin, Douan, and the Hmong children were "Poor Oudin, he does not have a clue," and about Douan, "She is like a little vegetable," and about the Hmong children "hopeless." Other comments regarding these twelve and other minority children were very explicitly pointing at the presumed mental ability of these children, almost echoing the psychologist's written comments in the files.

The researchers have some evidence that the children were going from a state of deep depression and mental isolation to a state of panic. This was shown in the decreasing attempts to participate and respond to questions, and to their inability to focus on simple directions. Undefined fears, physical restlessness, unfocused changing gaze, uncontrolled feet and hand movements, frequent need to go to the bathroom, and other signs of emotional turmoil increased during times of performance in front of large groups and caused serious embarrassment to these children, especially if they were reprimanded for them. In my field notes on Rosita, Emilio, and David, there were instances in which the teacher asked specific questions about reading, math, or their homework which the children could not answer. Any time Rosita was asked to read in front of the class, she would be physically upset and had to excuse herself to go to the bathroom. During the break she would explain that she had stomach problems. Emilio would just lower his head and wait till the teacher picked someone else. David and Oudin would respond "I don't know" in an angry way that discouraged the teacher from asking them again. The teachers interpreted this response as a challenge to her authority and her control of the class. Carlos would typically lower his head, get red-faced, and smile. On one occasion, after an incident which resulted in being sent to the principal for not bringing his homework and for not paying attention to teacher directions, he failed to attend school for several days.

Narath, Tou, and Bou are very shy and hardly talk to anybody about their problems in school. But any observer can see how hard it is for them to show competence in their work. In contrast with their usual response in the main classroom, that is, of frozen attitude and avoiding eye contact, in our experimental interventions in small group interactions during ESL and reading sessions, in which stress was minimized by allowing these children to select the areas and pace of activities as well as the level of skill associated with each activity, all three were communicative. Some music, an informal (almost casual) learning environment, and a consistently affectionate, personal approach, brought wonderful results. Oudin was often uncommunicative in the main class and more open in the small class (ESL). An example from my field notes about Oudin:

> The ESL teacher is trying to help Oudin with his multiplication tables. He is very resistant after the 2s. Physically backed his chair away. He couldn't look at the teacher. He had a great deal of trouble with the 3s and was embarrassed. The teacher talked about how important knowing multiplication tables is, and she offered to take as long as Oudin needed to study them. He said he could not come next week because he was going to die. They talked more outside and the teacher said smiling: "Don't die; not just yet; we need to work together." Oudin laughed, but he continued his great resistance.

We observed Narath and Pao saying in contexts similar to the one above, "I'm dumb, I'm dumb" and talking about killing themselves. I have mentioned the anger of Oudin when a Vietnamese movie was shown in his class and when he engaged in an argument during ESL class. I also mentioned how Douan preferred to remain quiet and resist passively when asked to answer questions about readings she did not understand. The same strategy was observed in Rosita, Narath, and Bou in reading classes which usually had materials unknown to them. Performing in another language, at a level of skill far above that yet reached, on areas and topics which required rather complex cultural knowledge, in the opinion of the participant observers, became a traumatic experience with detrimental psychological side effects.

We also saw children pretending to be unable to perform tasks they had already mastered in private or in a small group. A case in point was Oudin who, after he learned the multiplication tables, would refuse to answer by simply saying, "I don't know." Difficulties in the use of the English language during instructional activities had a seemingly cumulative demoralizing effect on these LEP children, to judge from the decreasing level of participation and productivity during written and oral assignments. The examples given earlier can illustrate this statement.

In summary, a close look at the compositions presented earlier would show that these children often could not distinguish semantic ranges in the use of words, that their syntax was incorrect (verb tenses, order, etc.), and that they could not articulate descriptions of incidents. Most importantly, they could neither understand nor generate concepts (environment vs. space), taxonomic differences between classes of objects (types of flowers), and gifts and activities associated with diverse holidays (Christmas and Halloween), and other relationships expressed through text. Their knowledge of the language and/or the subject remained approximate, at the surface of the central issues and concepts. The quality of their communication for academic purposes was clearly set apart from their peers. In essence, these children could not for the most part communicate in English for academic purposes in ways that would demonstrate an ability to see logical relationships in specific language structures.

The most disturbing finding to the research team was that most of the children stopped trying to learn and accepted their "disabilities" as personal attributes, not as a consequence of dysfunctional instructional arrangements or lack of responsibility in our political, social, and educational leaders. Evidence of this fact were the statements made by Oudin and other Indochinese children regarding their inability to learn the math tables or to write compositions as good as those of their peers. The decrease in participation is another piece of evidence that some of these children did not see much hope of improving their performance. To confirm their conviction that "disabilities" were always a personal failure, the 12 children and others suspected of being "disabled" (the original 40 students which constituted the pool from which our small sample was taken) were tested by the school psychologist. All 12 were officially declared "handicapped" or special education cases in instances where the testing took place in a language most of the children did not understand (English), and even when the child's performance in domains not requiring sophisticated linguistic or cultural knowledge (for example, in art or mathematics) was above average (Robert in 5th grade has a math level of 4.9, David in 3rd grade has a math score of 3.4, Tou in 3rd grade has a math score of 3.5; Chou is known in the community as an expert drawer of Hmong scenes).

LEARNING TO SUCCEED AND FAIL IN SCHOOL: TOWARDS A CULTURALLY-BASED THEORY OF ACHIEVEMENT SOCIALIZATION

Research on linguistic minorities' academic failure has attracted more attention than research on their success (McDermott, 1987a; Ogbu, 1974, 1978, 1987; Trueba, 1983). Gradually, criticisms of such an emphasis has modified the focus of the research to one of differential achievement across minorities and across all student populations (Ogbu, 1987; Trueba, in press). The liberal position of the earlier sociologists of education (Sorokin, 1927), who questioned the "leveling" and "democratization" effects of schooling in the U.S., has been welcomed by the radical reformist Neo-Marxist and liberal anthropologists who view success or failure as a function of structural societal factors, and less on the part of school treatment. This seems to have emphasized the focus on failure. More recently, the focus on success is consistent with an overall recent trend in the social sciences to look into the school treatment as a complementary explanation for success or failure. Bidwell and Friedkin state:

> To take the U.S. as a case in point, one would expect that after so many years of public and professional debate about equality of educational opportunity, American elementary and high school would have taken effective steps against ascriptive biases in educational opportunities and achievement. Instead, American common schools seemingly transmit these biases, strengthening them in the process (in press).

McDermott goes a step further in his implied criticism of social science research:

> Now I am trying to move beyond the problem of school failure that has grown into a small industry involving millions of people measuring, documenting, remediating, and explaining the habits, values, and skills of minority groups that contribute so heavily to their ranks of school failures. There is a preoccupation among us: Because we claim to offer good education to all and because many minority people seem to reject it, we are plagued with the questions of "What is with them anyway?" or "What is their situation that school seems to go so badly?" Their situation! . . . The breakthrough comes when we realize that their situation is not theirs alone; it is ours as well. We help to make failure possible for our successes. . . . Failure is a culturally necessary part of the American scene. We do not need to explain. We need to confront it . . . ; explaining it will only keep it at a distance, making us its slaves (1987b, pp. 361–363).

Recognizing the intimate relationship between language, culture, and cognition, and the significance of socially and culturally-based theories of cognitive development as proposed by the sociohistorical school of psychology (Diaz, Moll, & Mehan, 1986; Schribner & Cole, 1981; Vygotsky, 1962, 1978; Wertsch, 1985), a number of important questions can be raised from this study: (a) Is the relationship between language and cognition mediated by the culturally-based emotional response of students? (b) What is the significance of symbolic interaction in the context of academic activities, which are instrumental for the overall adjustment of children to a new culture? (c) Is it enough to use the child's mother tongue, or should there also be a culturally appropriate learning environment (congruent with the values of home culture) to maximize cognitive development of children?

If we are to take McDermott's advice seriously, one way of facing the culturally-based dichotomy of success and failure is to examine the organization of activities, which seems to create school failure, and suggest ways of changing it. Thus, we must face the practical issue of the role of language use in instruction (first-and/or second-language vis-à-vis the purpose and nature of instruction). The other deals with the role of language and culture in the acquisition of literacy skills:

1. What is the most effective use of language in the classroom, if the primary goal of instruction is to foster cognitive growth in children?
2. If some of the literacy problems faced by LEP children are related to their different experiences, cultural knowledge, values, and overall background, could the use of the native language facilitate the cultural adjustment of children to school?

The English-Only movement reflects the political clouds that have obscured the discussion of fundamental pedagogical principles that are applicable to all children. These principles must be stated and applied, even if political pressure and racial prejudice become an obstacle. One is prompted to ask: What has historically been behind such strong political movements which attempt to curtail the use of non-English languages in educational and other public institutions? From the early 1880s, when Connecticut, Massachusetts, Rhode Island, New York, Wisconsin, and other states declared English as the mandatory school language, to the late 1960s, when the Bilingual Education Act was approved, there have been important changes. Yet the memory of jailing and subsequent trials for speaking other languages is still fresh in the memory of some older minority persons.

Racial prejudice, as manifested in the La Playa community and school by mainstream teachers, parents, and children, may be best interpreted and understood as a conflict in cultural values, or even as genuine xenophobia, a profound anxiety about sharing physical space and engaging in social intercourse with people exhibiting different cultural, linguistic, and/or physical characteristics. The isolation of some ethnic groups in school may be related to emotional responses and behavioral patterns on the part of mainstream teachers and children, rather than to some well articulated racist philosophy. Many mainstream Americans have felt in the past, and still feel, that this country cannot rapidly assimilate such large numbers of immigrants, refugees, and other minorities, and they see minorities' presence as a real threat to national unity and economic progress. A sad example of this position appears in history from time to time; the period between 1880 and 1930 was characterized by legislation intended to curtail the voting rights and general participation of linguistic minorities in social, political, and economic institutions. The ongoing English-Only movement, which began in California two years ago, has now spread to twelve other states and repeats history.

One of the central issues raised by field-based studies such as the one reported here, is the importance that precise, logical, and sophisticated use of language has in effective classroom instruction and in the acquisition of literacy skills. One of the main goals in the education of linguistic minorities is to help students acquire high levels of literacy so they can process information and develop their thinking skills. The assumption (Cummins, 1986) is that cognitive skills (the ability to structure knowledge and to approach learning tasks effectively) can be best acquired through the native language and then easily transferred to a second language. Use of native language is best because critical thinking skills and cognitive structuring are conditioned by linguistic and cultural knowledge and experiences that children usually obtain in the home and bring with them to school (Cummins, 1986).

A second central issue, linked to the first, is that the nature of literacy problems faced by linguistic minorities is deeply related to their lack of cultural knowledge that is presumed by the instructors and writers of textbook materials. There is a serious ignorance and pervasive insensitivity of school personnel and textbook writers regarding the inherent inaccessibility and confusion for minorities in text written with mainstream middle-class American children in mind. Such insensitivity to the obvious cultural and linguistic gap between minority home cultures and mainstream cultures paves the way for school personnel to stereotype and underestimate minority children's learning potential.

If we are going to pursue a socialization approach whose main purpose was to understand the actual home cultural background and previous experiences of LEPs, in order to design interventions which would open the door to academic success, we must first understand better the social context of school failure and the conditions of failure, as well as the process of socialization for failure.

School children, particularly LEPs who are not achieving well in school, may need extra time and flexibility to place themselves in a new cultural ecology in which the interactional experiences they face daily in the home, school, and community, as well as their own intrapsychological processes, can permit them to make the transition to the new culture and language. Children's adjustment to school is often impacted profoundly by the prearrival experiences they face, the loss and separation from relatives, the feeling of guilt associated with this loss and separation, as well as the many degrading and traumatic incidents (DeVos, 1984) experienced by refugees and low-status immigrants. These experiences are often reinforced in school encounters and may easily lead to a profound anxiety about self-worth and personal safety.

In each of the four main interactional layers there are certain antecedents which seem to lead to experiences of individual and collective failure and which result in additional stress, ultimately creating a cumulative sense of impotence, isolation, and low self-esteem. Because the acquisition of academic knowledge, particularly towards the end of elementary school, requires a very sophisticated use of the instructional language, minorities are set up for failure, a failure which becomes devastating for some LEP children. Also, because learning, at least if viewed from a socially- and culturally-based perspective integral to the theory of learning postulated by the sociohistorical school of psychology led by Vygotsky (see Goldman & McDermott, 1987; McDermott, 1987a, 1987b; Ogbu, 1978, 1987; Trueba, 1987a, 1987b; Trueba & Delgado-Gaitan, in press), requires that the learner play an active role in determining the whats and hows of the learning process, LEP children, as shown in the study reported here, find themselves cognitively isolated and lost.

CONCLUSION

... If indeed cultural conflict is at the heart of illiteracy among minority students, and if illiterate minority students have been socialized to fail by an insensitive educational system, there must be ways to (a) sensitize the school system to develop culturally-based instructional models which are effective for minorities, and (b) socialize minority students to achieve academically. The resolution of cultural conflicts associated with school interactional contexts is deeply rooted in a better understanding of the opposition between the conflicting sociocultural systems which advocate different cultural values. In a very subtle but real fashion, these values affect students' ability to engage in literacy activities and draw meaning from text. Change in language and culture can be devastating in circumstances where the change was unexpected and/or unwanted. Socialization for academic success involves sensitive and creative approaches on the part of teachers and principals.

REFERENCES

1. Au, K., & Jordan, C.: Teaching reading to Hawaiian children: Finding a culturally appropriate solution. In Trueba, H., Guthrie, G. & Au, K., (Eds.): *Culture and the Bilingual Classroom: Studies in Classroom Ethnography.* Rowley, MA, Newbury House, 1981.
2. Bidwell, C., & Friedkin, N.: The sociology of education. In Smelser, N., (Ed.): *The Handbook of Sociology.* Beverly Hills, Sage Publications (In Press).
3. Cummins, J.: Empowering minority students: A framework for intervention. *Harvard Educational Review, 56:*18–35, 1986.
4. DeVos, G.: Ethnic persistence and role degradation: An illustration from Japan. Paper presented at the American-Soviet Symposium on Contemporary Ethnic Processes in the USSR, New Orleans, LA, 1984.
5. Diaz, S., Moll, L., & Mehan, H.: Sociocultural resources in instruction: A context-specific approach. In *Beyond Language: Social and Cultural Factors in Schooling Language Minority Students.* Sacramento, Bilingual Education Office, California State Department of Education, 1986.
6. Dunn, L. M.: *Bilingual Hispanic Children on the U. S. Mainland: A Review of Research on Their Cognitive, Linguistic, and Scholastic Development.* Circle Pines, American Guidance Services, 1987.
7. Duran, R.: *Hispanics' Education and Background: Predictors of College Achievement.* New York, College Entrance Examination Board, 1983.
8. Erickson, F.: Qualitative methods in research on teaching. In Wittrock, M. C. (Ed.): *Handbook of Research on Teaching.* New York, Macmillan, 1986.
9. Goldman, S., & Trueba, H. (Eds.): *Becoming Literate in English as a Second*

Language: Advances in Research and Theory. Norwood, Ablex Publishing, 1987.

10. Goldman, S., & McDermott, R.: The culture of competition in American schools. In Spindler, G. (Ed.): *Education and Cultural Process: Anthropological Approaches.* (2nd ed). Prospect Heights, Waveland, 1987.

11. McCarthy, K. F., & Burciaga-Valdez, R.: *Current and Future Effects of Mexican Immigration in California.* Santa Monica, CA, Rand Corporation, 1985. (Series R-3365/1-CR).

12. McCarthy, K. F., & Burciaga-Valdez, R.: *Current and Future Effects of Mexican Immigration in California.* Santa Monica, CA, Rand Corporation, 1986. (Series R-3365-CR).

13. McDermott, R.: Achieving school failure: An anthropological approach to illiteracy and social stratification. In Spindler, G. (Ed.): *Education and Cultural Process: Anthropological Approaches.* 2nd ed. Prospects Heights, Waveland, 1987a.

14. McDermott, R.: The explanation of minority school failure, again. *Anthropology and Education Quarterly, 18:*361–364, 1987.

15. Mohatt, B., & Erickson, F.: Cultural differences in teaching styles in an Odawa school: A sociolinguistic approach. In Trueba, H., Guthrie, G., & Au, K. (Eds.): *Culture and the Bilingual Classroom: Studies in Classroom Ethnography.* Rowley, MA, Newbury House, 1981.

16. Moll, L., & Diaz, E.: Change as the goal of educational research. *Anthropology and Education Quarterly: 18:*300–311, 1987.

17. Ogbu, J.: Cultural discontinuities and schooling. *Anthropology and Education Quarterly, 13:*290–307, 1982.

18. Ogbu, J.: *Minority Education and Caste: The American System in Cross-Cultural Perspective.* New York, Academic Press, 1978.

19. Ogbu, J.: *The Next Generation: An Ethnography of Education in an Urban Neighborhood.* New York, Academic Press, 1974.

20. Ogbu, J.: Origins of human competence: A cultural-ecological perspective. *Child Development, 52:*413–429, 1981.

21. Ogbu, J.: Variability in minority responses to schooling: Nonimmigrants vs immigrants. In Spindler, G., & Spindler, L. (Eds.): *Interpretive ethnography of education: At home and abroad.* Hillsdale, Erlbaum, 1987.

22. Ogbu, J., & Matute-Bianchi, M. E.: Understanding sociocultural factors: Knowledge, identity and school adjustment. In *Beyond Language: Social and Cultural Factors in Schooling Language Minority Students.* Sacramento, Bilingual Education Office, California State Department of Education, 1986.

23. Rueda, R. Social and communicative aspects of language proficiency in low-achieving language minority students. In Trueba, H. (Ed.): *Success or Failure: Linguistic Minority Children at Home and in School,* New York, Harper & Row, 1987.

24. Schribner, S., & Cole, M.: *The Psychology of Literacy.* Cambridge, Harvard University Press, 1981.

25. Sorokin, P. A.: *Social and Cultural Mobility.* New York, Harper & Row, 1927.

26. Spindler, G.: Change and continuity in American core cultural values: An anthropological perspective. In DeRenzo, G. D. (Ed.): *We the People: American Character and Social Change*. Westport, CT: Greenwood, 1977.

27. Spindler, G.: *Doing the Ethnography of Schooling: Educational Anthropology in Action*. New York, Holt, Rinehart & Winston, 1982.

28. Spindler, G. Schooling in Schoenhausen: A study of cultural transmission and instrumental adaptation in an urbanizing German village. In Spindler, G. (Ed.): *Education and Cultural process: Toward an Anthropology of Education*. New York, Holt, Rinehart, & Winston, 1974.

29. Spindler, G., & Spindler, L.: Anthropologists' view of American culture. *American Review of Anthropology, 12:*49–78, 1983.

30. Spindler, G., & Spindler, L.: Cultural dialogue and schooling in Schoenhausen and Roseville: A comparative analysis. *Anthropology and Education Quarterly, 18:*3–16, 1987.

31. Spindler, G., & Spindler, L.: *The Interpretive Ethnography of Education: At Home and Abroad*. Hillsdale, Erlbaum, 1987.

32. Suarez-Orozco, M.: *In Pursuit of a Dream: New Hispanic Immigrants in American Schools*. Stanford, CA, Stanford University Press, in press.

33. Suarez-Orozco, M.: Toward a psychosocial understanding of Hispanic adaptation to American schooling. In Trueba, H. (Ed.): *Success or Failure: Linguistic Minority Children at Home and in School*. New York, Harper & Row, 1987.

34. Tharp, R. G., & Gallimore, R.: *Rousing Minds to Life: Teaching, Learning and Schooling in Social Context*. Cambridge, Cambridge University Press, 1988.

35. Trueba, H.: Adjustment problems of Mexican American children: An anthropological study. *Learning Disabilities Quarterly, 6:*8–15, 1983.

36. Trueba, H.: Organizing classroom instruction in specific sociocultural contexts: Teaching Mexican youth to write in English. In Goldman, S., & Trueba, H. (Eds.): *Becoming Literate in English as a Second Language: Advances in Research and Theory*. Norwood, Ablex Publishing, 1987b.

37. Trueba, H.: *Success or Failure? Learning and the Language Minority Student*. New York, Newbury/Harper & Row, 1987a.

38. Trueba, H.: *Raising Silent Voices. Educating the Linguistic Minorities for the 21st Century*. New York, Harper & Row, 1989.

39. Trueba, H., & Delgado-Gaitan, C.: *School and Society: Learning Content Through Culture*. New York, Praeger (In press).

40. U. S. Bureau of the Census: *1980 U. S. Census. Current Populations Report*. Washington, D. C., U. S. Government Printing Office, 1984.

41. Vygotsky, L. S.: *Mind in Society: The Development of Higher Psychological Processes*. (Cole, M., John-Teiner, V. Scribner, S., & Souberman, E. (Eds.), Cambridge, Harvard University Press, 1978.

42. Vygotsky, L. S.: *Thought and Language*. Cambridge, MIT Press, 1962.

43. Wertsch, J.: *Vygotsky and the Social Formation of the Mind*. Cambridge, Harvard University Press, 1985.

Chapter 19

MEETING HMONG STUDENTS'
EDUCATIONAL NEEDS

Joan Thrower Timm

Like all students, Hmong students' performance in the classroom is affected by their cultural experience prior to coming to school. In an earlier chapter we assessed cultural reasons why Hmong early childhood socialization is conducive to a field-sensitive cognitive style and how that socialization impacts the way students approach a learning situation. In this chapter, some issues specific to Hmong students' needs are addressed and some suggestions for working with them in American classrooms are provided.

Field-Sensitive Learning

General guidelines for working with a field-sensitive cognitive style are relevant for working with Hmong students, but there are additional considerations, arising out of Hmong culture, which need to be taken into account as well. Like other field-sensitive students, Hmong students are attuned to social cues and the responses of their classmates as well as their relationship with teachers. Working with students on a one-on-one basis obviously enhances the teacher-student relationship.

Hmong students orient to situation-specific guidance, demonstration, and instructions. Directions in traditional Hmong culture were situation specific and based on observational learning. For this reason, teachers should be precise in their instructions and in describing their assignments. All homework assignments should be given in written form and explained in class. Hmong students should be encouraged to ask questions about homework assignments before they leave the classroom.

Teachers may take advantage of this cognitive style by using cooperative peer groups, as Lert (1979) has suggested. Traditional Hmong culture employed a field-sensitive socialization but cooperative learning

208

procedures were unknown in formal educational settings that focused on memorizing. In employing field-sensitive methods in the classroom, educators may utilize procedures which fit with Hmong students' need for contextual and social referents. (It is possible, of course, to employ both memorizing and cooperative discovery learning in the classroom.) Hmong students work well in groups. In mainstream classes, it is important to include non-Hmong students whenever possible in order to avoid isolating the Hmong from other students. This practice has been reported in some classrooms (Goldstein, 1990). When other students work with Hmong students, however, it is crucial that teachers monitor the process. Some teachers have reported that non-Hmong students sometimes believe that they are helping their Hmong classmates by doing the work for them (personal interviews). (In ESL classes, peer tutoring is obviously useful, but again needs to be monitored in order to avoid the same problem.) Finally, in assigning students to work together, at least two Hmong students should be included in a group if possible, in order to avoid isolating single students. In other words, in placing students in groups, teachers should avoid both types of isolation: that which separates Hmong students from each other and from non-Hmong classmates as well.

A factor arising out of Hmong culture, which teachers should consider in assigning students to group projects, is the relationship among the Hmong students. Students with the same last name are considered to be of the same clan, and therefore close relatives. Because of the strong family orientation in Hmong culture, Hmong students with the same name would regard each other as "brothers and sisters" and would, therefore, feel a special responsibility for helping each other.

Other factors, which teachers should consider in assigning students to cooperative groups, are the gender and age of the students. Teachers should avoid assigning Hmong boys and girls in high school to work with each other unless the Hmong students have the same last name. If they have, then they are considered to be clan-related and therefore are not potential marriage partners. Assigning students with different last names would be assigning potential marriage partners to work together. From a Hmong cultural perspective, it is considered inappropriate for potential marriage partners to work in such close association. From an American cultural perspective, this avoidance may appear sexist, but it reflects an important Hmong gender value.

Language and Thought

Two areas in Hmong students' school performance that are noticeably affected by Hmong culture are concept formation and the transition to English as a second language. Indeed, linguistic issues lie at the heart of educational problems for Hmong students. The transition to English is far more complex than the learning of a new vocabulary. There are two basic problems involved—the forming of conceptual categories and the mastery of two very different syntax systems. As in all cultures, Hmong concept formation is directly related to linguistic issues.

Hmong is spoken in most households because many older people have very limited English proficiency and because parents believe that their language is essential for the preservation of their culture. Many educators assume that if a Hmong child was born in the United States then he or she is more familiar with both English and American culture than those who recently immigrated but this assumption is not always valid. Xiong (1991) reported that when Hmong children enter school, many do so with very little knowledge of English, depending upon how much contact they have had with television and non-Hmong playmates. Thus, children born in the United States may have no better command of English than recent immigrants. When they enter school, many Hmong students do so with very little knowledge of English. A less obvious problem, however, is that their analytic skills are directly related to some limitations in Hmong language.

Hmong Concepts

One of the mental abilities, or logical operations, which Jean Piaget described is the ability to classify or categorize. Culture defines categories and concepts for all students and Hmong students are no exception, but Hmong culture affects students' understanding of concepts and categories which are taken for granted in American culture. The first of these is color.

Color categories. A Hmong educator has reported (personal interview) that color terms are not so extensive as American designates but are limited to red, green, black, white, blue, and yellow. There is no designate for purple. The name of a purple flower would be used instead. There is no term for brown, which would be identified as "the color of coffee." Tan is referred to as "a sort of coffee color." Burgundy would be "dark red" and pink would be "light red." Orange would be identified by the name of that fruit in Hmong. Because color is one of the earliest categories addressed in American education, teachers cannot assume knowledge of all color terms, as they do with other children, but rather need to call Hmong students' attention to a color and specifically teach them the term directly.

Cognitive comparison of categories. Another concept which is addressed early in American education is that of sequential comparisons, such as long, longer, or longest. Hmong language, however, accommodates only two-way comparisons such as big or small, long or short. When teachers ask young students whether a row of eight, six, or three marbles is the longest, Hmong students tend to disregard part of the array. Similarly, when asked whether a cup which is filled to the brim, half full, or a quarter full, has the most in it, Hmong students ignore one of the examples. Temperature is also interpreted in dichotomous terms of hot or cold. Again, the notion of "coldest" or "hottest" is difficult for Hmong children to understand. Culturally, they have learned two-way comparisons but find three or four way comparisons confusing. Teachers need to be aware of the absence of terms such as longest, fullest, or coldest, which accommodate multiple comparisons. In other words, they need specifically to demonstrate and provide the English terms which they traditionally take for granted.

The lesson for teachers in the forgoing examples is that Hmong students need experience in sequential and three or four-way comparisons which should be taught directly and early in their education. These comparisons should also include height, area, weight, volume, and area in order for students to become familiar with comparative categories that are common in American culture.

Procedural concepts. A third difference between Hmong and American thinking is the contrast between a procedural and a categorical approach to the conceptualizing of relationships among objects. A good example was reported by Marshall (personal interview). Many of her Hmong students chose incorrect responses among an array of pictures in a sorting test. The directions for the test were to "draw a circle around the object which does *not belong.*" One question included pictures of a hammer, a hatchet, a saw, and a fire. The Hmong students circled the hammer. The "correct" answer was the fire because it is not a tool. Fortunately, the teacher asked the students why they chose the hammer. They replied that a hatchet and a saw can be used to cut the wood to make a fire, but that you don't use a hammer to do that. The lesson is obvious. When teachers work with Hmong students, they should ask the reasons why the students respond the way they do, rather than assuming that they have "missed the point." In order to assess accurately students' cognitive processes, teachers should discuss Hmong students' errors with them and not simply note mistakes. Marshall (1991) has suggested that teachers should explain the concepts underlying the classifying and sorting problems so common in early elementary education and use pictures which provide visual associations with unfamiliar English words. Finally, *teachers should not assume that as students acquire a greater knowledge of English that they also acquire a more categorical and less procedural approach to learning.*

Hmong Language

There are profound difficulties in students' acquiring English which are far more complex than the obvious mastery of vocabulary because of specific linguistic differences from English. The first of these differences involves syntax. In Hmong there is no verb equivalent for the verb "to be." A more active verb must be used. There is no plural modification of nouns. In Hmong, the English "three books" is expressed as "three book" or "a lot of book." There is no possessive case. "Ler's book" is expressed as "Ler book." There are no gerunds. The phrase "barking dog" cannot be expressed in Hmong. There are no adjectival forms of numbers. "First street" would be expressed as "one street." In Hmong, pronouns are not used or are limited to adapting this concept from English. The English phrase "He hit him" would be expressed in terms of "the boy" or "the girl" or specific names would be used instead. The term "one" is used as a pronoun, but it could refer to "he" or "she" or "me" or "you." In Hmong, the noun precedes the adjective, such as "barn red." Verbs are not modified for past or future tense. Tense is determined either by context such as day of the week or the insertion of a single word which indicates tense. For example, the word "yuav" before a verb connotes future tense. In learning English, the concept of modifying a verb for tense is new to Hmong students. Irregular verbs are even more confusing. Taking these differences in order, Hmong expressions appear to be grammatical errors when they are transferred into English. Given these differences, it is little wonder that Hmong students struggle in two linguistic worlds. Mistakes in English are not mistakes in Hmong.

In addition to syntax, there are three other important differences between Hmong and English. First, Hmong is a tonal language. Slight differences in tone, which are often very difficult for non-Hmong to distinguish, express totally different words. In written Hmong, the pronunciation of a word is indicated by a final consonant which is not pronounced. As a result, Hmong students may ignore a final consonant when spoken in English. A middle school teacher reported an amusing example: when she asked a Hmong student to get her (audio-visual) cart in the next room, she looked out the window a few minutes later to see him wandering around the parking lot looking for her car (Timm, 1994).

Second, there are fewer synonyms in Hmong than in English to express the same idea. As a result, Hmong students are sometimes confused by English synonyms. For example, one of our students understood the verb "to help" but did not realize that "to assist" expresses the same idea.

Third, in Hmong there are fewer words with subtle differences in meaning than there are in English. Therefore, Hmong students have a tendency to interpret English words with these subtleties as meaning the same thing. A principal reported that when a radio announcer broadcast that school was postponed two hours due to weather conditions, her Hmong students either did not come at all or they came at the usual time. Neither they nor their parents understood that "postpone" means "delayed." The students who were absent told her the next day that they thought the announcement meant "no school" (Timm, 1994).

When these linguistic issues are considered as a whole, it is clear that Hmong students encounter major conceptual shifts in their transition to English. Teachers should use basic English and be aware of using synonyms which can be confusing to students with limited English. Even at the college level, we have found errors on tests which Hmong students made because they simply did not know the English word. Teachers should avoid speaking too fast. They should also avoid slang and colloquial expressions which are confusing. They should avoid using long sentences with embedded phrases.

Placement Issues

Even with television and perhaps American playmates in the neighborhood, Hmong children do not have an early cultural experience which "fits" with mainstream culture unless they have attended a preschool which few Hmong children do. If Hmong children have not had some prior experience with wider American culture before entering elementary school, their culture shock is great. Xiong (1991) reported that Hmong children's experience generally has been in a Hmong setting and that when they enter school, they do so with no frame of reference about what to expect. McInnis-Dittrich (1991) reported that Hmong children have no preconceived ideas about school. They respect their teachers and try to please them but are confused by classroom procedures. They have been taught to accept the teachings of adults and that silence is respectful. The question for educators, of course, is what procedures and placements are most likely to benefit Hmong students the most?

Placement in Mainstream Classrooms

Goldstein (1990) has reported two types of segregation in the sociocultural context of Hmong education: (a) academic, whereby they are placed in a limited English proficiency program (LEP); and (b) social, whereby they are placed in regular classes but remain isolated from American classmates. Despite enrollment of Hmong students in regular classes, the within-classroom social contact between American students and Hmong students was severely limited, due partly to language and partly to cultural differences. In other words, the mere placement of Hmong students in regular classes does not ensure increased interaction and cultural understanding among American and Hmong students. Educators need to consider ways of implementing changes in this social segregation.

In addition to cultural and linguistic differences when they enter school, Hmong students may encounter ignorance and misunderstanding about the Hmong which other children bring to school with them. Many Americans do not know who the Hmong are, why they are here, or anything about their history, culture, or struggle for survival. The attitudes of non-Hmong students are difficult to predict. A few teachers reported (personal interviews) that students sometimes ignore their Hmong classmates in a manner similar to that reported by Goldstein (1990). On the other hand, some students may "adopt" Hmong students and try to help them by doing their work. While well-intentioned, this assistance does not help Hmong children to acquire the skills necessary for success in American classrooms.

ESL Programs

Trueba and his associates (1990) have reported a higher success rate in English acquisition and fewer stress responses among Hmong students who were placed in smaller ESL classes where they were allowed to pace the activities in comparison with those who were placed in regular classrooms where teachers may be at a loss to know how to help them. There are continuing reports from around the country of Hmong children with little or no English simply being placed in regular classrooms where both these students and teachers are at a loss to know what to do. The advantages of ESL classes is that they work toward preserving the Hmong language and also help Hmong students to integrate the language at home with English at school. In order to be effective, however, these classes must occur regularly and be an essential component of Hmong students' education. An urban elementary teacher reported (personal interview) her frustration over a poorly implemented program in her school where the ESL classes are used as a reward for Hmong students if they do well with their classroom work first!

Placing students in ESL classes may serve their linguistic needs but a disturbing practice has evolved regarding language minority students including the Hmong. Sometimes these students are identified as having special needs, based on their limited ability to communicate, read, and write in English. Trueba (1990) has addressed this issue.

> If we start with the assumption that in general all (minority) children are competent enough to handle difficult learning tasks in the home and out-of-school setting, including the acquisition of their language and culture, then we are pressed to search for more rational explanations that lead to individual attributes of deficiencies such as 'learning disabilities.' . . . Because English literacy will continue to affect the future educational level and socioeconomic status of large numbers of minority students, it is important to explore ways of optimizing the sociocultural context of English literacy acquisition (pp. 91–92).

The question whether to place students in regular or ESL classes has elicited debate on both sides within the Hmong community. One Hmong educator has reported that in her opinion ESL programs offer advantages but that placement should be on a voluntary basis rather than forced on students proficient in English (personal interview). She also reported that preschool programs help prepare children for school both culturally and linguistically and expressed a wish for Hmong teachers and aides at the preschool level. Another Hmong ESL teacher reported that she believes ESL should be required in the primary years, especially if students have not had preschool experience (personal interview). Still other Hmong ESL teachers expressed a preference for compromise or "pull out" programs which isolate Hmong students from others on a limited basis (personal interviews). All expressed a concern about grouping too many Hmong students together in programs that segregated them from other students. In other words, they were concerned about Hmong children learning how to relate to both of their cultural worlds.

Additional Issues

A few additional pedagogical issues remain. Teachers should not assume that Hmong students always understand their explanations or instructions. They should avoid the question "Do you understand?" because the Hmong in general have a tendency to nod and reply in the affirmative, in order to show good manners. In order to be sure that Hmong students understand, teachers should ask students to rephrase both instructions and curricular content in their own words.

When they enter school, Hmong students are not accustomed to asking questions or to being singled out to speak. Teachers need to instruct them directly to ask questions.

Hmong students respond to encouragement rather than to personal recognition. Teachers should avoid singling out Hmong students to recite in class before they feel comfortable in doing so. In encouraging students to recite or to express their feelings, teachers should remember that in Hmong culture, children are not socialized to do this.

Many Hmong children are taught to avoid looking directly at an older person. This reticence is a sign of respect. Teachers should not expect eye-to-eye contact until the student has learned this is a behavioral expectation in American schools.

Perhaps most importantly of all, some Hmong educators have expressed concerns in regard to academic standards and reported that some courses that are offered to Hmong students are, in fact, simplified. There appears to be a concern that courses should maintain rigorous academic content in order that Hmong students may be adequately prepared for a variety of occupations. The general consensus is that the focus should be on linguistic issues early in the school years and that once English and its relation to mainstream concepts are acquired, Hmong students who are motivated to do so will succeed.

SOME FINAL THOUGHTS

Trueba et al. (1990) have suggested that learning experiences in the home prepare children for acquiring concepts, developing inquiry strategies, building taxonomies, and making logical inferences. Hmong students' academic success is affected by both their cognitive style and their culturally derived conceptual frames of reference. By becoming familiar with Hmong culture and its relationship to cognitive style, educators may gain insight into ways for implementing effective methodologies, programs, and teaching strategies that focus on group support, mutual cooperation, and a sensitivity to field-sensitive learning.

In working with Hmong students, teachers need to understand the relationship between Hmong language and concept formation. They need to distinguish between Western cultural categories and Hmong cultural categories and to refrain from assuming that "incorrect" responses are in fact "wrong."

Finally, teachers need to know the differences between mainstream American social values and traditional Hmong values. These differences have been analyzed elsewhere (Timm, 1996).

By becoming familiar with these issues, educators may build cross cultural conceptual bridges to enable Hmong students to succeed in both their Hmong and American cultural worlds.

REFERENCES

1. Goldstein, B. L.: Refugee students' perceptions of curriculum differentiation. In Page, R., & Valli, L. (Eds.). *Curriculum Differentiation: Interpretive Studies in U. S. Secondary Schools.* New York, State University of New York Press, 1990.
2. Lert, E. N.: Adult second language acquisition: Laotian Hmong in southland. Master's thesis, Brown University, 1980.
3. Marshall, H.: Techniques for effective work with oral cultures. Paper presented at the conference on Educating the Hmong Student, Oshkosh, WI, University of Wisconsin-Oshkosh, 1991.
4. McInnis, K. M., Petracci, H. E., & Morgenbesser, M.: *The Hmong in America: Providing Ethnic-Sensitive Health Education and Human Services.* Dubuque, IA, Kendall/Hunt publishers, 1990.
5. Piaget, J., & Inhelder, B.: *The Psychology of the Child.* New York, Basic Books, 1969.
6. Timm, J. T.: *Four Perspectives in Multicultural Education.* Belmont, CA, Wadsworth Publishing, 1996.

7. Timm, J. T.: Hmong values and American education. *Equity and Excellence in Education,* 27:36–44, 1994.
8. Trueba, H. T., Jacobs, L., & Kirton, E.: *Cultural Conflict and Adaptation: The Case of Hmong Children in American Society.* New York, The Falmer Press, 1990.
9. Xiong, M.: School links to the community: Involving Hmong parents. Paper presented at the conference on Educating the Hmong Student. Oshkosh, WI, University of Wisconsin-Oshkosh, 1991.

Chapter 20

MAKING SCHOOLS WORK FOR ALL STUDENTS

Barbara J. Shade

The psychologists of the 1900s perpetuated a major war on equality by promoting the concept of inferiority using "intelligence tests." Not only did they provide an excuse for individuals to be treated differently, they established a myth which evolved into an inherent belief within American culture that skin color makes people different and difficult. The fact that all of the groups which have poor academic performance in schools today have a different skin hue reinforces this myth and making schools work will remain particularly problematic until America comes to terms with the extent to which race is a major social-psychological problem, social issue and social barrier in this country. As Cornel West (1993) states, "race does matter" and it has a major impact on many decisions, attitudes and behaviors of everyone in this society. Unless there is a change in perception about race, educators will continue to give credence to the theory that students-of-color do not have the ability to learn and perform, need not be taught, and do not deserve to be taught.

There is little doubt that people of color who are the major participants in the schools of today bring challenges—but these challenges are not the result of their skin color. Instead, they emanate from the social and economic barriers which have been established to promote inequality. They also are the result of the development of different coping mechanisms which are necessary to adapt to the environments in which each of the groups find themselves. More important, all of the students about whom concerns are raised are from communities previously ignored and whose history of schooling is one of deprivation, alienation and denial.

African-American families and communities remember the history of segregated schools, of laws which denied their children the right to an education, of poorly funded and poorly staffed schools, of schools with high suspension and dropout rates, and of schools in which their chil-

219

dren are discouraged from taking courses which prepare them for careers and higher education. More important, African-American parents and scholars are painfully aware of the demolition of African-American self-identity, self-esteem and lack of recognition of their strengths within the educational setting (Shade, 1990, Fordham & Ogbu, 1989).

Similar perceptions are shared by American Indian and Mexican-American students, families and communities. As far back as 1860, European-Americans developed boarding schools to which American Indian children were sent as a way of "acculturating" the Indian people which meant eliminating any vestiges of American Indian culture and behavior. This required the elimination of their traditional names, dress, hair, religion and languages. The American Indian people resisted this cultural annihilation and as a result developed a psychological resentment toward "white education."

Mexican-American children, too, were subjected to segregated schools with very limited funding, poor teachers, as well as the lack of respect for their language and previous culture. As they became more involved in schools in this country, the suggestions that they must give up their native language and culture led to the belief that they must relinquish a part of their identity. New immigrants, particularly those from Southeast Asia are finding similar experiences. More important, they are not having assistance with the cultural shock and grief process which is an important aspect of readjustment to a new land and new culture while they are also subjected to rather harsh criticisms of their language and standards.

Overcoming this history and making schools work for racially different students is the primary challenge being faced by educators today. To meet the challenge requires a major shift in the belief system which overrides the concept of inferiority and advocates the basic tenet of democracy that **ALL CHILDREN DESERVE THE OPPORTUNITY TO REACH THEIR MAXIMUM POTENTIAL.** This is a major attitudinal change which must be addressed by teacher preparation programs, by school districts, by individuals entering the profession, by society, and particularly by the media which seems to be a major conduit of the negative message of inferiority. In addition to this psychological shift, there are rather direct behavioral changes which can be made in the classroom which can lead to the success of all students. Some suggestions for modifications are as follows:

1. *A shift in the perception of the students that being different is being deficient to one which recognizes and celebrates diversity.*

Our cultural experiences shape our motivation, our interpretation of events and the way we respond to people, events, and things in our environment. Our students, therefore, are not passive robots who come to school for us to program them. They are human beings who bring with them capacities, attitudes, and even mental pictures of how schools and teachers should function. Although it is important that individuals are not stereotyped based upon their group membership, educators must recognize the possibility that individuals respond differently than they expect because the child's "vision" of what is being asked is being interpreted from their cultural perspective. This is also true of words being used and behavior being demonstrated. Rather than considering differences as an indication of deficiency and inability to learn, educators should embrace the diversity of their students and work to develop a sense of belonging, a congruency of expectations, a bicultural set of values and norms. This suggests that teachers must begin to talk with students early, to ask for interpretation of their behavior, to ascertain their vision of what they believe is happening, and together develop a mutually approved way of working together. Children expect to be taught and they also recognize that it is the adult role to help them acquire behavior which will facilitate their growth and development. The conflict emerges when educators demean the behavior, language, ideas which emanate from the home culture and demand that students ignore and give up part of their identity by changing their style.

2. *A shift in the perception of the role of the teacher from being the controller to being the guide.*

The promotion of the idea that classrooms and schools must become more student-centered rather than teacher-centered is consistent with the idea that the final power over learning rests in the hands of the students— not the teacher. To acquire the important information or new skills or behavior, an individual learner must invest mental energy and involvement in both the learning process and the task. This means that the role of the teacher will be different than one of merely presenting information to a group of passive receivers. Instead, the teacher will devise activities which entice the student to interact with the information, provide the opportunity for the learner to explore the ideas in ways which are important to him or her, and find ways for the student to make the information meaningful to him or her in ways match their learning style preferences. In other words, the teacher establishes the parameters for learning—i.e., the environment, the context, the concept, the modalities but it is the learner who interacts and finally processes the information into a form which produces understanding and adds to the person's knowledge. This suggests that teachers will need to be aware of the different approaches to information processing, different modality preferences, different techniques for presentations and various contexts into which the concepts can be transmitted.

The teacher who is most successful with all students becomes a "Peter Pan" for learning and uses the experiences, prior knowledge, cultural orientation and learning style as a bridge to entice the student to persist and engage in the learning process. Gloria Ladson-Billings (1990) describes this type of teacher as a person who sees teaching as an art and a process of "mining" or pulling knowledge out of the student. Most important, the teacher in this role believes all students can learn and succeed and becomes intent in helping students accomplish the task regardless of their individual differences. Successful teachers further recognize that effective teaching results in effective classroom management.

3. *A change in the goals and outcomes of instruction from one which focuses on acquisition of facts to one which facilitates the development of thinking and reasoning and teaches students the joys and process of learning.*

Although learning is the responsibility of the learner, students must be taught how to engage in this process. To meet this particular objective requires teachers and educators to approach the teaching-learning process from a new philosophy. Instead of the traditional behaviorist (tell-repeat) approach, it has become very clear to cognitive psychologists that the ability to learn by any individual rests in their ability to reconstruct the ideas into one's own reality. If individuals can explain the idea, there is every possibility that they know it. This is referred to as constructivist learning theory.

Teaching from this philosophical perspective requires a different approach which begins with the understanding and acceptance of the child and their cultural background which includes a culturally specific way of learning. The brain is always seeking to impose order on incoming information and generate models of understanding and predictions. The student initially has learned how to impose this order within the framework of their family, their peers, and the community in which they live but as they develop within academia, they must learn different ways of transforming ideas which will be useful for them in life and society.

When using this instructional orientation, teachers guide students through the process of understanding and representing problems, in discerning mathematical and environmental relationships, in organizing information, in formulating conjecture and generalizing the results. The goal of teaching and learning will not be the regurgitation of previously defined facts but the development of a means of communication, self-organization and reorganization. Active or engaged learning is further facilitated when the students perceive themselves as a part of a team or learning community in which adults and their peers are engaged in assisting in the process of inquiry, discovery and knowledge development.

4. *A modification of the curriculum from being European-dominated to one which is inclusive of all groups who are a part of this society.*

The basic premise of multicultural education promoted by scholars such as James Banks, Carl Grant, Geneva Gay and others is that the curriculum within the schools offers a monocultural perspective which ignores the existence of racially different people and their contributions to the development of this country (Branch, Goodwin & Gualtieri, 1993). Moreover, ideas, explanations or contexts with which the students are familiar and with which they have a relationship are more likely to enhance the learning process. When students encounter new information, it is important that they perceive some similarities and differences with other ideas, events, people or concepts with which they are already acquainted. The curriculum materials used must provide this type of bridge if students are to add to their knowledge base and become good academic performers.

5. *An increased use of a variety of teaching strategies which enhance the student's learning styles and encourage their involvement in the material.*

The basic premise of this book, particularly the section on the educative process, is that students do not approach information in the same manner. There are individual and group differences on how they wish to have material presented, the extent to which they seek help or will use resources, and how they will reconstruct the idea so that it has meaning for them. To facilitate this process, teachers will become adept at using a wide variety of teaching strategies from peer tutoring, projects, experiments, technology, group discussions, etc. Furthermore, teachers will be creative in their approaches. Implicit in these new strategies is the ability to engage in dialog, have pleasant interpersonal interactions, and plan activities which probe and lead students through the process of thinking about and constructing their own reality. As noted by the various authors, there are some strategies which seem to be more culturally suited than others and these should be incorporated whenever possible. When a person is venturing into an "unknown" territory such as found in new material, being allowed to use an approach which gives comfort and with which the child is familiar from their previous experiences or which matches their particularly preferred intellectual approach is more likely to guarantee the motivation to engage in the learning process.

THE CHALLENGE

Change is not easy. The types of changes recommended are so fundamentally different from the policies and practices currently used by educators and schools that the change is uncomfortable. However, the recognition that these transformations must occur is prevalent throughout the literature and in the new educational practices being promoted. Increasingly, scholars and practitioners are advocating the use of technology, the move toward encouraging the embracing of the constructivist learning theory, promotion of multicultural and bilingual education, use of cooperative learning and changes in the way science and mathematics are taught. These pedagogical practices are based upon the premise that individual differences have a cultural base and must be addressed in the teaching-learning process. If the changes are to occur, they must begin with teacher preparation programs, continue with the hiring process to ensure that the teachers who can meet the challenges are members of today's faculties, and lead to staff development programs to help teachers become aware and implement the new approaches. Not only is this transformation important for students of color, it has the potential for making an impact on all students.

REFERENCES

1. Branch, R. C., Goodwin, Y., & Gualtieri, J.: Making classroom instruction culturally pluralistic. *The Educational Forum,* 58:57–76, 1993.
2. Fordham, S., & Ogbu, J. U.: Black students' school success: Coping with the "burden of 'acting white.'" *The Urban Review,* 18:176–206, 1986.
3. Ladson-Billings, G.: Culturally relevant teaching. *The College Board Review,* 155:20–25, 1990.
4. Shade, B. J.: *Engaging the Battle for African-American Minds.* Washington, D. C., National Alliance of Black School Educators, 1990.
5. West, C.: *Race Matters.* New York, Vintage Books, 1993.

NAME INDEX

A

Abrahams, R.D., 136, 138, 139
Adler, A., 169
Aiello, J.R., 19
Albott, W.L., 85
Allerhand, M.E., 5
Alper, W., 15
Amidon, E.J., 153
Anderson, J.R., 71, 82
Anderson, L., 182
Anderson, L.M., 81, 83
Anderson, R.C., 94
Arbess, S., 172
Aschenbrenner, J., 16
Attneave, C., 29, 30
Atwood, B.S., 155
Au, K., 188
August, 82
Ausburn, F.B., 63
Ausburn, L.J., 63

B

Backman, M.E., 84
Bacon, M., 16
Banks, J., 223
Barbe, W.B., 74
Barrett, R., 22
Barry, H., 16
Barsch, R.H., 73, 74
Battle, E.S., 21
Bauer, E., 19
Baxter, J.C., 19
Begishe, K., 32
Bell, 102
Bellet, W., 183, 184
Benitez, M., 140
Bennett, M., 134, 135, 139

Berman, J.J., 21
Bernard, H.W., 71
Berry, J.W., 7, 70, 93, 96, 97, 111
Bieri, J., 63, 65
Billingsley, A., 23
Black, H., 78
Blackman, S., 65
Blackwell, J.E., 23, 24, 70
Blaha, J., 65
Blassingame, J., 14, 16
Bopp, J., 29, 30
Bopp, M., 29, 30
Borkowski, J.G., 147
Bower, E.M., 55
Boykin, A.W., 15, 79
Branch, R.C., 223
Bright, H.A., 85
Brim, O.G., 163
Brody, G., 19
Brophy, J., 145
Brown, A.L., 63
Brown, F., 85
Brown, J., 31
Bruner, J.S., 71, 77, 80
Bryson, J.A., 18
Bulk, J.D., 107, 109
Burciago-Valdez, R., 188, 189
Buriel, R., 37, 118, 119, 121
Butler, B.W., 85
Butterfield, R., 182

C

Cabezas, A., 42, 43
Campion, J.C., 63
Canavan, 119
Carlson, R., 20, 79, 81
Carpenter, 77
Castaneda, A., 36, 37, 39, 118, 119

SUBJECT INDEX